the communications revolution

the communications revolution

frederick williams
Annenberg School of Communications,
University of Southern California

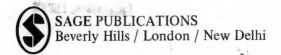

SAGE PUBLICATIONS
Beverly Hills / London / New Delhi

For information address:

SAGE Publications, Inc.
275 South Beverly Drive
Beverly Hills, California 90212

SAGE Publications India Pvt. Ltd.
C-236 Defence Colony
New Delhi 110 024, India

SAGE Publications Ltd
28 Banner Street
London EC1Y 8QE, England

Printed in the United States of America

Library of Congress Cataloging in Publication Data

Williams, Frederick, 1933-
    The communications revolution.

    Bibliography: p.
    Includes index.
    1. Telecommunications. I. Title.
HE7631.W54   384   81-18498
ISBN 0-8039-1782-1   AACR2
ISBN 0-8039-1783-X (pbk.)

FIRST PRINTING

*This book is dedicated to
Marie Elder Williams,
woman, bookseller, librarian,
poet, and indefatigable
bridge player.*

CONTENTS

THE NEW SOCIETY

PREFACE

Writing *The Communications Revolution* has been a labor of love.

For over 20 years I have had a growing curiosity about the invasion of communications technologies — everything from $5.95 radios to giant computers — into our lives. At first I used to wonder why we communications academics did not spend more of our time studying these wondrous gadgets. Soon I began to discover that the ultimate impact of these revolutionary technologies is not so much in their razzle-dazzle but in their combined effects on our lives. *The* "revolution" is ultimately a social one.

Our lives will never be the same again.

A little over a year ago I was given the first sabbatical research leave of my career to pursue a book on this topic. For this leave I am most grateful to the trustees of the Annenberg School of Communications, especially Ambassadors Walter H. and Leonore Annenberg.

Although I am an academic writer, teacher, and researcher by profession, I have chosen to write *The Communications Revolution* in a nontechnical style. This is in deference to those many members of public audiences who can bring a professor back down to earth with their point-blank, clear, and pressing questions about why television must be so mediocre, whether we are all now suffering "information overload," or why their kids know more about computers than they do. I hope that I can share this book now with them.

I am also indebted to those many individuals in business, industry, and government who have so freely shared their opinions with me on this newest revolution. And I owe much to my professional colleagues in the academic fields of communications, especially to a very unique group of them (particularly Richard B. Byrne) who as Annenberg School faculty and students set off on a great adventure in 1973 to explore the ongoing revolution in human communication.

Acknowledgments

Permission granted by the following persons and publishers to use quoted material is gratefully acknowledged.

Macmillan Publishing Co., Inc. (in Chapter 12): quoted from Joffre Dumazedier, *Toward a Society of Leisure*, translated from the French by Stewart E. McClure. Copyright © 1967 by The Free Press, a Division of Macmillan Publishing Co., Inc. David L. Wolper, for a quote from *EMMY Magazine*, Summer 1979 Supplement (p. D-25), used in Chapter 12. *Los Angeles Times* (in Chapter 12): quoted from Barry Siegel, "Television: It's Changing Life in Samoa," *Los Angeles Times*, June 14, 1979. © 1979, Los Angeles Times. Reprinted by permission. Dow Jones & Company, Inc. (in Chapters 12 and 15): quoted from "TV Comes to Town: Fads & New Wants Come Along with It," by L. Leff, *The Wall Street Journal*, October 2, 1979, and from "To Raise a Politician to the Heights, Try Helicopter and Music," by James M. Perry, *The Wall Street Journal*, September 24, 1979. Reprinted by permission of *The Wall Street Journal*, © Dow Jones & Company, Inc., 1979. All rights reserved. Universe Books (in Chapter 18): quoted from *The Limits to Growth: A Report for The Club of Rome's Project on the Predicament of Mankind*, by Donella H. Meadows, Dennis L. Meadows, Jørgen Randers, William W. Behrens III. A Potomac Associates book published by Universe Books, N.Y., 1972. Graphics by Potomac Associates. Basic Books (in Chapter 18): From *The Coming of Post-Industrial Society: A Venture in Forecasting* by Daniel Bell. © 1973 by Daniel Bell. By permission of Basic Books, Inc., N.Y.

Frederick Williams
Los Angeles

INTRODUCTION

We are changing.

Not just in our institutions, the automobiles we buy, nor the fashions we wear, but in how we behave as human beings. The fundamental premise of *The Communications Revolution* is that the contemporary explosion in communications technologies — computers, satellites, tape, disc, microprocessors, and new telephone and radio services — are perceptibly changing the nature of our human environment. As we have done so many times in the history of our species, we are in the process of adapting to environmental change. This is not so much a "future shock" type of thesis as it is one of recognition and observation of change. After all, change is nothing unique or new to us humans. We are already the consequences of many millenia of environmental adaptation. Change is the name of our game.

Nor is it the thesis of this book that communications technologies are a sole cause of change. On the contrary, there are many forces of change in our contemporary world — the threat of nuclear confrontation, Third World countries calling for their fair share of the earth's resources, the shift of advanced nations toward a "post-industrialism," as well as the looming recognition that our earth has finite limits to industrial and population growths. Within this grand context, the communications technologies are more a catalyst or intensifier of change than they are a sole cause of anything. They are a part of our problems and they are a part of our solutions.

Given these assumptions, an initial objective of *The Communications Revolution,* and the topic of the first section of the volume ("The Communications Explosion") is to observe the communications technology revolution in its broadest possible view — as it distinguishes our planet and us as humans in the known universe, as well as the place of this revolution in our history as a species. Against the 35,000 or so years which separate us from the Cro-Magnons, the current explosion in communications technologies occupies hardly more than a final instant on our human time scale. Yet this same development is accelerating at a rate which portends a near "communications" metamorphosis of our environment. Increasingly we are living and working in an environment that is artifactual and electronic. We are rapidly fabricating a total psychological environment for ourselves.

What is contributing now to that environment? What are the next developments? These questions are the basis for the second section ("The Electronic Environment") of the book. We need not resort to soothsaying to answer them because most of the technologies which will fill our homes and offices in the next several decades are already on the planning boards. We need only to have a look.

Despite the glitter, promise, or threats of the new communications technologies, nothing is so important as is their consequences upon our daily lives. These consequences do not tend to be entirely new activities for us, but appear more as changes in traditional services and the institutions which supply them. Accordingly, the third main section of *The Communications Revolution* ("Living in the Communications Future") explores the impact of the new technologies in such traditional areas of our lives as leisure, transportation, health, politics, work, and education. No matter whether in your role as a professional in one of these areas or in your roles as a consumer in all of them, life will never be the same again.

Finally, we must also attempt to have some conception of the longer range future of these changes if we are going to make good decisions in the present. Long-range forecasts, of course, are hazardous. However, in our era we have improved upon our capabilities for understanding something about the forces of change. We have learned to think about the future in terms of likely alternatives (although there is the probability, of course, that none may happen). And we are beginning to improve upon our abilities for considering the management of those forces over which we in the present do have some degree of control. All of this as it applies to the communications technology revolution is the topic of the final section ("The New Society") of the book. What are the main vectors which seem to be propelling us toward our future — post-industrialism, world power shifts, the "doomsday" theses? In this same broad view, how might our advances in communications technologies interact with these vectors? What choices do we have today? What are some of the alternative scenarios? And if we could most fully use communications technologies for a highly positive human future, *what would we want?*

Whatever choices we make within this newest technological revolution are likely to have global effects for as we enter the decade of the 1980s, the United States is the world leader in computer and telecommunications technologies. But if present trends continue — if we go without aggressive national and international policies, if we try to prop up aging manufacturing industries while subjecting the world's largest computer and the world's largest telephone corporations to constant litigation — we will surely lose this lead. Moreover, there will be a reduced chance to employ the contributions of these new technologies to solutions for world problems. We cannot afford to continue a policy which at best has been "muddling through."

On the other hand, if we replace our muddling with a clear policy of "managed change," we could bring these technologies more rapidly to bear upon world challenges. We could also provide the United States with a rich opportunity for post-industrial growth and continued world economic leadership. We might also gain more control over our psychological environment than we have ever had in the history of our species. It could be stultifying or enlightening. The choice is ours.

That we see these alternatives and that we — both personally as individuals and collectively as citizens — begin to make good choices with these most powerful new technologies is the ultimate objective of *The Communications Revolution*.

THE COMMUNICATIONS
EXPLOSION

Galactic Prime Time

CHAPTER 1

Intelligent?

If our earth were being systematically observed from deep space by an advanced civilization, our speck of a planet would certainly have done something to draw attention to itself. We are at the center of an electronic explosion that is now bulging beyond a radius of 80 light years. To our remote observers this ever expanding spectacular is surely a sign that a profound change has taken place on this small bluish planet. Perhaps this explosion would signify the creation of life, the termination of it, or some great evolutionary step.

Should the observers have the capability to explore this environment, they might detect Guglielmo Marconi's experiments with radio telegraphy in the outer layer, or in an inner one our first commercial radio broadcasts in the 1920s. At about 40 light years out from the center would be evidence of regular television broadcasting. Near the earth's surface the observers would encounter an electronic maelstrom of data transmissions, long distance calls, land and sea communications networks, and encrypted military messages, not to mention the glut of radio and television broadcasts. If all of these could be made visible, our earth's surface would appear as a dense and tightly interwoven network of communications channels, much as the surface of a baseball with its cover torn back.

That we are able to draw so much attention to ourselves might cause us to overstress the importance of what we have done with the miracles of electronic communications. For also in the older strata of this electronic halo are the face and sounds of Milton Berle. Somewhere out there Fibber McGee and Molly prattle on and on. And our long past but remembered "L.S./M.F.T." could be mistaken as our coded salutation for that important first encounter.

Given close scrutiny, there is little doubt but that this great nova surrounding us would be taken as a sign of life here. But whether it would be considered intelligent will probably remain a matter for speculation.

The Electronic Environment

Surely in the midst of these goings on, we here on earth also sense that something electronic in our environment is happening. In America our television sets are on an average of six hours a day. Between the ages of six and eighteen, our children will watch about 16,000 hours of TV and spend another 4,000 hours with radio, records, and movies. They will spend more time with media than with school or in talking with parents. We adults have witnessed most of the great events of our time on television, sometimes at the same moment as our leaders. Much of our local television news is programmed more for entertainment than for information. We are bombarded with 30,000 to 40,000 TV ads per year. We have learned to tolerate messages about sanitary napkins with our morning coffee.

We are buying video recording machines with all of the fervor that we bought color TV sets. When the images are better, we will buy wide screen television. The more venturesome of us have already bought sets which will show two programs at once, and soon we will be looking for voice controlled stereo and TV sets.

More and more of our entertainment dollars are being lured from theater to home entertainment expenditures in the forms of pay-TV, prerecorded cassettes and discs, and programs for our TV computer games. After we subscribe to cable, we will be offered broadcasting direct to our homes from satellites.

As if the revolution in home entertainment were not enough, our telephones have either become decorator items, small computers, or both. How many volleys of calls to answering machines are now necessary before you can get a friend on the line? Some of us have been invited to pay our monthly bills by punching in tones to our bank's computer via our push-button phones. British visitors tell us how they can hook their telephone to their TV set to get the news headlines, to order theatre tickets, or even for an updated horoscope. We can now buy our telephones in any shape or form, all of which is fun until they break down.

Over the last few Christmases those $15.95 plastic toys which looked so spectacular on TV but were so flimsy at home have been replaced by TV and hand-held electronic games. We learn that as many adults as kids play with them, that there are $69.95 versions which incorporate three or four different games, and that the $169.95 version will take as many different game cassettes as you are willing to buy. A friend in computers tells us that for $295.95 we can get one to program ourselves and take pride in saying that we have a *home computer*.

If we get serious about a home computer, we learn that a more expensive one will keep track of our checkbook and household budget, teach spelling, reading, and math, analyze our investment portfolio, and still be able to handle all of the games we would be interested in playing. For a few hundred dollars more we can use it to control household devices: turning on the oven, closing the drapes at night, and sprinkling the lawn on schedule. If we buy even more accessories, we can attach our home computer to our type-writer and write and rewrite letters in "memory" before we put them on paper. It's a good way to take the labor out of addressing all of the Christmas cards over again each year.

Radios do not look like radios anymore. Digital displays replace the old friendly dial (and the pulleys and strings) and most of our new small radios are clocks too. Radio paging devices allow us to be reached on the spot anywhere in a city. On the planning boards is a satellite and radio device capable of contacting us anywhere in the world. We hear that AM radio may be expanded, including the establishment of stereo stations.

Two-way cable communications services for the home have already been tested in several markets. This does more than bring you a better TV picture — it allows you to send messages back to the station. Using a keypad not much bigger than a hand calculator, you can do everything from participating in game shows to ordering shoes displayed on your TV. Someday you might even be able to vote via your television set.

Our offices are changing too. Ordinary typewriters are getting smart. They can remember dozens of pages typed into them, then rattle them back like player pianos. In fact, it is getting difficult to tell the difference between some of the new typewriters and small computers. That's because there isn't any. Something you might mistake for a new copying machine is actually a facsimile machine, capable via telephone lines of sending print or pictures anywhere another similar machine exists. Modern business executives are becoming increasingly adept at getting computers to do management tasks for them. The executive desk of the future may have much less room for paper and more room for pop-up screens where a busy manager can punch up anything from the corporation's monthly calendar of events to the weekly football pool. Many business trips may be replaced with teleconferences where individual participants meet electronically rather than travel across country to exchange notes and make plans. Message movement replaces people movement.

One of these days education might never be the same again. An inexpensive small computer can handle routine drills in spelling, reading, and mathematics far more efficiently than a teacher with pencil and paper exercises *and* it will never be driven to the brink of insanity after correcting 30 papers five times per day. With electronic two-way communications systems, there is little reason to travel across town, or even across country, to hear college lectures. New technologies allow instructional materials to be brought to the student rather than vice versa. Much education could be completed at home with time in school left for those activities which require face to face communication.

Modern communications are rapidly shrinking our world to distanceless dimensions so far as the communications environment is concerned. Once a satellite communications system is in place, distance is irrelevant. Three large satellites can bring television, radio, data, and telephone links to every square inch of our earth's surface. More than Marshall McLuhan's notion of uniting us into a "global village," international communications networks allow us to participate in many villages simultaneously, and as temporarily as suits our needs. Unfettered by space and distance, a "village" is now created when people, organizations, or nations come together for common communications purposes in the network.

As a citizen, you will pick villages from the communications infrastructure to meet your needs. Some will be for work, others for leisure, some for political activity, occasionally one for health services, perhaps even one for religious or philosophic motives. Where you dwell will be irrelevant to everything except your direct physical needs which, of course, include access to the communications networks.

We are moving into electronic space.

People Choices

The communications revolution is not the only symptom of profound change as we experience ourselves being thrust into a new century. We also seem to be at a point of economic, social, and value transitions. We are in some type of major shift, a discontinuity of change. We are on the cusp of something big.

For the first time in history we are facing identifiable limits to our capability for continued growth on this planet. These are limits in the earth's nonrenewable resources, limits in our ability to feed humanity if population growth continues at current rates, and limits of our earth to tolerate greater pollution. Not all theorists agree with the immediacy of these limits, especially the predicted collapse of industrial economies by the so-called "Club of Rome" group. But most agree that we are meeting limits that we should have been anticipating and preparing for several decades ago. How we should face such limits — by "doing more with less" or by hoping that technological breakthroughs will pull us through — is the focus of most intellectual debates on this issue. Meanwhile many of us have experienced gas lines, increasing inflation in fuel costs, and a general worldwide continuing pattern in cost increases for most of the basics of life. We are already feeling the effects of the era of limits.

The nature of advanced industrial economies is changing too. Some countries, including the United States, seem to be entering an era of *post-industrialism*. Service and information industries rather than manufacturing are the growth areas. Health, leisure, finance, communications, and computing are expanding areas of our economy. Highly labor intensive manufacturing is now profitable only in countries where labor is markedly inexpensive. Knowledge and information manipulation rather than raw materials and manufacturing technologies are at the base of the post-industrial economy. There is a greater acknowledgment of the importance of "intellectual" technology, the ability to understand a problem theoretically and to use this understanding as a basis for finding solutions. The "knowledge worker," the person who can exercise intellectual technology, will grow in influence in our post-industrial society. A more educated public will demand more social services; they will expect intellectual technology to be applied to human problems. They will be less inclined to allow their futures to be exclusively in the hands of politicians, especially those whose candidacies are mainly a product of media images.

We are also witnessing changes in social values. Value shifts abound in our personal lives in attitudes about marriage, family life, abortion, childbearing, sexuality, and individual goals. Yesterday's pornography is today's mass entertainment. Lawlessness, a good predictor of social change, is steadily increasing. Our political values have been uprooted by an unpopular war, a nearly impeached president, and governmental as well as corporate corruption.

Yet many of us cannot deny that we have access to a good life in terms of material goods, health care, opportunity for education and employment. The problem is our decreasing ability to associate what we think is right in modern life with traditional concepts of *good*. Our schools teach us nothing about value systems and our churches are becoming outbombarded in the electronic communications age. Our media, in fact, intensify this shift in values as we witness more life played out in prime time drama than in personal real-life experiences.

When our value questions become visible as in the student riots of the 1960s, there is often an underlying theme of dissatisfaction with technologically oriented values, a dissatisfaction with modernism itself. There is a questioning of the overapplication of corporate values to the operation of society. Do "cost-benefits," "objectives," "input-output-throughput," or "efficiency" become overwhelming when cast into the human equation? French philosopher Jacques Ellul holds that we have plunged our social order so deeply into technology that we have irreversibly technologized the human condition. Herbert Marcuse, the idol of the student radicals of the 1960s, sees technological society as so "one-dimensional" in values (such as "efficiency") that it is incapable of productive criticism or change. Even businessman-scientist Simon Ramo, whose whole career has been in the applications of technology, warns of the growing mismatch between the progress of science and the progress of society. Sociologist Daniel Bell, who has written the most about post-industrial society, anticipates value shifts paralleling economic ones.

The communications revolution is occurring simultaneously with these forces of change. It is not a cause nor an effect, but an intensifier or catalyst. New communications and computing technologies allow us to manipulate and distribute as never before our knowledge and information resources. At the same time, many in our population spend up to a quarter of their waking hours mesmerized by a medium unundated by programmed mediocrity. These same communications as well as computing technologies could raise the educational level of every U.S. schoolchild, yet our classrooms are administered in ways not unlike our own or even our parents' days in school. Education, which is our most valuable strategy for preparing a new generation for change, is the last to adopt the techniques of change. The same television which sells patent medicines so well could be used to promote resource conservation, family planning, and respect for the natural environment. Yet we have been unable to revise the basic 1934 legislation under which we operate most communications in the United States so we could begin to give more priority to social goals.

We have no plan for the development of our vast communications resources in such a way as to support effectively our economic transition to a post-industrial society. Just as the forces of change are causing us to ponder the meaning of *good* in contemporary society, the media environment, by catering to our immediate gratifications, adds to the confusion. Very little in our media is of a deliberative nature, nor does it invite intellectual interaction of the public. At the same time, communications technology has the capability to help us in many of our problems in making our way into the next century. It could support a form of democracy undreamed of by the signers of our Constitution.

How we use the miracle of modern electronic communications may well determine our success in creating a satisfactory if not enlightened future for ourselves.

If indeed we are being studied by remote observers, surely we are the best show on in galactic prime time!

CHAPTER 2

The 360 Century Day

"Communication is the distinguishing mark
of being human."

So might we translate and update a famous statement
attributed to Marcus Tullius Cicero, distinguished states-
man, orator and philosopher of pre-Christian Rome. Cicero
theorized how the human capability for communications
was the basis for civilization. Yet even Cicero was a comparative latecomer in philosophizing about human communications. Aristotle wrote a comprehensive manual on
techniques of persuasion 300 years earlier, although his
teacher, Plato, had relegated the topic to the domain of
"cookery." (Can you imagine Plato's response to an evening
of commercial television?)

The capability for speech, like the opposed thumb and
upright stance, is a unique biological inheritance of our
species. Its presence is interwoven with a brain capable of
symbolization and with a flexible jaw and tongue arrange-
ment capable of making the 40 or so sounds basic to any
human language. Complementing our capability for creating
these sounds is an auditory capacity for distinguishing
among them. No other species can create nor discriminate
among this range of basic speech sounds. (Monkeys who
"talk" use sign language. Parrots only mimic the superficial
features of speech.) If only in terms of our physiological
equipment, we humans are unique communicators.

The system which relates speech sounds to our meanings is *language*, the complexity of which far surpasses any known communication system in the animal kingdom or the most powerful computer systems we have been able to build. Even a severely brain-damaged human possesses a communication capacity far exceeding that of a highly educated ape. When a parrot learns a few words of a language, it does not adopt its sound system as a basis for mimicking; hence a parrot who usually mimics English would not, as we would, have a carryover accent in French.

A most unique feature of our language and one which gives us an infinite expressive power is our ability to combine words in different orders so as to represent different meanings. This power of combination, or *syntax*, moves human language from simple utterance of surprise, command, or invective to rich description, elaboration, argument or poetry. It also reflects the remarkable conceptual power of our brains. Since the times of the ancient Greeks, the capability to select and arrange words, or *style*, has been considered one of our greatest talents. It is the basis of literature, a distinctively human achievement.

The prehistory of human language is mostly a product of conjecture or myth. One theory holds that sound and referent relationships developed out of variations in noises early humans made as they lifted heavy objects, chewed, spit out seeds, or looked up suddenly (say "ah" while moving your head up and down as if to signal "yes"). Another holds that our speech began as emulations of the sounds about us. (There exists a doctoral dissertation which relates the hissing sound of "s" to the sound of urinating on rocks!) One Garden of Eden theory held that the world's main language originated with the inhabitants of that paradise, including a hypothesis that the serpent spoke French. Although the origins of language may be forever lost to us, there is some agreement that "Cro-Magnon" *homo sapiens* of the upper Paleolithic period (35,000 B.C. to 10,000 B.C.) were language users. The brain cage and flexible jaw observed in their remains suggest this possibility, as does the evidence of a village-like existence.

The only unequivocal evidence of early language, of course, is its representation in writing. The oldest examples of writing date back to approximately 4,000 B.C. as found in Sumerian inscriptions and a little later on clay tablets. Many examples of carvings, decor, or paintings which predate Sumerian writing do exist, but there is no way to relate them to language use. The quite elaborate cave paintings of Lascaux (France) are thought to have been completed sometime between 28,000 B.C. and 22,000 B.C. Their existence suggests a ritualistic use which in turn suggests the presence of language. The ancient form of writing best preserved for us is Egyptian hieroglyphics which date back to approximately 3000 B.C. As you have no doubt observed already, this is an ornate form of writing and lends itself well to the adornment of temple walls, jewelry, household implements, and the like. It was also extensively used along with papyrus to record business transactions, land deeds, and religious rituals. Hieroglyphic writing was supplemented by a simplified system around 1500 B.C. used more for everyday purposes than as an art form. Greek writing evolved sometime after 1000 B.C., the first two letters of which contribute to our word, "alphabet."

Human communication practices did not change so rapidly in prehistoric and ancient times. If we assume that language, like communication, took place in Cro-Magnon times, it was roughly 31,000 years before we humans got around to writing, a span of time almost incomprehensible to us. If the average human lifetime were around 30 to 35 years in those times, over 1000 lifetimes passed before writing was in any visible use. It was to be another 180 lifetimes before the printing press appeared in Europe.

The Acceleration Curve

Innovations in communication in our current century are quite a different picture. In the last 80 years, more new forms of communication have developed than throughout the almost 360 centuries which separate us from the first *homo sapiens*. Even since the dawn of the modern electronics communications era after World War II, more people have been put into contact with one another, more knowledge has been accumulated and recorded, and more people have access to that knowledge than ever before in history. Like the early evolution of human language, the development of writing, or the invention of printing, we are again swept up in something new. These monumental changes in our ability for communication as we approach the twenty first century may well bring about as great a wave of social changes as that associated with these earlier milestones in our history. More people are communicating in more ways than in any of our prior history, and this growth is exponential. Figure 2.1 illustrates this growth in the form of an *acceleration curve*. As of today we do not know the limits of this growth.

Even with the acceleration curve it is difficult to sense the remarkable compression of time scale in which recent communications innovations have evolved. For most of our history as a species, our methods of communications were very slow to develop. As a means to sense the rapidity of change, let us juggle our figures slightly so that the 24 hours of a single day could serve as a time scale for gauging change in the approximately 360 centuries since Cro-Magnon times to the year 2000. Figure 2.2 illustrates this analogy. Note the vast expanses of time in which we know of no communications innovations. For example:

New Day	12:00 Midnight	— *Homo sapiens*, language 34,000 B.C.
	3:00 a.m.	— Nothing
	8:00 a.m.	— Cave paintings
	12:00 Noon	— Nothing
	6:00 p.m.	— Nothing
	8:00 p.m.	— *Sumerians*, writing, 4,000 B.C.

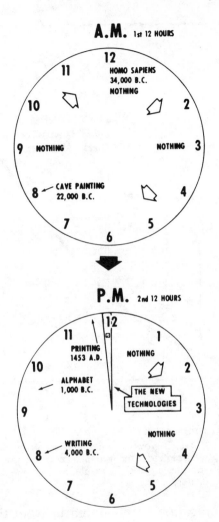

Figure 2.1   *The 360 Century Day*
NOTE: If the history of human communications were squeezed into the 24 hours of a single day, we would spend all of the a.m. hours with very little change, and with little change until the closing p.m. hours. In fact, most of the technologies which are inundating us today have been invented in the few moments before midnight.

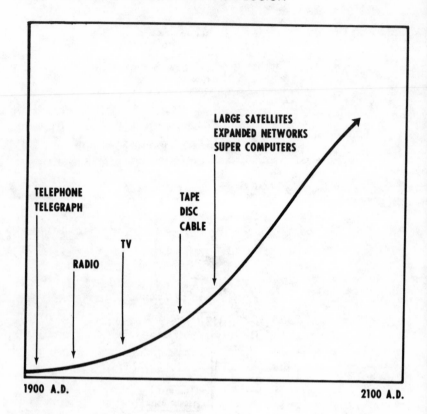

Figure 2.2   *The Acceleration Curve*
NOTE: If growths in the amounts of human communication were plotted in the form of a curve, this curve would surely be showing a marked acceleration as we enter the twenty-first century.

If our communication habits on earth were the subject of study by some outside observer, they could well conclude that on the average over these 360 plus centuries, we did little more than develop a capability for speech and use it alone as our communications medium for most of this time. About five-sixths of all of the time separating us from the first *homo sapiens* passed even before the invention of writing. Think about it. We have only been using writing for about one-sixth of the period for which we can trace our evolution from Cro-Magnon times. Relatively speaking, it is a new invention.

Things do not really start happening in our 360 century day until the evening. Egyptian hieroglyphics appear at 8:40 p.m., followed by the alphabet at 9:28 p.m. Then there is another lull until around 10:06 p.m. when the works of Homer appear, probably the most ancient literature that we read for more than historical curiosity. The four and one-half centuries of the Roman Empire (and Cicero) flash by between 10:38 and 11:01 p.m. Almost 96 percent of the 360 centuries has now gone by.

It requires almost ten centuries more and is rapidly approaching midnight when the Gutenberg Bible is printed at 11:38 p.m. The pace of communications innovations begins to quicken as the steam press appears at 11:53 p.m. The telegraph follows at 11:53 and 24 seconds and the first transatlantic cable at 11:54:38 p.m. The telephone (11:55:02) and phonograph (11:55:04) appear just a few seconds later in our day, which is now 99.6 percent complete as we approach the year 2000.

The last few minutes explode with new communications technologies. We are on an acceleration curve of communications inventions. Communication grows as a business in the forms of the telephone, telegraph, motion picture and commercial radio.

11:55:47 p.m.	radio telegraphy; motion picture camera
11:56:48 p.m.	commercial radio a reality
11:57:04 p.m.	sound motion pictures
11:57:40 p.m.	prototype electronic computer
11:57:50 p.m.	Xerography developed
11:57:52 p.m.	transistor invented
11:58:02 p.m.	color TV introduced

The pace of new communications technologies increases even more in the closing minute, which brings us to the decade of the 1980s. Commercial television grows overnight. Computers increase in power but decrease in price. Giant communications networks form. Satellite communications is a commercial success. New communications devices invade the home, including the computer.

The last two-minute countdown to the year 2000:

- −104 sec.   Sputnik launched
- −101 sec.   stereophonic FM broadcasting
- − 92 sec.   first commercial satellite
- − 87 sec.   computer timesharing feasible
- − 85 sec.   merger of telecommunications and computing
- − 78 sec.   portable TV camera
- − 74 sec.   microelectronic circuitry
- − 62 sec.   major advances in computer memories
- − 61 sec.   home TV recording equipment
- − 49 sec.   It is the 1980s and the communications revolution continues to accelerate

Table 2.1 fills in a few more details of the evolution of human communications from Cro-Magnon times until the present. Even a cursory glance over this table suggests several fundamental generalizations about our communications heritage. It illustrates, for example, how communications innovations have come in bursts: writing in the fourth and third centuries B.C., printing in the fifteenth-century Europe (600 A.D. in China), high speed printing, the telephone, telegraph, phonograph and photography in the nineteenth century, radio and television in the early and mid-twentieth century, and the convergence of telecommunications and computer technologies in the last part of this same century.

We can again see in the table also how the pace of communications innovations is quickening in our times. The older electronic media such as radio, the telephone, and the telegraph were all developed mainly in the past 100 years, only a speck of time in the history of human communications. The period during which we have seen computers grow from expensive and inefficient prototypes to both giant networks or cheap video games can hardly be seen on the time scale. The greatest growth of communications technologies has been in our lifetimes and it is still accelerating. This is in remarkable contrast to the approximately 180 lifetimes which separate the invention of writing from the invention of printing in our communications history.

We can also note how periods of human social change correlate with changes in communication technologies. For example, the rise of civilization itself is linked to the evolution of human language. The establishment of the great civilizations of antiquity is parallel with the development of writing. Printing and the Renaissance were simultaneous. The harnessing of energy in the industrial revolution correlates with high speed printing and cheap paper, both of which made the newspaper possible. The telegraph, telephone, phonograph, photography, radio and television mark the beginnings of the technological era in the Western world. Through research and development the science-based industries of our contemporary era have given us the computer, transistor, laser, fiber optics (glass "wire"), cassette, and disc.

When we examine the communications capabilities available to past civilizations, the correspondence between the limits of their communications systems and their social orders stands out. Societies formed and maintained without the capability for using the written word are severely restricted in space and time. Whether we speculate about the effects of this in pre-Sumerian times or observe it directly in the few tribes which live under Stone Age conditions today, an *oral* society has certain distinctive characteristics. The number of individuals involved in any form of simultaneous communication is limited by the range of the human voice. Because of its ephemeral nature, what is said orally is restricted to the moment in time unless it is subjected to the distortions of memory and repetition from individual to individual. Ritual is particularly important in primitive preliterate societies as a means for preserving a spoken tradition. It is difficult for knowledge to accumulate in an oral society since it is limited to the capacity of human minds to store and recall it. Temples, icons, pottery, and crude utensils no doubt complemented oral communication in ancient societies.

TABLE 2.1

Milestones in Human Communication

35,000 B.C.	Cro-Magnon period; speculation that language existed
22,000 B.C.	Prehistoric cave paintings
4,000 B.C.	Sumerian writing on clay tablets
3,000 B.C.	Early Egyptian hieroglyphics
1,800 B.C.	Phoenician alphabet
1,000 B.C.	Early Greek script
600 B.C.	Earliest Latin inscriptions
450 B.C.	Carrier pigeons used by the Greeks
130 B.C.	Library of Alexandria built
350 A.D.	Books replace scrolls
600 A.D.	Book printing in China
676 A.D.	Paper and ink used by Arabs and Persians
1200 A.D.	Paper and ink art in Europe
1453 A.D.	Gutenberg Bible printed
1562 A.D.	First monthly newspaper in Italy
1594 A.D.	First magazine in Germany
1639 A.D.	First printing press in North America
1642 A.D.	Early adding machine developed by Blaise Pascal
1709 A.D.	Copyright law in England
1791 A.D.	First Amendment to the U.S. Constitution
1819 A.D.	Flat bed press invented by David Napier
1827 A.D.	Photographs on metal plates
1830 A.D.	Koenig steam press invented
1834 A.D.	"Analytic engine" (computer) principles; Charles Babbage
1835 A.D.	Samuel Morse introduces the telegraph
1846 A.D.	Lightening Press; high speed printing
1855 A.D.	Printing telegraph; David Hughes
1866 A.D.	Transatlantic cable completed

1876 A.D. Telephone invented; Alexander Graham Bell

1888 A.D. Radio waves identified

1895 A.D. Radio telegraphy; Guglielmo Marconi

1895 A.D. Motion picture camera; Auguste and Louis Lumiere

1900 A.D. Speech transmitted via radio waves

1912 A.D. Motion pictures a big business

1920 A.D. Home television speculated upon

1927 A.D. American Telephone and Telegraph Co. demonstrates TV

1936 A.D. *Life* magazine founded

1942 A.D. First electronic computer in U.S.

1946 A.D. Xerography invented; Chester Carlson

1947 A.D. Transistor invented; Bell Laboratories

1949 A.D. First stored-program computer

1951 A.D. Color TV introduced in the U.S.

1957 A.D. Russia launches first earth satellite, *Sputnik*

1958 A.D. Stereophonic recordings in use

1961 A.D. Push-button telephones introduced

1962 A.D. Telestar satellite launched by U.S.

1968 A.D. Portable video recorders introduced

1970 A.D. Microelectronic chips coming into wide use

1975 A.D. Flat wall TV screen invented

1975 A.D. Fiber optic signal transmission now highly developed

1976 A.D. First wide marketing of TV computer games

1978 A.D. Videodisc system test marketed

1979 A.D. 3-D TV demonstrated

1980 A.D. Home computer available for less than $500

1980 A.D. New breakthroughs in space photography

1981 A.D. Two videodisc systems widely marketed

1981 A.D. Space shuttle "Columbia" has successful mission

1982 A.D. European consortium launches multiple satellites

1982 A.D. Major advances in implementation of digital telephone

They have been our only basis for detecting "messages" from the far distant past.

A society with the power of the written word can extend itself infinitely in distance and time. It is no coincidence that the hieroglyphics which cover the walls of the great Egyptian temples in Karnak and Luxor are mostly descriptions of the claims of the reigning pharaohs about their political conquests, treasures, and afterlife. The walls also tell us of the jealousy of pharaohs over their predecessors. A powerful new ruler often had his enscriptions carved over those of an earlier ruler.

Although we humans have been in possession of writing for at least 6000 years, literacy did not begin to spread to the masses until after the Renaissance in the Western world. Until a civilization is fully literate, the ability to write and read is a basis for power and influence. For many years in Western civilization, illiteracy was not so much simply the fact that people could not read, but also that there was little available *to* read. Before the invention of printing, books were expensive and scarce commodities.

Of all that has been said about printing, it should also be added that it is the great social equalizer. Whereas writing breaks the barriers of distance and time, printing multiplies our messages into these dimensions. It brings the written word to all who can comprehend it. It encourages those who cannot, to become literate. Cheap printing and cheap paper break down the barriers of social stratification based upon information and knowledge gaps. Cheap printing is the original mass communications technology, the dissemination of messages from "one" to "many," and the "many" need not be at one place in space and time. Certainly the invention of printing was a remarkable step in human history, but it was inexpensive and plentiful paper combined with energy-driven presses that eventually moved the world the most. This made universal literacy practicable. Invention of the linotype in 1885 was another important step. This removed the last highly labor intensive barrier to rapid production of print materials.

The shape of post-Renaissance European civilization owes much to developments in printing, not only in terms of literature, newspapers, pamphlets, or posters, but to textbooks which made possible the secularization of knowledge. The advanced industrial nations of today have their roots in a literate and educated middle class. If mass printing had evolved at a slower pace (say, without the benefits of the Industrial Revolution), we might all still be pursuing crafts and trades or farming the small acreage tilled by our ancestors.

The early electronics era of the telegraph freed communication from the speed of transportation, a limit imposed for most of the 36,000 plus years that we have deserved to be called human. Moreover, the emergence of the telephone, film, and radio allowed us to bypass the written word and to extend our communication senses and capabilities directly. Speech and images could now span distances, be preserved in time, and be multiplied almost infinitely. Television has added greatly to the capacity of these extensions. Although a telegram is just a telegram to us, and the newspaper just provides us with a snapshot of goings-on, a medium like television provides experiences that some users began to confuse with real life. As George Gerbner has reported, people who spent much time with television tend to overestimate crime statistics and to have stereotyped images of vocations often found in TV drama — for example, doctors, police and emergency personnel. Child viewers unfortunately may begin to believe that violence solves problems.

Virtually all of us have personally experienced the direct impact of major TV events such as the Kennedy funeral, moon shots, the Sadat-Begin meetings, the hostage crisis in Iran, or the shootings of Reagan and Pope John Paul II. As is stated several times in this volume, television has gone past the stage of simply being one of the communications media in our lives. It is an environment. Never before in history have 60 to 100 million human beings been in a position to experience simultaneously the same environment.

The computer is the first communications technology to interact intellectually with its users. Most technologies only transform light, sound, or data into electronic impulses for transmission, then reverse the process at the receiving end. Computers, by contrast, can accept or reject our messages, reduce or expand them, file them, index them, or answer back with their own messages. Computers are a programmable technology. We can tell them what we want ("program"), then expect them to carry out our instructions precisely. The merger of communications and computer technologies allows us not only to distribute the power of a computer anywhere the communications links can be established, but also to combine the power of individual computers.

If printing can be said to have planted the roots for formation of mass society, the electronic technologies bring it into full bloom. Society can now expand to the limits of the communications network in distance and time. Whereas for most of human history the communications flow which kept a society functioning moved at the speed of humans or animals, the electronic technologies have boosted this flow to the speed of light. The computer has allowed us to speed up our information processes and to automate many of our methods of information analysis. The new mass society is not only potentially distanceless and simultaneous, but for the first time in human existence our manipulation of knowledge and information need not be accomplished by manual labor. Just as ninteenth-century humans harnessed energy to multiply the printed word, we have harnessed it to gather, manipulate, and interpret information.

Surely in these years leading to the twenty-first century we will be witness to social changes every bit as profound as the technological changes exploding out of the communications revolution. We are on a social acceleration curve.

Meanwhile, my infant son is busy acquiring a language that has evolved throughout most of the existence of our species. His era may experience more changes in human communication — and human and machine communication — than any prior era in history. Certainly this will be accompanied by social changes not even imaginable by me.

At the same time, my son's Doberman puppy barks at birds in a manner identical to his prehistoric ancestors.

THE ELECTRONIC ENVIRONMENT

Prime Time Anytime

CHAPTER **3**

Friday, April 8, 1927 was not a particularly busy news day for the New York *Times*. The main international item was another in a series of insults between the Russians and the Chinese. This time Chinese police had raided offices of a Soviet bank and the Soviet-Chinese railway system in Tientsin, China. As for local items, the *Times* carried a page one story on an experiment set up by American Telephone and Telegraph Company to transmit sounds and moving images by wire and radio. The headlines leading into the article read:

FAR-OFF SPEAKERS SEEN AS WELL AS HEARD HERE IN A TEST OF TELEVISION

Like a Photo Come to Life

Hoover's Face Plainly Imaged as He Speaks in Washington

The First Time in History

Commercial Use in Doubt

Commercial Use in Doubt?

At the beginning of the 1980s nearly 99 percent of all American households had one television set and around 50 percent had two or more. We have more television sets (over 150 million in 1981) than home telephones or automobiles. Home entertainment equipment is currently the fastest growing consumer market area in this country. Within this field, television sets and new accessories lead the way. For example:

- Inexpensive black-and-white sets, some only 25 percent of the price that one had to pay two decades ago.
- Miniature size sets, some hardly larger than a cigarette pack.
- New higher resolution TV signals which may make your current set obsolete but will allow enlargement of TV screens with all of the quality of film images.
- Six foot diagonal TV screens specifically designed for home use.
- TV sets which will "zoom in" (enlarge) a portion of the picture.
- Multiple image TV sets, allowing you to monitor a second program in the corner of your main screen.
- TV sets with controls which respond to your voice commands for on-off, station selection and volume.
- TV with stereo sound.
- TV sets with built-in telephone answering machines.

But of all these innovations, nothing is matching the sale of videocassette recording (VCR) and playback equipment. By the 1980s sales were doubling annually in America with around 2 million machines in use during 1981. In that same year, the Japanese planned to produce 5 million videocassette machines for the world market. Americans have not been the largest relative market; the Saudi Arabians have. In the early 1980s there were probably more video movies watched per home in that Arab kingdom than anywhere in the world. Perhaps this is understandable for a country with no public theaters and (at that time) very little television broadcasting. World-wide estimates hold that one video camera is sold for about every 15 recorder machines.

Machines for recording television materials electronically have been widely available outside the broadcast industry since the mid-1960s. However, most of these were in the hands of educators, business personnel, or hobbyists. If you had any experience with them, you might remember that they were in the repair shop a lot, if you were even lucky enough to have such a shop nearby. You might recall, too, the underground TV movement of two decades ago. Small-scale video recorders were the forte of a generation of antiestablishment communicators affectionately known as *video freaks*. The idea was to break out of the Hollywood mold, which in one instance led to a two-hour show on nothing but bare feet!

With a little tinkering, most of the early tape machines could be used to record programs off the air, but few users chose to do so unless there was a reason for building arc-hives. These machines were not really home devices. Most were a small tape size black-and-white format. Reel-to-reel loading was cumbersome. Lack of standardization made it hazardous to assume that a tape recorded on one machine could be played on another. The machines could go out of adjustment easily so picture quality was often poor. Unless video was your hobby or you took the office machine home for a weekend, most people did not get into home video even though the machines were becoming truly portable.

By the early 1970s cassette versions of these machines became available, but the real breakthrough for home cas-sette (VCR) was the Sony Betamax introduced in 1975. Its mass marketing promoted standardization, although two formats (both developed by Sony) have evolved. Early ex-perience with the machines indicated their reliability. At the start of the 1980s, 20 manufacturers were in the VCR busi-ness. Machines were getting lighter and more compact. Soon cassettes could record programs up to four hours in length. Timers on newer model VCRs could be programmed to record up to four different selections over a week's period. Only two barriers loomed to slow the sales of the increasingly popular home videorecorder — a lawsuit which held that copying programs off the air constituted a copyright infringement, and the emergence of a new, more sophisticated, yet potentially less expensive home playback device, the *videodisc* machine.

As is the case with so much of communications law, the developments in technology exceed the ability of the law to keep up with them. Also, when legislation is promoted it is often highly protective of an existing business, as when broadcasters and theatre owners kept cable television from growing. The same problem arose with videocassette recorders in the 1970s when MCA-Universal (Music Corporation of America) and Walt Disney Productions filed suit against the Sony Corporation and several of its associates holding that home copying of television programs should be illegal because of copyright restrictions. It is no coincidence that MCA at the time was entering the videodisc business, marketing its vast movie and music holdings, or that Disney was remarketing its famous movies via a "family channel" for cable companies.

One key difference between disc and cassette machines is that the former have no home recording capability; but are for playback only. The general fiscal argument given for the legal case was that the value of original program materials to their owners — such as the ability to have advertisers sponsor them — is lost if the public can record programs at will. Late in 1979, a decision was handed down which favored the Sony Corporation and took the position that individuals could copy over-the-air materials for their own use. This was another example of the climate of deregulation in communications in the United States, the philosophy of allowing communications technologies and services to compete openly on the marketplace. An obvious practical reason for the desirability of this decision is that given the flood of videocassette machines in the hands of the public, restrictions on recording would be virtually unenforceable. But in late 1981, an appeals court reversed the 1979 decision and the litigants are prepared to see the case through the Supreme Court as this book goes to press.

> *Look for* further price reductions in VCRs as they are mass produced and eventually face competition from lower priced disc machines. Routinely expect features such as freeze action, fast-forward (where you can monitor the tape contents), improved editing capabilities, thin tape (allowing recordings over six hours duration), and extended capability for presetting the machine to record programs at different times over a week. Watch while theater owners and TV broadcasters squirm.

Programs and Pirates

The biggest business in VCRs is not selling the machines but providing programs for them. Although VCRs were first marketed for watching your favorite shows "when you want to see them" or for seeing them over again, the biggest program appetite has been for prerecorded movies. First-run films have been most popular, followed by classics, and then pornography. All of this, you might think, would be a boon for the movie business. Instead, it has been a nightmare for the marketing and distribution side of the film business. For one, theater operators are immediately cut out of the business which has already seriously been threatened by cable and pay TV. Worse is the problem of retaining proprietary rights over materials once they get into cassette circulation. Cassettes are easy to copy and this has led to the so-called "pirate" market.

When people first lined up to see *Star Wars* once, twice and even five times, it was possible in some parts of the country to purchase it in illegal cassette form for about $50. Other large-scale films, such as *Close Encounters of the Third Kind* and *Superman*, released shortly thereafter were out on pirate cassettes even before they were in the theaters. It has been reported that Cuban Premier Fidel Castro boasts of seeing cassette tapes of most American hit movies at the same time as their premieres in the United States. The TV program *60 Minutes* showed films of customers openly purchasing first-run movies on illegal cassettes in regular retail stores. In some Third World countries you can walk into a video store with a blank cassette and have the movie of your choice dubbed right on the spot. Copies of porn films abound and constitute an increasing share of the pirate market. There is the story of a team who regularly checked into hotels, plugged their VCR into their room's closed circuit television service, and obtained first-run materials for their thriving business in cassettes mailed in "plain brown wrappers." The rare and unusual are especially valued on the underground market. Among these is a pirate tape of the autopsy of Robert Kennedy.

One initial solution for movie makers was to get their own copies of first-run films out in the public marketplace before the pirate market could distribute them. At first, cassette distribution was delayed until a film had played a few months but this has been slowly shrinking to the point where some motion picture companies are releasing their films simultaneously on tape and in theaters. Now another problem has cropped up. People seem to prefer to rent rather than to buy their "legitimate" cassettes. This again cuts the original investor out of most of the distribution profits. Film companies can only charge a limited amount for their tapes lest they drive distributors and customers more deeply into the pirate market. When a cassette rental store turns the same cassette over and over in daily rentals, it is nearly impossible to find a workable way to funnel some percentage of the profits back to the production house. By late 1981 most major "rack sales" record and audiotape stores were in the videocassette rental business and so were thousands of small entreprenuers who were purchasing tape rental franchises.

Look for expansive growth in the prerecorded videocassette market, especially rentals, in Western countries, with prices so attractive that the pirate market will be slowed in its growth. In other countries where distribution networks are difficult to oversee, expect the pirate market to boom. Watch cassette clubs and exchange programs with dealers grow. Along with pay TV, the cassette machine is apt to make your living room the movie theater of tomorrow.

The Disc Invasion

In the mid-1970s there was a great amount of talk in home entertainment circles about the coming of "records" that would provide both sound and a picture. These soon became known as *videodiscs* and the company to watch was the huge entertainment conglomerate, MCA-Universal. Getting a lead on the disc business looked very logical for MCA because of their vast program holdings in feature films and TV series. The system was to be called "DiscoVision" and Magnavox was to build the players. The disc for this system was a plastic-like silvery record which contained some 55,000 concentric rings, each of which could store the information necessary to create a single, fixed television image and enough space for stereophonic sound. These discs are virtually impossible to wear out since a tiny laser beam rather than a needle "reads" them. This disc format, as compared to tape, allows you to move from one frame to any other of 55,000 frames almost instantaneously. Single frames can be combined with motion sequences. The disc has one great disadvantage for the consumer: You cannot record on it. This feature, of course, is of advantage to the manufacturer of discs because without highly expensive equipment you cannot make more discs yourself. (This is ideal for companies such as MCA, but there is still the availability of videocassette copying. No wonder MCA joined in the lawsuit against home copying!)

Although test marketing of the MCA system was supposedly successful at the end of the decade, the machines and the limited number of programs discs were slow (relative to videocassette machines) in catching on. The price was around $800 and discounts were hard to obtain.

The major mass marketing of disc machines was usurped by RCA in early 1981 when they introduced their own "SelectaVision" with a $150 million promotion campaign. The RCA system is simpler and less flexible than the MCA system, its chief disadvantages being a needle which touches the recording surface and the lack of sterophonic sound. The main advantage to the consumer is the RCA machine's lower cost — kept under $500 by the manufacturer. RCA began with the aim of selling about 200,000 machines and about 2 million discs per year. With a large and experienced marketing network, RCA has hoped to capture the disc market. They see that market reaching up to $8 billion by the late 1990s.

A third system was due in late 1981 from the Matsushita Company of Japan, the manufacturer of several well-known electronics lines (such as Panasonic). As the trend seems to be, it is incompatible with the other two.

In the meantime, the foregoing companies have been entering into partnerships with other giants at the rate of one or two a year, including with CBS, Inc., IBM, and General Electric, to name a few.

Disc systems, particularly of the optical (MCA) type, offer considerable flexibility in how an image is retrieved. In advanced versions, it is possible to request by number any of the 55,000 images encoded as each ring of the disc. (In "freeze frame" the machine simply repeats the same ring instead of moving to the next.) The playback apparatus goes across the disc directly to that ring, making it possible to locate and display the "pages" of a disk faster than is possible in thumbing through a book or catalog. It is also quite possible to combine on one disc selections where images are in motion with those that are only single frames. In 1981 Sears Roebuck and Company field tested a disc version of their catalog which included models strolling around in the latest swim fashions. Eventually it will be possible to freeze frame any instant of this sequence to provide a code number which would allow you to order the merchandise.

The capability for selecting 55,000 different images on the disc gives it a remarkable potential as an instructional medium. Production is already underway to create "how-to-do-it" lessons, ranging from auto repair to golf swings. As an academic instructional device, course materials can be programmed in sequence, as can intermittent quizzes.

Obviously tape and disc will not stand still in the next decade. Although the price has been coming down on videocassette equipment since the late 1970s, the declining value of the dollar relative to the Japanese yen (Japan being where much electronic equipment is manufactured) has slowed reductions. Also, unlike equipment which is nearly entirely electronic (such as pocket calculators) and still falling in price in tandem with increasingly less expensive electronic technology, VCRs and disc systems incorporate mechanical components which will keep them at certain minimum price levels.

Disc and tape may in many cases be vying for the same markets. If most uses are for only playback of available prerecorded materials, and eventually more complex interactive systems involving single images, quick access, or varying orders of materials, disc will be the appropriate equipment. Disc is also less expensive than tape. Where recording capabilities are required, disc cannot compete with tape. It is likely that in many instances educational institutions, businesses, and even enthusiasts in home entertainment will have both.

Market studies of videocassettes suggest a strong move into the home movie business. Although the one-time cost of a VCR and camera combination greatly exceeds that of a motion picture projector and camera, the cost of an hour of color video production is quite inexpensive as compared with the costs of individual movie films, the charge for processing, and considering the fact that the films run only a few minutes. Moreover, the tape can be monitored as it is shot, stopped, reshot, and eventually the cassette can be used over again if desired. Home movie makers will certainly invest in tape before disc.

Some market analysts have felt that aggressive marketing of disc machines will result in increased sales of cassette machines, perhaps even more so than disc. The reasoning is that individuals who have not yet invested in home video systems will see tape as more to their advantage once they have decided to buy equipment. The Sony Corporation, not yet in the disc business in the early 1980s, advertises this proposition widely.

Look for both tape and disc to grow in the 1980s and 1990s, especially tape in home installations and disc in institutional settings. Competition between them as well as among disc formats is likely to be fierce with some large corporate losers. Disc use should grow also in combination with computer applications (certain disc systems and computers can "talk" to one another). In the long run, home entertainment may take the way of LP and 45 rpm records of yesteryear. People may go the "components" route and have both. Anyway you look at it, a lot of us will have more video options in the home. Are you ready for prime time *anytime*?

CHAPTER 4

Down to the Wire

The "wired society" notion so bandied about in the 1970s is becoming a reality in the 1980s and 1990s with the explosive growth of cable television in this country. Although the telephone long ago literally wired us together, its carrying capacity is restricted and until recently we have used it in a limited fashion. The new growth of cable, with 20 to 40 and more channels and the potential for two-way communications, promises us a range of services from the latest entertainment to buying shoes.

The history of cable TV would make the basis for a great soap opera. It has all the ingredients of prime-time drama, from small town businessmen who wired up community TV antenna systems to giant corporations now buying up cable franchises in the $100 to $200 million dollar range. The same TV network executives who were supporting regulation against cable in the courts and belittling it in public are often now found heading new cable programming services. Down in Louisiana they are watching a lot more porn movies than ever before — right in the living room.

Discovering the Communications Business

Many experts thought that cable TV would grow significantly in the late 1960s. Before that period, regulatory barriers to development raised by theater owners and broadcasters, the lack of investment capital, and the high costs of delivering program materials around the country all had inhibited the growth of cable. Much of the prior attitude toward cable TV is summed up in its acronym CATV, which stands for "Community Antenna Television." An anecdote attributes its beginnings around 1949 to a TV repairman near Philadelphia who solved his community's poor reception of a single channel by wiring the homes to a master antenna on a nearby hill. As cable slowly but steadily developed in the 1950s and 1960s, subscriptions were mainly sold to improve TV reception. Entrepreneurship was mainly in the hands of individuals who, although they knew the transmission technology, never understood that they could be in the communications business. They failed to realize that bringing multiple channel "broadband" telecommunications right into a home only scratched the surface of the marketing opportunities for communications services.

Although cable did grow throughout the 1970s, the picture did not come close to the expectations of planners, consultants, and writers who foresaw a whole new range of program services available to all, "public access" channels open for use by diverse groups in our society, and a "new rural society" whereby businesses could decentralize using telecommunications networks. But by the end of that decade things were opening up. Broadcasters were defeated in their attempt to restrain cable as an economic threat to their industry. The Federal Communications Commission, after a major study of the matter, denied that threat and gave all signs that open competition would be the name of the game. By the beginning of the 1980s, cable was finally a big and expanding business. Estimated total revenues were $2.4 billion in 1980, up about twice the $1.4 billion in 1978. Reflecting an "if you can't fight 'em, join them" attitude, CBS, RCA, and ABC have all moved aggressively into the cable TV business. They are joined by such other giants as Westinghouse, American Express, Times-Mirror, Time, Inc., and the New York Times Co., to name a few. Cable franchises which were set up 20 years ago for a few hundred thousand dollars are now going for over $100 million. Owning a cable franchise has been compared to having a franchise on a city's streets.

Estimates of the growth of cable are that 50 percent of about 95 million projected households in 1990 will be purchasing cable services. In the early 1980s cable penetration was a little over 20 percent of 77 million households. This projected threefold increase is combined with an expanded range of services which can be delivered over the hookup. The problem of getting programs to cable operators has now been largely solved by satellite distribution, which is in itself a big business (see Chapter 6).

The expansion of cable programs and services may be more exciting than the explosive growth of the subscriber lists. After two decades of mainly retransmitting existing TV signals — the old "antenna" notion — we are witnessing a whole new range of program material. These include:

- an all news network
- special arts and cultural channels
- an all sports channel
- special movie channels for classics to soft porn
- religious channels
- a woman's channel
- channels for children's programs
- foreign language channels
- programs from the BBC
- programs from out of town independent stations
- a "pay" legitimate theater channel
- coverage of Congress in session
- special stereophonic continuous music channels
- stock market reports

The foregoing do not include the diverse services which can be offered when the cable hookup has a "two-way" capability; that is, when you can send signals from your house back to the station.

The best known example of a two-way system has been the "Qube" service initiated by Warner Communication (now Warner-Amex) in December 1977 in Columbus, Ohio. A push-button response pad allows you to participate in "live" audience surveys, to answer quiz show questions, to "vote," to bid in auctions and even take tests for college courses. You can view setups of football plays, then vote on what you think the coach should do. In one demonstration, Qube's subscribers had the chance to register their opinions about food labeling practices with an official of the U.S. Food and Drug Administration. Warner-Amex had yet to turn a profit on Qube by late 1981 but the service has drawn international attention to the potential of two-way cable services. Some of the services which now exist or are on the planning boards include:

- shopping via TV, including ordering from home
- emergency warning systems for fire, police, medical aid
- burgler alarms
- banking
- travel reservations
- consumer and political polls
- games
- text information services
- interactive instruction
- stock market transactions
- home computer services
- theater and sports event ticket purchasing

Look for continued explosive growth in the "wiring-up" of cable television networks in this country. Cable is rapidly becoming the business of any large corporation that sees communications networks as part of its expansion plans (watch American Express) or can afford a long range investment (watch petroleum companies). Now that the federal government is deregulating communications and the traditional networks are further threatened by the new technologies, expect the big communications companies to move into cable from all directions. Watch how cable franchise dollars heat up local politics. As a consumer, expect to be wooed by everything from blockbuster movies to burglar alarms from your newly aggressive cable operator. But also watch the industry question the market viability of complex services. The next decade will determine whether the public is truly interested in spending their time with two-way TV activities. The new leaders in the cable business definitely know what business they want to be in.

Why Cable?

Why not send some of these services over the telephone lines? AT&T would love to get into the information-providing business but two things stand in their way. First, telephone companies by law are regulated as carriers, not providers, of communications content. The laws would have to change but they are being bent already (see Chapter 5). Then there is the technical problem. Cable television systems and telephone networks are just about as different as two wired systems could be. Relatively speaking, the telephone wire in the home has only about one-thousandth the information carrying capacity of an average TV cable. The former is designed to transmit sufficiently intelligible speech, the latter is particularly designed to carry multiple and broadband signals. (Broadband, as the name implies, is a high capacity communications channel, technically one that can carry more than a voice signal.) For example, one television channel on a cable can carry up to 600 different telephone conversations or 100 stereo music programs. Many existing cables carry 20 television channels, some up to 40. A 40-channel TV cable could replace over 24,000 telephone lines.

On the other hand, why not run the telephone through the cable TV system? The problem here is that telephones are connected by *switched* networks, meaning that every point on the network can be linked for two-way communications with every other. In early telephony, individual phones were wired to each other, but if you think for a moment that gets to be very complicated (if not impossible) very early on. Instead, phone wires all meet at central points where they can be interconnected and disconnected at switchboards. This is a much more complex system than feeding TV signals down a main trunk line with branches into subscriber's homes. Even two-way cable systems like Qube are much simpler than the switching systems required in a telephone network. If the telephone network were upgraded to much greater signal carrying capacity, then you could receive television programs via your home phone line (see Chapter 8). If cable systems were to serve telephone users, this would require replacing the entire network with a switched one; very impractical. But as for the opposite, keep your eye on the telephone company.

Why send broadcast signals over cables, rather than over the air? One answer is the reason for the early development of cable TV. People wanted to use TV sets in remote areas where no signals could be received, or in crowded urban areas where there was too much interference. A more important and long-range answer is that we are running out of channel space in the broadcast spectrum. TV signals, as we have already said, consume much more channel space than voice signals, which themselves use much more space than digital data signals. If television programs could be disseminated via cable networks, then much over-the-air space could be effectively used for other rapidly growing types of communication, mobile telephones, for example. Also, if interactive types of programming, like the Qube system discussed earlier, are to grow in use, the costs for setting up two-way broadcast communications links, including the equipment needed in the home, are very much greater than if done with a wired system. Another particularly business-oriented reason for cable is that it protects the proprietary nature of whatever is sent over the system.

Satellite communications have been both a boon and a threat to cable television. One long-standing problem in cable operation was the cost of importing program packages to put into the system. Transmission was costly over commercial communications networks, as were delivery services for films or videotapes. Satellite communications have allowed cable operators to bypass these problems by offering economically feasible as well as dependable transmission services to virtually anywhere. "Home Box Office" (HBO) was the first major program origination and dissemination pay TV service that used a satellite network for transmission.

The threat posed to cable comes from the fact that we have reached the point where direct broadcasting from satellite to home is quite feasible. Because of their frequency characteristics, the communication channels used by satellite still have some room to grow. Why should a program distribution company sell its wares to a cable operator or even a local TV station when they could deliver them directly via satellite to the customer in the home? Again there is the problem of protecting the proprietary nature of the program and the likely use of scrambling and decoding systems. Cable entrepreneurs argue that their ability to offer 20 to 40 channels of programs and services, including interactive ones, is far more attractive to the home customer than one or two pay-TV channels received via direct broadcast satellite.

> *Look for* clash of the giants in competition to deliver telecommunications services to your home. If telephone deregulation continues — and once it is fully started, it will be impossible to stop — look for telephone companies to become information providers. (Electronic Yellow Pages and ads will be a good first step.) Satellite networks will not be content to sell transmission time only to cable operators when they could broker programs direct to you. Bear in mind also that it may be most convenient to watch movies from tape or disc. Given continued deregulation, the consumer will no doubt decide the winner among these delivery systems. After all, consumers couldn't care less how they get a program or service. They only want it to work and to be the best they can get for their money. Worry if you are an investor in a traditional TV station.

Corn, Porn or ?

What about the *content* of cable television programming? Some of the altruistic dreams in the 1960s and 1970s were that cable could bring us a rich array of culturally and intellectually rewarding programs. It could bring us a rich array of culturally and intellectually rewarding programs. It could also make television more a medium of the people than of the networks. In the early days of cable, many community activists hoped that some of the many channels would be given over to local, even neighborhood, broadcasting. Given that mass communications are typically in the hands of big business and reflect that view of society, there was a movement to require as part of franchise agreements that cable operators save channels for local programming, including access by groups wishing to get their "messages" on the air. Civil libertarian organizations won a legal battle to include such requirements in regulations handed down by the Federal Communications Commission. Presumably, if the everyday population could "get on TV," we might begin to have a clearer image of our culture.

A number of major cable operators subsequently opened up "public access" channels, thus extending this mass medium to use by local groups as well as filling out a regular program schedule. The problem, however, has been that with only some exception the public use of such channels never really got off the ground. Production quality of public access programming, as compared with the usually glossy fare of network prime time, was so poor that few people ever watched (including the people who produced the programs). The most frequently watched public access programming has often been the weird, the outlandish, or outright lewd.

Mostly in the 1960s and 1970s, cable television brought us just more of what was already available over the air if you were in a major broadcast market and could receive a good signal. Public access and other types of local or special programming were never supported with much enthusiasm by cable operators nor would they be unless they became the basis for new revenues. But the dream of cable television offering us high quality, specialized programs may become a reality. The only hitch is that you will have to pay for them. Two commercial uses of cable TV will probably shape its future programming more than any other factors: "pay cable" and the selling of advertising time.

Paying for the programs you see is, of course, not restricted to cable television. Such programs can come over the air, as they do in many cities; you gain access to them by using an unscrambling device. The problem for companies selling over-the-air pay television is that these devices can be duplicated by people who have a modest degree of electronics knowledge. (Diagrams and parts can sometimes be found on the open market.) Also there has been some disagreement over whether people who make or sell "unlicensed" scrambling devices are actually violating the law. One small manufacturer openly advertised his "pirate" television decoder system. The argument is that once something is broadcast, it is there for anybody to use, even if they have to use special means to "decode" it. So why should selling decoders be illegal?

Pay TV over cable is much more secure in terms of program theft. Moreover, with two-way cable systems in the wings, the cable network can automate billing systems based upon records of programs or services which are ordered.

At the beginning of the 1980s, Home Box Office (owned by Time, Inc.) dominated the pay-TV business with about half of the near eight million subscribers in the United States. Most of their business has been with movies so it was not unexpected that they (along with Showtime [Viacom International, Inc.] and Teleprompter, Inc.) objected when the Getty Oil Co. and four movie companies started "Premiere," a movie channel that would exclusively distribute the films of those producers. The films would be kept off other pay-TV systems for a period of nine months. The Premiere venture was short lived, however, because it ran afoul of antitrust laws — both on its likely effect on price-fixing and withholding the films from market. Although Premiere never got on the air, it illustrated both the desire of a high-revenue,

investment-seeking company to get into a new type of communications business, as well as the attempt of major film
companies to regain control over the distribution of their
products by a new technology. In the meantime, CBS and
ABC have inaugurated arts and culture programming services, there are new sports channels, and even the Public
Broadcasting Service (PBS) has proposed getting into the pay
cable business.

Although the advertising revenue of cable operations
was only about $30 million in 1981 compared with the net-
works' $11 billion, the potential for cable as an advertising
medium is brightening. It has three advantages. One is that a
well organized cable company will know the market characteristics of its subscribers and be able to offer an advertiser
an opportunity to reach specialized markets as contrasted
with mass marketing. Advertising can be even more
specialized for the particular program channel — for example, cultural events as against sports.

A second advantage is that cable companies do not have
to operate under the advertising restrictions of over-the-air
broadcasters. Ads can be as long as an operator thinks people would watch them. They can be "ad-informational," a
combination of promotion and information, as in how to do
a home repair job.

Finally, there can also be entire programs which may
indirectly support a product. The ultimate may be channels
devoted solely to the selling of goods. When two-way cable
reaches a sufficient number of subscribers to make it
economically viable, chances look good for the development
of "electronic catalogs," where you can "thumb" through
pages of electronic pictures and text, then place your order
right from your television set.

The specialized interests of cable subscribers is leading to
what those in the industry call "narrowcasting," or assignment of a distinctive type of programming to each channel,
somewhat akin to the way urban radio has its all-news, hard
rock, soft rock, classical, or religious stations. Qube has a

large number of movie channels but they distinguish among them for showing adult films, action and adventure movies (called "Drive in"!), "Classics and Encores" where old greats are shown, and several channels showing only first-run movies. There is a children's channel, a news channel, and so on.

Currently the communications trade papers almost weekly describe new "packages" available for cable systems. We already have a total news channel including a two-hour live newscast at prime time. Others are collections of children's programming, including packages offered by Disney and Warners. Also there are "all sports" services which will sell signals to cable owners. We have already mentioned the programming services of Home Box Office and Showtime.

Another trend is to import signals from distant stations, which leads the originating stations, or "superstations," to program in ways attractive to disparate regions of the country. Superstation signals are easily distributed to operators via satellite. The cable operator's fee is small, on the order of ten cents per cable subscriber per month. There are proprietary problems arising from such questions as whether the original producers of program materials, including performers, should be compensated for further sale of their materials to cable owners. Also there are problems in determining schedules of compensation to a station whose signal is further transmitted by satellite and cable.

Some of the services available through cable television are attracting investment capital from cities and from institutions (such as universities) interested in being wired into homes. Developers of apartment or condominium units and planned communities are interested in closed circuit channels for their own local use. There have been plans to wire all homes in a community to a cable network which in addition to usual TV programming would link to fire, police and emergency medical centers. Smoke and heat sensors would alert fire department personnel. Detectors for break-ins or unauthorized entry could send signals directly to computer monitors in police headquarters. Emergency medical instructions would be available almost instantaneously over the network. It is estimated that homeowner fees could pay off the initial debt in approximately seven years. Also there would be reduced costs of fire and police services and homeowner insurance rates.

We have already mentioned shopping services over a cable system. When viewers see a product on TV that they would like to buy, the purchase can be signaled by feedback into the system. In more sophisticated systems, the viewer should be able to call for catalog "pages," many of which could be short video segments in color and motion. Orders would then be signaled directly from the home.

Another promising use is information service. Here the user signals a request, say, for airline schedules to be fed into the home TV set in text form. Such systems operate by storing the information in large computer data bases to which the cable subscriber can be linked. Whether these systems will develop under the auspices of cable operators or telephone companies (see Chapter 8) is a matter of current debate. The largest experiments with them, as with "Prestel" in Great Britain, have been conducted by telephone companies.

Not all experts on the cable market agree that such services as purchasing or textual information will be popular with the public. Such services could be more a novelty to the public than anything else, and might be rejected in any large-scale marketing effort. Moreover, it is hard to conceive of an individual spending great amounts of time reading information from a home-size TV screen.

Nonetheless, current or planned services with cable television include:

- continuously broadcast sports "scoreboard"
- public libraries offering reference services
- simple coverage of local government meetings, school boards, and the like, somewhat the way Congress now covers its sessions

- late, late or very early morning feed of programs meant for home videotaping and playback at convenient times
- price comparison services for shoppers
- regular educational offerings which allow the student to interact with the materials (for instance, exam taking)
- electronically organized "town meetings" where participants can register their opinions by button pressing
- up to 100 music channels continuously available over a cable system
- electronic classified ads which you can respond to via interactive cable
- general as well as customized news services, eventually competing seriously with traditional newspapers (Why shouldn't the newswire go directly into the home?)
- quiz games developed around electronic participation of the viewers
- channels with programming developed for major religious faiths
- channels which will provide computer programs or will interact with the new breed of small, home computers

Look for growing competition in cable services, especially a wide mix of programs vying for the pay cable dollar. Current estimates indicate that there may be more programming and special services coming than the public will buy. If so, look for cable TV content to regress to many of the characteristics of current over-the-air television, ads and all. The same TV network executives who warned us that cable would have us paying for what we have gotten "free" may be the same ones planning just that future for us in their new cable jobs. If deregulation continues, look for telephone companies to get into information and purchasing services over phone lines. The race with cable TV for your own communications dollars may literally get down to the wire!

Goodbye POTS

When you think of "big" in business you inevitably must think about the American Telephone and Telegraph Company, affectionately known as "Ma Bell." AT&T is the world's largest corporation with assets around $115 billion in the early 1980s. With its over one million employees, it is second only to the U.S. government as an employer. Income on annual revenues works out to an average of about $15.5 million *per day.* To its critics, AT&T is an out-of-control corporate behemoth capable of squashing everything in its path. To its praisers, AT&T has brought the United States the world's best telephone service. To most people (about 80 percent) in this country it *is* "the telephone company." Whatever happens to telephone services in this country will also be a description of what happened to AT&T.

Times are changing. New communications technologies have far outdistanced the Communications Act of 1934, which set up the telephone monopoly in this country. It is now more the hoped for breakthroughs in obsolete regulation than the advances in technology that will govern the future of telephone and related services in the United States.

The old monopoly is being chipped away as new companies have used antitrust arguments to win a share of the telephone business. Even the U.S. government has taken AT&T to court with the objective of breaking it up into smaller companies so as to open up competition in the telephone and telecommunications businesses. AT&T, in turn, is proposing new, unrelated businesses for itself. Joking, some say that if the Communications Act ever is revised, it should be called the "AT&T Act." Now it is all breaking loose. As they say in the trade, it's goodbye "Plain Old Telephone Service."

Take it or Leave it?

The revolution in communications technologies — satellite, computers, data transmission systems — has for over two decades antiquated the monopolistic structure of the telecommunications business in this country. Arguments for maintaining, if not strengthening, the monopoly draw heavily upon the necessity to protect massive investments in existing facilities and incentive for their upkeep. Another persuasive argument to politicians is that protection of the monopoly will keep home telephone service reliable and inexpensive. Yet these laws have hampered the growth of new telecommunications services. Telephone companies both here and abroad have been among the slowest of modern institutions to adopt a consumer-oriented marketing strategy. "Here's the service, take it or leave it" has been a long time attitude, not unlike that of a typical utility such as the water or power company.

Part of the recent changes date to when telecommunications planners saw numerous new advantages in interconnecting different communications devices — such as mobile radio, computer systems, intercoms — with the existing telephone system. Until 1968 nothing could be legally connected to telephone lines or even indirectly linked with telephone sets in this country unless it was the property of the telephone company. (Litigation on "foreign" devices even once extended to dust covers which a company wanted to market for telephone books!) You could not buy accessories such as answering devices nor purchase decorator phones from the local department store.

In the early 1960s the Carter Electronics Corporation, which manufactured a device for connecting a mobile radio system to the telephone system, was cited by AT&T for violating the tariff prohibiting "foreign" equipment connections. Carter retaliated in 1966 with an antitrust action against AT&T. The resolution was left to the Federal Communications Commission, which in a 1968 landmark decision in the Carter Company's favor declared interconnections would be allowed so long as they did not adversely affect operations of the telephone system.

The Carterphone decision as well as several others have reflected the latest U.S. philosophy that competition would be beneficial for the advancement of telecommunications in the United States. Virtually overnight new markets were created for communications equipment. This has nudged the world's largest telephone company along faster into the *communications* business. AT&T created a marketing department in 1973 and by 1978 had a $2.1 billion budget earmarked to advance its products and services.

If you think that the Carterphone case was a David-and-Goliath encounter, consider the MCI Communications Corporation's victory in an antitrust suit against AT&T. MCI had charged that AT&T had used illegal practices to bar them from entering into the long distance telephone market. MCI won and was awarded $1.8 billion in damages. MCI's annual revenue that same year was only about $144 million!

The telephone business has gotten more lively for the American consumer now that there is more than one phone company in town. In the 1970s and 1980s, a great many new services and gadgets became available to the telephone user. One of the most burgeoning markets has been in telephone answering machines, some of which have broken well below the $100 barrier. Since incoming calls can be heard over the loud speaker of most answering devices, many people find themselves using the machine even when they are home simply to screen out which calls they prefer not to answer on the spot. More sophisticated machines allow you to call in from another number, then trigger a signal which will activate the playback mechanism allowing you to check for phone messages without ever coming home. The machines are also useful for leaving "voice-grams" for the other party. On the negative side is that you can wind up calling back and forth between answering machines for days before you get the real person!

Another popular market has been in decorator and specialty telephones. Although department stores and electronics shops have moved heavily into the decorator phone market, AT&T's Bell System has not stood idly by. They have their "Phone Center" stores, usually located in mall or high traffic areas so as to promote impulse buying. One very popular specialty phone is cordless, having been designed to operate on a radio linkage so it can be carried anywhere, or as they say in the ad, "out to the pool."

Services currently or soon available to subscribers include:

- *call forwarding:* your incoming calls can be routed to another number.

- *call waiting:* when you are already on the line, a signal will indicate that somebody is trying to reach you; you can interrupt your conversation to acknowledge the caller.

- *speed dialing:* allows you to call your most frequent numbers by using only the first several digits.

- *conferencing:* whereas the operator can bring a number of people on the line for a conference call, you will be able to set up a three-party call by yourself.

- *international direct distance dialing:* available for a few years now, this will be constantly extended to new areas.

- *funds transfer:* now offered by some banks, this allows you to pay bills by phone (on some systems this can be done by pressing codes on push-button telephones) or to transfer funds from one account to another.

- *repeat dialing:* now available on some commercially available instruments, this will redial a number at regular intervals if it is originally found busy.

- *remote dictation:* several word processing systems are available now which allow you to phone in to a dictation system which can be controlled by push-button telephones.

- *personal number:* you, not just your telephone, will have an address number; you will be able to easily change where your number can be reached.

- *mobile services:* new technologies will greatly increase current capacities for mobile telephone services.

Look for aggressive marketing of telephone services by companies competing with AT&T. ("If you want to reach out and touch someone, why not do it cheaper with us?") This is already happening with long distance rates. Expect also to see continued growth in aggressive sales of telephones with special features, not only for services such as assistance in dialing, call holding, and the like, but for decorator purposes with as much variety available as in dishware or home furnishings designs. Anticipate significant marketing efforts to have customers "invest" in their own telephones, to have them "rent free." Selling just the phones is getting to be big business. POTS is long gone.

Vanishing Videophones

Even as far back as the 1870s and the invention of the telephone, there was the expectation that someday people would be able to communicate over wires visually as well as by voice. Many of the major early advances in the science of sending moving images electronically had been the work of engineers of the American Telephone and Telegraph Company. In 1927 when President Hoover's image and voice were (simultaneously) transmitted from Washington to New York City, there was speculation that "television" might complete what Alexander Graham Bell had started with his telephone.

One of the star attractions of the 1964 New York World's Fair, 37 years later, was AT&T's *Picturephone*™. Accompanying publicity packets heralded it as the next great step in home and business communication service. A company vice-president declared its development as equal to the invention of the telephone itself. Yet over the next two decades very few *Picturephones* were ever put into use. Mostly they could be found in demonstration or business environments; none went into home use.

One reason for lack of growth was the high price, about ten times the rate of normal audio service. Another is that at first people are uneasy when they are suddenly "on camera." Seeing women poke at their hair or men constantly tweaking their noses when trying out video telephones is remindful of natives shouting "Are you there?" when telephones are demonstrated in remote areas of developing countries. Nobody, it seems, ever thought much about whether people really wanted to see each other when they talked on the phone or what types of adaptation it would take to be comfortable in doing so.

Home use of the video telephone, if it ever develops, is likely to be a bit different and evolve more slowly than most experts would have predicted 20 years ago. Some scenarios show it developing along with integration of television, video recording, and telephone components into overall home entertainment and communications systems. Videophone will probably never be important for those everyday telephone conversations with close friends, for making (or breaking) appointments, or telling the kids to come home. On the other hand, there are situations where the exchange of images is important, such as in shopping from catalogs, or attending meetings via a video link. Surely those monthly calls to parents or grandparents would benefit from a video exchange. Family members could catch up on how much the children have grown, photographs and videotape segments could be shared, and all images displayed lifelike on a wall-sized television screen. All these are yet to come.

Where the video telephone seems to be catching on now is in business and organizational settings where it is among the communications devices used in *teleconferencing*. This allows groups to gather in two or more locations and be linked by audio, video, facsimile, and data communications, or any combination of these. AT&T's version of this is called their "Picturephone Meeting Service." For some time now you could arrange with the telephone company or other telecommunications providers to link up meeting places for conference services. Some companies have already installed their own systems. In 1981 AT&T's service could be installed on your premises for a little over $100,000 and a monthly charge of about $12,000. Or else you could set your teleconferences up in sites operated by one of the Bell companies. It will be interesting to learn over the next decade how successfully you can conduct meetings over teleconferencing facilities. Already there are many success reports but the widespread use of teleconferencing has yet to happen. Perhaps rising transportation costs more than the attractiveness of video telephone links will bring the change (see Chapter 13 for more on teleconferencing).

Don't *look for* much in the way of home video telephone services for a long time to come, if ever. Until they become so inexpensive that customers cease to feel that price is a barrier, the added video link to a telephone call probably will not be worthwhile to most people. On the other hand, indications are that video teleconferencing is on a growth curve in business and government. If you are in one of those kinds of offices, be ready to smile when your phone rings.

An Uncommon Carrier

As you probably know, telephone service in this country is regulated as a *common carrier*, the business of transporting signals — anybody's signals. Many of the services which AT&T would like to offer, and which they could bring to market rapidly and efficiently, are beyond the range of the common carrier business. For example, AT&T is a developer and world leader in uses of electronic computers, yet they have been barred since 1956 from getting into the data processing business. Such a business would not fit logically nor legally under the current interpretations of "common carrier." However, what if AT&T simply started some business branches which were not regulated? The problem is that the incredible financial clout of AT&T would allow it to monopolize nearly any business it wanted to enter, and it would be doing this with profits earned and protected under its status in the regulated telephone business.

The way around this impass, and the one passed by the Senate in late 1981 (but still pending in the House as this book goes to press), is to allow AT&T to set up "fully separated, affiliate" companies — "Baby Bells," as they say on Wall Street — which, although unregulated, could have a "regulated" amount of investment flow from AT&T. Some form of this legislation seems destined to make its way into law. No matter the consequences on the pending antitrust suit or revision of the Communications Act, we are in for a profound change in the telecommunications and allied businesses in this country. The "Baby Bell" plan is discussed also in conjunction with allowing AT&T to enter into the data processing business.

You probably have never thought of the telephone company as a "publisher," but by the time you count up the number of telephone books in homes, AT&T ranks among the largest. Moreover, the "Yellow Pages" are a significant source of advertising income, which puts the telephone company into competition with newspapers, magazines, and broadcasting. Although it is doubtful that AT&T wants to do more of this traditional publishing, it is very clear that they could become almost instantly the nation's largest "electronic" publisher. The first obvious candidate would be to make the *Yellow Pages* available over telephone lines so entries could be displayed on your television screen (or a screen which AT&T might sell with an entire home communications center). If they offered such services, why not add news headlines, sports scores or classified advertising (all to the horror of newspaper owners)? In fact, why shouldn't they offer a comprehensive range of wired services, including remote shopping, banking and emergency warning systems? (Pity the newspaper owner who bought into cable TV to survive!) As a common carrier, AT&T is supposedly barred from selling what they might put into the communications system. But by 1982 they had attempted field experiments in the delivery of textual information services and were already advertising themselves as being in the "knowledge" business.

Even more underway is the expansion of mobile telephone service, a regulated area where AT&T has been given the lion's share of the market. Calling from your car has traditionally involved making a radio connection with a transmitter-receiver which covers a large area and is restricted in the number of conversations which can be handled at the same time. In New York City, for example, only 24 calls could go on simultaneously. New broadcast and switching technologies have made it possible to blanket a mobile service area with many low-powered radio links, each covering a relatively small area or "cell." The cellular grid is served by switching equipment which allows a caller to move from area to area without interruption. This makes it possible to increase the number of calls many thousands-fold, to several hundred thousand, for example, in New York City.

In early 1981 the Federal Communications Commission approved the development of cellular services and awarded half of the available broadcast frequencies to AT&T. Their reason for the award was that AT&T had the capital and know-how to get the service going rapidly, yet the remaining 50 percent of the frequencies would leave enough room for sufficient competition. AT&T plans to have cellular mobile telephone service operating in 70 cities by the mid-1980s. There is already talk of a portable "pocketphone."

Look for a steady flow of new and competing products and services from AT&T and its competitors. The odds are overwhelming that parts of the Bell system will be deregulated and this will drastically alter the telecommunications scene in this country. You may receive two or three simultaneous phone bills in the future — one for your regulated service, one for competitive services, and one for equipment. Look for change, too, in the long-running antitrust case against AT&T as well as in attempted rewrites of the Communications Act of 1934. The logjam is now breaking. If deregulation is restrained, the United States will begin to lag even further behind the other industrialized nations of the world in the flow of telecommunications innovations from lab to market. (You can bet this would make the Japanese the happiest manufacturers in the telecommunications world!)

CHAPTER 6

Rockets, Birds, and Dishes

In ancient times those who controlled the roads and caravan routes held the power. In the fifteenth through the nineteenth centuries, control of the seas was a basis for power. In the twenty-first century whoever controls the international electronic networks will surely wield the power. The key to those global networks is the communications satellite, three of which, if properly positioned, could communicate with every square inch of our earth's surface.

Already we have earth satellites carrying our telephone calls. Perhaps you have already experienced the momentary lag in an international conversation while your voice is making a 44,600 miles round trip into space. Satellites photograph weather patterns and defense installations. They are the bases of international computer and data networks. Now that the United States Space Shuttle is operational, we may soon see the construction of giant satellites which have already been dubbed "communications platforms." Some of the services made possible by large satellites include:

- a worldwide communications network linking all individuals on earth by means of wristwatch-sized communication units;
- improved broadcasting of radio and television directly from satellite to rooftop dishes on homes or apartment buildings;
- communications networks for business and government, significantly reducing costs of teleconferences, electronic mail, and sharing of computer data;

- greatly improved electronic aids to navigation including hand-held ones;
- monitoring systems for weather, air pollution, energy usage, military movements, animal migrations;
- the teaming up of large computer and data systems for computer assisted management or design;
- linkage of small hand-held computer terminals, like pocket calculators, with sources of information such as banking records, the stock market, transportation scheduling, a library of games, or useful computer programs;
- movement toward electronic mail systems where electron movement replaces paper movement;
- nationwide educational communications network, one capable of supplying instructional materials from a central library, of supporting computer-assisted instructional systems now too costly for schools, even systems which can link into the home.

From "Echo" to "Intelsats"

Satellites alone do not make all of these advances possible. It takes large rockets to put the "birds" into orbit and for many years the size of our satellites was limited by the size of the available rockets. It also takes earth stations or "dishes" to send and receive the satellite signals. The bigger the satellite (broadcasting power) the smaller the dish.

The history of communications satellites is very recent, intense in events, and as dramatic as were the first "beeps" from Sputnik in October 1957. You may recall that very shortly after Sputnik the Russians had a dog in orbit, his life functions being monitored by the world press. The United States, smitten by these events, stepped up its satellite development program and got into space by January 1960 with a grapefruit-sized satellite called "Vanguard."

During those early years of the space race there was little public talk of what satellites would do for us. To most of the public they were spectacular firsts as well as heightening the anticipation of putting humans into orbit. Little coverage was given in the press about using these artificial "moons" to relay communication signals on earth. Yet in the next several decades, *communications* became a major growth area for satellites and the first such use to become commercially successful.

In the spring of 1960 many of us stood on our front lawns and caught glimpses of "Echo I," an aluminum-coated plastic balloon some 100 feet in diameter orbiting 1000 miles above earth. Echo I was an experiment in relaying broadcast messages between the United States and Europe. Although it was only a passive surface for reflecting broadcast signals back to earth which otherwise would escape into space, Echo I was a kind of "communications" device. Perhaps more significant, however, was the fact that it could be seen in the night sky. It was only a bright speck, but watching Echo move against a background of well known stars and knowing that it was an object of human making gave one a direct and personal sense of its reality. Knowledge of its presence did not depend on newspaper accounts. It was there for everyone to see; it was visible evidence of what we could do with space technology. Although Echo I (and Echo II in 1964) was so technically unsophisticated that some would not include it as a consequential step in the evolution of communication satellites, it was a spectacular public show.

In the same period there were experiments with small, "active" (that is, able to receive and send signals rather than just reflect them) satellites — "Score," "Courier," "Relay" and "Telstar." Of these, AT&T's Telestar received the greatest publicity. Using power from its solar cells, Telstar could receive, amplify and retransmit signals for television, telephone, and data. Telstar was an important step for a number of reasons. It was a first major example of satellite communication technology that could complement or compete with the operation of land-based transmission networks.

Telstar could be conceived of as a powerful extension of existing earth-bound communications facilities which were the product of monumental financial investment and yearly upkeep. It could improve upon that existing investment. Moreover, studies indicated that more advanced versions of a Telstar-type satellite could replace land-based equipment for long distance communications at a fraction of the cost. Another significant feature of Telstar was that it was the first commercial venture into space, the result of government-business cooperation. This message was as aggressively communicated in public promotion of Telstar by AT&T as were the capabilities of the satellite itself. It was the first satellite to be the object of a Madison Avenue advertising campaign.

The next technical advance came in 1963 with "Syncom," a National Aeronautics and Space Administration satellite. Orbiting some 22,300 miles above earth and moving at a speed equal to the earth's rotation allowed this satellite to fix its position for continuous coverage of almost half of the globe. At that distance, three such satellites could cover most of the earth's surface. Being in a "stationary" orbit meant that, unlike Telstar, it would not be out of contact when it disappeared over the horizon. Symbolically, if not technically, this marked the emergence of the satellite as a potentially worldwide, mass communications technology. Whereas earlier conceptions and even some subsequent experiments treated the satellite as a device for getting signals to remote areas, its greater significance was as the foundation of a new generation of world-spanning transmission technology. Satellites can bring advanced communication distribution networks to areas where development of terrestrial networks — wire, microwave relay — would be impractical in terms of population density or economics. It is not unusual for emerging nations to have their eye on the acquisition of satellites.

The next major growth in satellite communications came with the organization of the Communications Satellite Corporation (COMSAT) in 1962. Their "Early Bird," the first commercial satellite, was launched in 1965, followed by the "Intelsat" series which continues today. In 1974, after legislation made it attractive for private industry to get into the satellite business, Western Union went into space with its "Westar" series, followed by RCA's "Satcom" in 1975. By the mid-1970s the communications satellite business was well underway in this country. Less in the public eye are even more advanced military and surveillance satellite systems.

By the decade of the 1980s we were approaching around 75 communications satellites in orbit, most of them built and launched by the United States. "Intelsat V" (nine satellites in all) of the 1980s represents spectacular advances over its predecessors in the Intelsat series which date back to 1965 ("Intelsat I" and "Early Bird" are the same). The number of two-way telephone circuits increased from 240 to 12,500 and the cost per circuit decreased per year from $30,000 to $700.

Look for the emergence of many new commercial satellite communications systems as well as international competition over the use of certain broadcast frequencies. Some such systems will be large platforms constructed and serviced in orbit by space shuttles. Deregulation in the United States will open up competition among traditional message carriers using satellites. Watch for technical debates as to whether satellite design should move toward more sophisticated versions of current equipment (such as Intelsat V) or toward the development of "communication platforms" to be constructed in space by use of the space shuttle. Imagine the consequences of satellite communications for large countries such as China or India or the countries of the Arab world. They can be "wired" as never before in history by the positioning of a satellite and a ground network of earth stations. Satellite communications will have amazing economic, social, and political implications for developing countries.

The Demise of Distance

A unique feature in the economics of satellite communications is that transmission costs do not vary with distance. Any earth station within a satellite's coverage has the same transmission costs to any other earth station in the system. If, for example, a major corporation wishes to install a computer system which will be linked via satellite to its offices throughout the country or the world, distance is *not* a communication factor so long as its location is within satellite coverage. This is a remarkable thought when we consider how geographic proximity has governed the development of most of our institutions throughout history. Satellite services make it possible to instantly "wire" a city. If that city is very much tied to an information economy — as in insurance, banking, research, government — then it becomes less important for its major institutions to be crowded physically into a central area. These institutions can decentralize in the direction of employees' homes and thus lessen commuting times. Some work can be done directly in employees' homes.

Another important factor in satellite communications systems, often overlooked in the enthusiasm over space technology, is the terrestrial-bound facilities, or "earth stations." The first earth stations were large, complex, and in the $10 million cost category. Large antennas were necessary as were intricate tracking systems for following the satellite in its orbit. The large tracking stations, such as those associated with space missions — Goldstone, for example — are in this category. Several factors, however, have allowed dramatic decreases in the size, complexity, and expense of earth stations. Deployment of stationary satellites alleviated the need for earth stations to have a complicated tracking capability. Further, as satellites themselves have become able to receive weak signals and to rebroadcast increasingly powerful ones, the need for antenna size on earth has been remarkably reduced. These factors, coupled with a satellite system providing proper coverage and signal strength, makes an era of rooftop antennas feasible, where every home or apartment building could receive its own radio and television programs.

Direct broadcasting from satellites strikes fear in the hearts of those who now hold monopolies on broadcast signal distribution, namely radio and television stations, not to mention the national TV networks. The costs of two-way, send-receive earth stations have also reduced drastically, thus making it feasible for businesses, schools, and any other institutions who can use two-way communications to get directly into the satellite network. And as we mentioned at the outset, the emergence of large and very powerful communications platforms will allow certain types of fixed use earth stations to be reduced to nearly wristwatch size.

Even at 22,300 miles it takes three satellites to cover the entire earth, thus necessitating an earth station relay of globe-wrapping signals. Practical methods for intersatellite communications are now well along in development. This alleviates some of the relay traffic between earth stations and satellites, as well as cutting down on the slight delay caused by the 44,600 miles relay time in satellite-earth-satellite transmissions.

Additional important technological advances in satellite communications are reflected in the ability to compress more information transmission into communications channels and the ability of different ground stations to share a single satellite or "multiple access."

Barriers to the advancement of a satellite communications system have often been more political than technological, and this is bound to continue. For example, the U.S. Communication Satellite Act of 1962 protected domestic land-based communications industries by restricting satellite development to the Communications Satellite Corporation for only international transmissions. Burgeoning developments and markets for satellite communication eventually overwhelmed this legislation, opening the way for deregulation and competition. Thus is late 1979 it was the same corporation which proposed to open a satellite-to-home subscription television service by 1983 in the United States, a system already in experimental use in Japan. Almost simultaneously, this announcement was met with a whirlwind of objections from conventional broadcasters and cable operators.

International barriers abound too. At the World Administrative Radio Conference of 1979, where negotiations over

allocation of broadcast frequencies were taking place, several nations located along the equator maintained that their sovereignty extended to the 22,300 mile orbits of satellites stationed above their territories, and that users would have to rent or buy "slots" in this space.

When the previous conference was held, in 1959, the communications satellite did not exist.

Look for great growth of satellite communications in business and home applications, including someone knocking on your door expecting to sell you a "home dish." (Perhaps you have already seen them on display.) A business which deals mainly in information — such as banking, insurance, product design — can easily decentralize given the direct broadcast satellite services, to meet head on in the home entertainment market with traditional broadcasting — that is, if protective legislation for broadcasters and cable-casters can be avoided. (In a study of the opinions of experts, Francis Ford Plude found that nearly 83 percent fully expected direct broadcast satellite services to be economically viable.) Watch also for the development of dedicated commercial communications networks such as "Satellite Business Systems." Although it has lost money getting started, its president, Robert Hall, predicts $1 billion in revenues by 1990. (That should make you upset if you own AT&T stock.)

CHAPTER 7

Life on the AM-FM Dial

Radio is alive and doing extremely well. The image of the family huddled around a huge, floor model, mahogany-veneered living room radio waiting for Jack Benny to come on hardly exists in the minds of anybody under 30. Instead, "radio" conjures up images of $5.95 transistor sets cluttering up household drawers like so many pocket combs, AM-FM stereophonic outfits that encompass more electronic gadgetry than the old radio stations, a place on your car's dashboard that would be absolutely naked without a dial, kids by the thousands carrying around AM-FM cassette stereo "music boxes," and joggers shielded from the outside world by stethescope-like earphones pumping music into their heads from cigarette-size units. Nor does what resides on the dial bear any resemblance to the days of Lux Radio Theater or Jack Armstrong. Radio is now "narrowcasting" for the most part. Most stations have a "format" — hard rock, soft rock, all-news, all talk, classical, quiet sounds, and for a while, all too much disco. Formats or "images" are what's marketed now, not individual radio programs. (Some say that this will also be the future of 100 channel TV systems.)

"Radio Is Red Hot"

So said the signs scattered throughout the 1980 meeting site of the National Radio Broadcaster Association. The big word for commercial radio in the late 1970s and 1980s was "deregulation." The Federal Communications Commission had dropped requirements on broadcasting news, dropped limits on the time devoted to commercial messages, and dropped a variety of regulations concerning studies of community needs and evaluation of how well stations were meeting them. The commercial radio market had grown so large and programming services so varied that competition rather than regulation would be the new policy. If the policy continues, radio for all practical purposes will be entirely deregulated.

This policy, of course, delights the nation's slightly less than 9000 station owners, for the sky is now the limit in trying out new formats and in halting spending on services that were not profitable. For example, in markets which have all-news stations available, it is fruitless for a music format station to try to compete for news listeners. This has resulted in token news operations which serve nobody, least of all the listener.

This period of deregulation also happens to be a time when station profits are on the upswing. Advertising revenues in 1980 were up to around $3.5 billion, about 20 percent over the previous year.

There is also the prospect of making room for more radio stations on your AM dial. When standards were originally set so stations would not drown one another out, it was agreed to have a certain amount of broadcast spectrum set aside to divide each station from one another. Most of the world's AM stations use less dividing space than we do. If we moved to their standards there would be room for as many as 1400 new AM stations in this country when taking into account new space in the broadcast spectrum and the geographic separation of their locations. There would also be more room because an international agreement was reached at a World Administrative Radio Conference to expand slightly the total band allocated for AM broadcasting. Added to the above room for expansion is the distribution of radio program material, especially stereophonic music, on cable-TV systems as well as the linkage of cable systems by communications satellites.

Look for spectacular growth in everyday AM and FM radio programming alternatives, including more AM stations and possibly AM stereo. Expect to see some of these alternatives show up in your cable TV system, including the reemergence of "network" programming in specialized formats. Anticipate that narrowcasting will increase to the point where you switch from station to station for your "program" — everything from call-in chatter about sex problems to what the kids now jokingly call "Safeway" music.

"Where'd You Go, Rubber Duck?"

Remember that one? "Breaker . . . breaker . . . smokies . . . your home twenty" and all that? It was the Citizen's Broadcast Band ("CB") craze of the 1970s. It came in so fast that the Federal Communications Commission never could keep up in granting licenses. It went out so fast that a lot of marginal manufacturers lost their shirts in the CB business.

In 1958 the Federal Communications Commission ("Uncle Charlie" to CB'ers) allocated certain broadcast frequencies for a citizen's radio service with a very relaxed set of requirements for licenses. (One license was good for everybody in the family.) CB grew slowly at first. It wasn't until mid-1974 that a total of one million licenses were issued, and the number doubled in 1975, and quadrupled in 1976. Then, almost as abruptly, things slowed down.

In its heyday, CB radio demonstrated how new electronic "communities" can spring up overnight when a communications network is put into place. Besides the usual trucker exchanges, all kinds of gab fests filled the airways. Teenagers chewed the rag with night watchmen. Retired folks gave weather reports and handled emergency calls from motorists. Fishing parties set up communications networks like naval expeditions. Hippies in communes chatted with drivers of six-axle rigs. Licensing requirements become even more lax as the Federal Communications Commission could not keep up with applications. Nobody has ever had an accurate count of all the CBs in use, least of all the government.

The CB explosion also demonstrated another point. Radio is used for far more purposes than the stations which occupy the spots on your AM-FM dial. There are almost 50 distinct uses for radio, ranging from mobile telephone, police communications and paging systems, to air control, navigation and radio astronomy. The uses are so extensive that one of the greatest technological challenges in radio today is in how to squeeze more space out of a very crowded broadcast spectrum.

We have already mentioned in Chapter 5 how the new system of "cellular" radio transmitters will increase thousands-fold the number of mobile telephone conversations in a single urban area. Another popular growth area is in the use of radio to extend telephone systems either by a paging device or by "cordless" telephones around the house or business. A radio paging system allows a signal to be sent to a "beeper" or any other type of alarm device that you can conveniently carry in a pocket or hook on your belt. When you get a signal, you go to the nearest telephone and dial a predetermined number. These instruments are in increasingly wide commercial use (look for them on repair or service personnel). We may well have them also as personal "pocket" phones.

Cordless telephones are simply small transmitter-receiver stations built into your telephone handset which broadcast to a unit directly in your home or business. This unit is in turn connected to the telephone network. Cordless phones are becoming widely available as more electronic manufacturing firms get into the telephone market. Their cost is now down to a few hundred dollars. If it were not for the already overcrowded broadcast spectrum, the technologically possible combination of paging and remote telephone devices would be expected on the market soon. Although there are some devices that are moving in that direction, there are no known major marketing plans in the early 1980s. The crowded spectrum is the problem.

Even our everyday, around-the-house radios are changing, particularly as computer-type technology is used in their design. Included in the innovations is replacement of old tuner mechanisms, the design of which had not changed much in 50 years. Tuning can now be totally computerized, resulting in improved sound quality. Digital readouts also replace all of the mechanical pulleys and strings or rotating dial faces of traditional radios. Push-button tuning is a much simpler possibility, as are "memory" features which allow you to scan preselected stations or even to program your radio to play certain stations at different times of the day. While these features add to the sophistication (and expense) of home radios, the manufacture of small hand-held radios is reaching the point where cases and packaging are more expensive than the inner workings. Who ever thought radios would sell for less than five dollars even in a double digit inflationary period? Radios pretuned to certain frequencies could be manufactured now for less than one dollar. Perhaps we will see more special purpose radios mass manufactured which give us weather, time, newsheadlines, stock quotations, or other information valuable or necessary to some of the public. An AM or FM station might even find it worthwhile to distribute "free" pocket radios pretuned to their frequency.

Look for more radio-linked home and business telephones and for the price to come down. Look for paging devices to be practical for home use. Some paging systems may be able to receive data and some sophisticated ones to transmit. Look for changes in the design of personal radios, ranging from computer tuning to inexpensive hand-held models. Assume there might be a chance for more services to be available via radio, such as weather reports are now. Despite more efficient use of the existing broadcast spectrum, expect problems of crowding to increase.

Who Owns the Airways?

We not only have problems in overcrowding in our own uses of the radio broadcast spectrum, but now we and other advanced industrial nations face claims from Third World countries for a greater share of it. Many countries now wish to expand their radio communications services and argue that the industrial nations which have only about 10 percent of the world's population are using 90 percent of the broadcast spectrum. Although there are many innovations which allow us to pack more broadcasting in the same amount of spectrum space as well as the possibility of substituting wired communications systems, there are still more uses for radio than we have room for in the airways.

Many policy makers thought that international competition over crowded airways would come to a head at the World Administrative Radio Conference held in late 1979 in Geneva. International cooperation in broadcasting dates back to formation of the International Telecommunications Union in the last century and agreements made over telegraphy, including adoption of the Morse code. Cooperation over the years chiefly has been among the advanced industrial nations who controlled most of the world's radio services except for the national radio systems of individual nations. Meetings were mainly for technical agreements such as standardization of procedures, avoiding interference among different uses and users, and cooperating for development of new services. Since the previous conference in 1959, membership in the International Telecommunications Union had increased from 84 to 154, mainly the addition of third world nations.

As the time for the 1979 meetings approached, the political atmosphere heated up over demands of the developing countries for use of the broadcast spectrum, including a call for a new "world information order." The industrial nations who had controlled most of the world's broadcasting were accused of perpetuating colonialism. But the 1979 confer-

ence did not come to be the political battle that most anticipated. A great variety of minor technical agreements were
reached. Political arguments were postponed as a result of
the industrial nations advancing the position that new
technologies will allow better use of existing spectrum allo-
cations. Developing nations were persuaded that "there will
be room." Confrontations were thus put off for the time
being, but they will certainly emerge again in this decade and
in the 1990s as specialized uses of broadcasting, including
military applications, increase in developing countries.

> *Look for* international political debate over radio broadcast
> frequencies in the next two decades. Expect Third World
> nations to argue for a greater share of the "broadcast pie."
> This will not only threaten some of the advanced nations'
> anticipated commercial uses of broadcasting but will cut into
> military networks. The argument that new technologies will
> make better use of the existing spectrum allocations cannot
> be expected to solve the problem totally.

Are You Ready for Data Radio?

One of the most promising uses of radio and one which
allows us to make more efficient use of the crowded spectrum is for the transmission of data. Suppose, for example,
that the spoken weather reports which we can obtain by
tuning in to a certain station were transmitted only in terms
of the relevant figures involved. These could include the
temperature, air pressure, relative humidity, wind direction
and speed, probability of rain, with forecasts of these available for 6, 12, and 24 hours. The amount of data involved in
transmission of these figures is trivial. It could fit easily within
one of the very brief pauses in the stream of normal speech.
The broadcast of this information could be received by a
device not much larger than a wrist-watch (and could serve
as one too). The weather report would be presented to you
in a small digital display as on a watch face. Forecasts could

be triggered much the way we now call for the date on our electronic wristwatches. More broadcast channel space could be saved because this weather information need not be sent continuously. It might be sent only once per hour and in a manner whereby your wrist receiver would put the information in its memory until you call for it. This is all technologically possible right now.

It would also be possible to consider further information services which could be made simultaneously available such as stock market quotations; times of sunset and sunrise; tidal information; coded descriptions of freeway traffic levels; arrivals of airplanes, trains, or ships; or emergency warnings of weather, air pollution, earthquakes, or national defense.

This use of broadcasting is usually called "data radio," and when information is sent in bursts, often including information which allows the burst to be identified or "addressed," this is called "packet" radio.

Packet-type distribution allows many different types of data to be mixed in the same broadcast network, since each burst can be sorted out or routed by its identifying information. All of the services mentioned above could easily be made available in one broadcast frequency. Your "weather watch" would only register information received in packets addressed to it for this service. A more complex "communications card" similar to the card-sized calculators of today might have simple function buttons which would allow you to display commodity prices in one mode, the weather in one, and your horoscope (if you so desired) in another. All could be received and stored in different tiny memories according to the packet "addresses."

Data and packet designs also make possible a great number of radio-based information systems. Police communications are already moving in this direction in the form of small computer terminals located in patrol cars which are linked by radio to a computer at headquarters. Reports or inquiries are thus made in "data" rather than voice form which is faster, more reliable, can be partly automated, and takes up less space in the broadcast spectrum. Checking out license plate numbers, for example, goes much faster than when called for by the old-fashioned voice communications system.

It is possible also that many types of information gathering will eventually employ radio data transmission, especially where wired communications are impractical. For example, your water, gas, and electrical meters could have small radio transmitters which periodically would send readings in packet-coded bursts to a receiving station. The station could be a mobile one with equipment for interrogating via radio commands your meter readings. When received, these would go directly into a computer where eventually your monthly statement would be automatically calculated. (And you might use your remote radio-linked telephone to signal payment of this bill while you lounge at poolside.)

There are hundreds of other conceivable uses of radio as either an information or control system, for example, in burglar and fire alarms, earthquake detectors, smoke alarms in remote forests, and for personal message systems. There has already been a feasibility study of a worldwide personal data communications system which via communications satellites could link every individual in the world who carried a wrist-size communications unit. This is technologically possible with modern radio right now!

Look for innovative uses of radio for control and data services which you might see first in business or government and eventually in the home. Hand-held "information centers" are a possibility, including ones which can accept small computer programs broadcast to them. Anticipate that satellite communications wil add greatly to the range of such devices. (Have you picked out your worldwide personal digital address yet?)

Television for "Reading"

CHAPTER 8

Fingertip Information

Imagine it is a Friday evening in Chicago and you have decided to combine your business trip to Denver with a day of skiing. You press a telephone dialing code for travel information and turn a switch to link in your TV. Almost simultaneously the screen blinks on with a simple text message:

Thank you for your travel inquiry. Please enter desired dates, times, destinations, and desired modes of travel. City and town codes are in your service guide or can be seen here by pressing "5."

You enter the requested information in a simple format displayed on the TV screen. With a little give and take to fit your desired schedule with what is available, you are told:

Your air travel Chicago-Denver, United 48, seat 7B, 8:30 a.m., 9/7/85, return United 50, seat 8C, 10:15 p.m., 9/11/85 confirmed. Tickets are charged to your account. Do you wish them mailed (press "2") or will you pick them up at the airport ("6")?

You ask that they be mailed, after which the screen blinks back a confirmation and some further questions:

Your tickets are now being processed for mailing. Do you wish to rent a car in Denver? (yes = "1"). Can we help with your lodging reservations? (yes = "3")

Since you already have local transportation and lodging, you press the telephone "off" button, then switch your television set over to the football game. You pour a drink, then settle in to watch the game. About an hour later a message in small text coming via your TV signal is superimposed across the bottom of the screen.

> The weather forecast is for snow in Chicago tomorrow. For details, press "75."

You press the digits on the same small keypad as you used to make your flight reservations. This service is coming directly from your TV set; the telephone is not involved.

> The low pressure region moving in from Minnesota is expected to bring snow to the Chicago area about 8 a.m. Central Standard Time. Temperature will drop to -3 Celsius, sleet to follow the storm about 11 a.m. For local weather chart, press "6." For long-range forecast in local area, press "8." To check on air traffic at O'Hare, press "10."

You switch back to the game and hope silently that it will snow in Denver too.

"Videotext," "Teletext" . . . Next?

Some of the largest scale experiments in new uses of television in the late 1970s were in services involving the printed word, or *videotext,* which has come to be the generic term. As in the above scenario, these experiments have moved in two directions. One type of text service comes over wire lines to the user. The largest try-out of such a system is *Prestel,* a service of the British Post Office. Another type includes "pages" of textual information which are broadcast piggyback with television images but which cannot be seen on the TV without special equipment. Early examples of the latter type of system have been in the British Broadcasting Corporation's *Ceefax* or the Independent Broadcasting Authority's *ORACLE* (certainly simpler than

"Optional Reception of Announcements by Coded Line Electronics").

Broadcast text services differ in several capabilities as compared with wired ones. The text information is piggy-backed on the TV signal in a limited amount of channel space between TV images. (This is the bar you see when your TV set gets out of alignment.) A device added to your conventional TV set can "grab" and display a page of text or simple graphics tucked in this signal space. A sequence of pages can be broadcast so rapidly that, say, up to 800 different pages could be transmitted in a brief period and depending upon when you called for a page, the delay time would be any-where from a second or so up to two minutes. A small pad of pushbuttons allows you to control the system. While this system is essentially simpler than a wired one, there are some practical limits to the number of pages involved be-cause the time delay becomes frustrating if not prohibitive. In Prestel, a wired system, the number of pages is limited only by the size of the computer memory; after a year or so, the system had 250,000 pages. Another difference is that broadcast text services are more difficult to charge for than ones the wire where requests can be tallied and billed automatically.

Videotext systems are not truly a new communications technology but a combination of existing ones — the TV set, telephone system, and computers. As discussed in Chapter 9, computers are remarkably able information storage and communication devices. Text information can be fed in via keyboard, then appropriate computer programs will edit, format, and index this information in ways which will facili-tate its subsequent use. Small displays, or "pages" of infor-mation can be constantly updated. Users of such a system can be "routed" from one page to another according to their information desires.

Whereas to read a newspaper you either go page by page or use a very simplified index, this same information stored in a computer could be retrieved by subject matter codes, proper names, dates, or by anything serving as a useful label or index item. Since many people will want to be working at the same time with such systems — putting in new information, updating, retrieving — systems of simultaneous use, called *timesharing,* become an important part of development.

Now, giving your imagination free reign, think what it would be like if much of the information you used in daily living — news items, shopping ads, encyclopedia entries, airline and train schedules, new laws — were available in one big computer system. Instead of having to dig through the newspaper, call the airline, or wait for the news to come on TV, you could have any of this at your fingertips, and when you wanted it, rather than when it was published or broadcast. Perhaps the first sobering thought to threaten this fantasy is that most people, having no direct experience with computers, would not expect to be able to use, or even want to use, such a system. These were some of the dreams and challenges facing the developers of Prestel.

Obviously people are not going to rush out and buy expensive and complicated looking computer terminals. But if their telephone and TV sets combined with a keypad about the size of a pocket calculator could gain them access to a vast number of information resources, the prospect for wide public use would look a little more promising. Also if use of the system required no training, no learning of "computerese," it would likely be much more attractive to the public. These were all early decisions in the development of Prestel, a service of the British Post Office (which also runs the telephone system).

Prestel is now a publicly available information service in the United Kingdom. Its essential features are as follows. To gain access to Prestel you purchase or lease components which adapt your existing television and telephone to the system. There is the option of Prestel TV sets with all this built-in. When put into use, costs to you include the price of a local phone call, a modest per-minute charge for the service, and a possible payment to whomever provided the information "page" in the system. In practice, advertising information is free, civic or consumer information is negligible in cost, but important business information or entertainment features range upward in costs paid to the "information provider." Some of the diverse types of information services include:

- theater schedules
- horsewinning tips
- horoscopes
- recipes
- train schedules
- restaurant guides
- weather
- stock market
- price and shopping guides
- business data
- credit card information
- jokes and entertainment items
- classified advertisements
- show reviews
- games
- educational items

The "information provider" is an important component of the Prestel system. Such individuals or organizations pay an overall annual subscription fee to be in the service plus a per page cost for whatever information they have booked into the systems. Providers have a direct input capability to Prestel so they can fill in their pages and update them as desired. Depending upon the market demand for their items, providers then are compensated by the users of that information. As already mentioned, some information is free since it is in the information provider's interest to have it used. This essentially is the "advertising" in the system. Small information providers can use Prestel under the auspices of larger organizations that "broker" pages in the system.

Another interesting problem posed by Prestel is who has control over its content. As much as possible, the British Post Office has wanted to avoid becoming an "editor." Just as telephone companies and data carriers consider themselves only "conduits" for messages, or *common carriers*, Prestel has sought only to operate the system, not to become a "publisher." Anybody can enter anything so long as problems of libel, pornography, or copyright are not involved. Formats, types of information, accuracy, and taste have all been left to be regulated by the marketplace. Successful information providers, however, have come to recognize the importance of "house styles," accuracy, clarity, and other characteristics which enhance the marketability of their pages.

> *Look for* competition everywhere between wired and broadcast systems, especially when the marketplace rather than a government will have to support them. Expect this competition to extend especially into advertising revenues in free enterprise countries. Not only will the text services be challenging one another but the traditional media will not want to give up their advertising dollars. Based upon the brief experience with Prestel, after the novelty wears off, payment for service may only come from individuals who have a special need for the service or information. Otherwise more traditional and less expensive sources may be consulted. Also do not expect the average individual to spend hours "reading TV." It's too uncomfortable.

Phone, Cable, or TV?

Joining company with the development of Prestel have been *Antiope* (France), *Telidon* (Canada), *Bildschirmtext* (West Germany), and *Captain* (Japan). Text services in all of these countries, including Great Britain, are still undergoing development.

What about the United States? Obviously there was no rush to the market in the 1970s nor was it clear *who* would make the attempt. AT&T would have except for their antitrust problems, their restriction to common carrier status which would bar them from being any type of information provider (remember that they would like to sell electronic Yellow Pages advertising), and their desire to get into the business in an *un*regulated status. There was no major move to bring Prestel services to the United States, although General Telephone and Electronics Corporation (the second largest telephone company) held the license in this country for it. At the time the few newspapers who had even awakened to the fact that their publishing technology might be radically changing were terrified of electronic services. (After all, many papers were just getting used to having computers around for typesetting.) Finally the U.S. Postal Service has no talent nor funds for such innovations on a large scale.

Some text information services had developed, however, that were more in the form of specialized computer information files ("data bases") which an individual or corporation could call into on a timesharing basis. Dow Jones and the New York *Times*, for example, have had a news-retrieval service since the 1970s. Or, more for the general public, you could join the "CompuServe" information network in 1981 and connect into it with a computer terminal available from Radio Shack for under $500. Also, a number of cable systems had channels with textual information available. However, except for systems with a two-way capability, such as Qube, you could not call for selected files.

But by 1981, there were a variety of videotext experiments in operation in the United States and many on the planning boards. CBS, Inc. and public broadcasting station KCET in Los Angeles, after testing for signal interference for text broadcasts in 1980, began test services in 1981. In Murray, Kentucky, the Murray Ledger and Times leased a cable-TV channel to broadcast news texts as well as advertising. Public station WETA proposed a try out of the Canadian Telidon system in Washington, D.C. AT&T and Knight-Ridder News-papers, Inc. were partners in tests in Coral Gables, Florida. Time, Inc. plans a cable-TV 24-hour news service.

The potential giant in development of the U.S. system is, of course, AT&T. Although they have been secretive about it, it is well known that substantial planning has gone into ways the existing telephone network could be the basis of a nationwide textual information system. As mentioned in Chapter 5, AT&T could have a service already well developed in the form of the Yellow Pages. It would be a few simple steps beyond this to provide "call in" shopping services and further information on products. Obviously at some point providing "information" would spill over into providing "news." This gives newspaper owners the shudders, so much so that they have been able to halt (probably temporar-ily) a proposed AT&T experiment in Austin, Texas for textual information. (Media history buffs might recall that the first "newspapers," or *advices* were mainly advertising coupled with news announcements.)

Look for major growth in most industrialized countries of videotext systems. The decade of the 1980s will see the birth of either a major system or two in the United States or a host of small, more specialized systems. How AT&T fares in anti-trust litigation and how successfully newspapers and broad-casters can lobby to keep them out of the "information busi-ness" will decide whether you'll be getting much in the way of text services from your phone company. Surely they will try to push through electronic directories and some form of the Yellow Pages. Don't expect much more than is being tried now from individual cable systems or newspapers unless they get into some type of national alliance with systems that are technically compatible. Expect some type of national stand-ards in this decade (this began to happen in 1981). Better move your favorite reading chair over to the TV.

Whither the Printed Page?

Will videotext systems alter traditional types of publishing? Will the printed newspaper be the dinasaur of the twenty-first century? One key point made by those who have seriously studied these systems in prototype form is that they are much more of a *new* communications medium than something to replace traditional ones. Uses are much more likely to cut across many communications activities — such as visiting the library, looking in the paper for the weather report, calling offices for information, tuning in the news headlines on the radio.

The display of text on a TV screen does have several unique characteristics likely to affect usage. First, only limited amounts of text are on each "page" because of screen limits, space needed for page labels, as well as space for the "menu" for what can be chosen next. Prestel pages take about 150 words of material in addition to the administrative items. Your eye can skip over many more headlines on a printed newspaper page and browse much faster than with a videotext system. If you want to read at a fast clip, say 500 words per minute, too much time is taken up ordering new TV pages.

It is not particularly comfortable to stare for long periods at a TV screen of current vintage and at the distance necessary to read detailed text. Technology can alleviate this problem in part, perhaps leading to much higher resolution screens, either wall-sized or hand-held. Some users of the British systems report frustration in trying to locate their television sets (and themselves) in positions which are comfortable for both program viewing or reading text.

In the foreseeable future, then, it does not seem likely that videotext systems will replace print where the reader wants to browse through a great deal of material or read at a steady and fast pace. It is hard to imagine being comfortable if you knew that the charge meter was running while you were trying to wake up with the morning newspaper or settle down in the evening with a good novel. Videotext systems will probably grow much more for services dealing with information which has a good market if it can be constantly updated, easily indexed, and usable in modest-sized amounts — for example, stock reports, news headlines, directories, schedules, sports results, weather forecasts. In competition with newspapers, videotext is efficient for news headlines, movie and theater guides, daily personal items such as horoscopes, and especially classified advertisements. Studies indicate, as you would expect, that most of the classified pages are seldom read. They are used more as a file. If such advertising is put into a computer file, it can be rapidly retrieved by simple indexing systems. In an advanced type of wired two-way videotext system, prospective buyers could send their bids directly into the computer for eventual follow up. Loss of classified ad revenue would be a disaster for most newspapers.

Commercial broadcasters are known to worry about broadcast videotext systems not so much because they will draw viewers away from programs, but because the time during the commercial would be convenient for dialing up text reports on the weather, sports, or stock market. It appears that some commercial interests are ready to get into videotext operation as an advertising-supported medium. You may tune away from a program to catch the update on gold prices, but it will be brought to you courtesy of your local gold dealer.

Another natural for videotext systems is broadcast program schedules. Perhaps your *TV Guide* of the future will be elctronic. The publication's programming schedules are already put together in electronic form before they go to press, so why bother putting them on paper?

Don't *look for* the printed page to vanish overnight. It's a still much too convenient communications technology. (No plugs, transistors, phone line charges, and very, very portable.) Yet do expect certain types of information services —

where selected information is to be retrieved and where information is frequently updated — to be a natural for video-text services. Simply the costs of printing will also encourage more electronic publishing. You may still be reading those lengthy, in-depth articles from newsprint in a much thinner New York *Times,* but scanning headlines, stock quotations, and classified ads on a TV screen. If Dow Jones has done their planning right, and as their ad says, their *Wall Street Journal* may well be your first "own private newspaper" — electronic that is. (Think of the trees we'll be saving.)

CHAPTER 9

The Digital Connection

From Looms to Computers

In 1801 the French inventor J. M. Jacquard introduced a semiautomatic loom which allowed you to choose the pattern of the weave by selecting a loop of cards with holes arrayed in them. Each card, by the presence or absence of a hole in certain positions, controlled a specific section of the weave and the result was "control" of the overall pattern. Although it probably never occurred to Jacquard, his "cards" represented the fundamental reduction of information to what we in modern times call *bits, binary* decisions, or *digital* information. In a broad analogy this is the way electronic digital computers store and manipulate information. They do it in terms of vast arrays of miniature "off-on" electrical switches. We humans convey information into computers by methods which eventually reduce it to a digital storage form. We can also give our computers special forms of information ("programs") which set up patterns of switches so that they will do things with further information that we have already given, or will give, them. In this way you can "tell" a computer to add, subtract, multiply, divide, or take the root of any numbers you give it or have stored in its memory. In fact, in 1823 another inventor, Charles Babbage, planned to use Jacquard's card system in a "calculation machine" which he designed (but never built) to perform the operations just mentioned.

Although we often think of modern electronic computers as giant calculation devices, they can also qualify as a *communications technology*. They are capable of taking our messages and giving them back to us or others, as does any communications device. But unlike any other communications device, they are capable of *acting upon* them in a manner defined by an extension of our own human intelligence. While other communications technologies extend the range of our human messages, the computer allows us to extend our human capability for acting upon messages. When we combine these two types of technologies — we have at our disposal an extension of human communication powers that far exceeds any other communications invention. In centuries to come, historians may look back upon the invention of the printing press as a novelty, an interesting wayside en route to the "intelligent" electronic communications networks that are already with us in the last years of the twentieth century.

We experience these intelligent networks when we make airline reservations, when we engage in remote banking transactions, when our business computers "talk" to one another, when we read those now experimental textual messages displayed on our TV screens, or when some of us hook computer terminals up to telephones so we can get information in to or out of the company computer.

At the heart of most of these networks is the large computer, the "electronic brain" or, in computer circles, the "mainframe," that we have heard so much about since the early 1950s. In the 1980s we are forced to say "most" and "large" because we now have evolving networks of small *home* or *personal* computers (the topic of the next chapter). To do justice to the large computer would take several books the size of this one. But there are a few key points that can be made simply.

(1) The main feature of computers is not so much their intelligence as their ability to manipulate exceedingly large amounts of information at near incredible speeds. If you

think of a "bit" of information as the binary information stored as the presence or absence of one hole in a position of Jacquard's loom card, a silicon chip one-tenth the size of a postage stamp could store 65,536 bits of information in 1980. The Japanese have demonstrated a chip that will store 262,144 bits but which will not be on the market until the mid-1980s. Taking the maximum number of memory chips into account, the IBM Model 3081 can accommodate up to 256 million bits of internal, accessible memory. In addition to this is the virtually unlimited storage capacity of magnetic tapes and discs which can be used in conjunction with the basic computer.

As for speed, consider a numerical problem that might take you or me a minute to do by hand and would take a 1965 state-of-the-art computer about .3 microseconds (one-millionths) to complete. Computer engineers are currently talking in terms of *nanoseconds* (or billionths). By the mid-1980s we may have demonstrations of "supercomputers" which will only take 2 to 2.5 nanoseconds to do a computations step. A goal is to reach one nanosecond. In order to lessen the distance that electronic signals have to travel (their speed is 6 inches per nanosecond), components would have to be highly compressed in supercomputers, perhaps to a total contral unit smaller than a basketball. But this would be impossible for several reasons, one of which is that the heat generated by the circuits would melt the unit. The key is a "switch" that gives off little or no heat, and that is what researchers are concentrating upon.

(2) In addition to advances in their central processing unit capacity, the growth direction of large computing systems is also in the direction of distributed services. One version of this is the computer network, where large machines of varying designs can be linked when necessary. For example, a problem may be too large for one machine, so two are linked together to process it. Or a computer in one research center may not be the optimum machine for a particular problem so the network is used to transfer the

problem to another, more appropriate machine, which could be a continent away. Such networks are also useful as a basis for "electronic message" systems, computer tele-conferences, and the like. The best known example is the "ARPANET" (the Advanced Research Projects Agency is a part of the U.S. Department of Defense).

The other version of growth is in distributing a large computer's services to many remote terminals. Because computers operate so much more quickly than we humans can give them tasks to do, they can serve many of us at once. We can "timeshare" with them, so to speak. Large computer installations which require many user terminals — as in banking or ticketing — can support very large and complex timeshare systems. Bear in mind also that there are constantly new small portable terminals on the market which allow you to timeshare from wherever you can find a telephone. Sometime in the 1980s we should see a portable terminal on the market that is not much larger than a hand calculator.

The coming of the microcomputer also makes new types of timesharing possible. For example, you could work out parts of a problem on your small, stand-alone computer, then "upload" it for further processing through a timesharing system to a large machine. Similarly, you could call into a main computer for programs, data, "mail," or instructional packages for subsequent, independent processing on your small machine.

(3) Computer experts generally agree that the electronic architecture of large computers probably will exceed in sophistication the "programming" available to operate on it for many years to come. Or they say: "Hardware is way ahead of software." At the outset of this section we said that computers are the first technology to allow humans a major extension of their intellectual problem-solving capabilities. "Extension" is an important word here for even though we use computers for so-called "artificial intelligence" research, the intellectual capabilities (not the memory or speed) of

computers so far as we know cannot exceed what we put into them.

The design of computer programs moreso than the architecture of the computer itself incorporates these human intellectual extensions. The more that programs precisely fit our intellectual style for solving certain kinds of problems, the better we and the computer perform. The problem is that we and computer programs often must compromise with one another in translating our problem-solving style into the computer's extension of it. If the computer is ever to become a fully utilized intellectual extension for all types of human problem solving (in medicine, the law, even in the arts), we will have to make great advances in the theory and practice of software development.

Look for startling advances in computer memory and processing speed capabilities but do not expect them to affect your lives very directly, at least not for now. They will only make more efficient the very large-scale operations that are now already being accomplished. Expect some "trickle down" consequences of memory and disc storage technology for use in small, personal, or home computers (Chapter 10). As a consumer, your next type of contact with large computer systems will likely be in electronic banking, remote computer-based services over your cable TV system, and the constant upgrading of the telephone network (and new services). In your professional life, expect to experience computers of all sizes moving into the office and performing services ranging from word processing, managing information, doing accounting to receiving, storing and forwarding electronic mail. Better learn how to manage computers as well as people!

"Going Digital"

Although the transistor was not such big news to the public when it was announced in 1948, it became a household word with the mass availability over the next several years of palm-sized inexpensive radios that most of us simply called "transistors." The transistor did not do anything very new in electronics. It controlled current flow much as did the large vacuum tubes in the old radios of the 1930s and 1940s or even the miniaturized tubes developed in World War II. But the transistor did offer some very desirable advantages. It was much more compact and durable than its fragile glass counterpart. It generated less heat, used less electricity, and held promise of being manufactured more cheaply than the tube.

As transistors began to replace vacuum tubes, the chassis on which everything was wired together began to shrink in size, especially when mostly transistors were involved. Eventually, around the late 1950s it began to make sense to combine several different circuits on single silicon chips since there was no reason anymore to spread them around on large circuit boards. This was the "integrated" circuit and the beginning of adding more and more circuits to a single chip until we reached the era of "large scale integration" (now "very large scale"). When most of the key circuits needed for computer-like processing were eventually integrated on a single chip, this was called a *micro-processor.* Small computers which use these as the basis for their operation are *microcomputers.*

Microprocessors are initially very expensive to develop, literally in the millions of dollars. Yet once the manufacturing process is set up for a design — the etching process is something like photolithography — mass production makes them very inexpensive. In 1980, some of the microprocessor chips in the heart of small computers had a retail value of just under $20. There is little reason that this price could not shrink to $1 or under by the year 2000. Much of microprocessor design and manufacture is computer-automated, thus bringing costs down. More complex circuits are being reduced to single chips. New circuits are being developed which can correct themselves if there are design flaws or breakdowns. There is even talk of three-dimensional chips and circuits which could lead us to *superintegration.* Further integration is limited only by our ability to work with circuits narrower than the bandwidth of light waves.

Maybe you have already heard the phrase "going digital." This means not only the stored binary form of information in computers, as we discussed, but the conversion of all types of information into that form for transmission. Traditional radio, television, or telephone transmissions use an amplification form of message encoding where "analog" circuitry modifies electron flow in lesser or greater amounts. When your voice is sent along a conventional telephone circuit, the patterns are an analog of your vocal patterns. When we use microprocessors to sample these patterns they convert them into a stream of coded on-off pulses, a "digital" transmission. Obviously, you need another microprocessor at the other end to convert these pulses back into sound. Because they work with digital information in the first place, computers naturally "talk" to one another in digital codes.

Beyond computers, is there any advantage to going digital? There are indeed many. If we considered only the telephone system, great advantages accrue from digital technology. When telephone circuits and switching systems are converted for use of digital transmission, very high speed data transmissions, even among computers, can be easily mixed with telephone conversations. Because microprocessors are less expensive to manufacture than conventional analog switching equipment and last much longer, digital installations are especially economical and reliable. American Telephone and Telegraph's immediate problem, however, is that the great share of its equipment is still in analog form.

Digital transmission lends itself well to automation. In more traditional types of communications systems, messages are routed by changing the circuits, not unlike the old-fashioned telephone switchboard. Although these are now highly automated with many messages combined in the same circuits, consider a method called *packet switching* (similar to packet radio [Chapter 7]). Here the network of circuits is connected all the time, but at each of the junctures on the network is a computer which will send the message by the most direct and open route. Messages are divided electronically into "packets," each of which has its own "address." This system is something akin to the postal network. The addresses of electronic packets are "read" and routed at each juncture in the network. This network is totally automated.

Virtually any "message" — voice, moving images, music — can be transmitted, stored, or manipulated in digital form. In addition to its compatibility with computers and computer-automated transmission systems, digital transmission offers the advantage of distortion-free transmission. In recording or transmitting traditional analog forms of communication, its distortion or "noise" portions are cumulatively amplified along with the signal. The encoded digital form of a voice message is like a recipe for it. When reproduced from its recipe-code, it is an identical copy of the original. Traditional phonograph records are an example of storing music in analog form. Irregularities in the record grooves cause the pick-up needle to vibrate in patterns replicating what was recorded. Even with the advanced state of hi fidelity, stereophonic long-playing records, some sound quality is lost. Every step from an original recording, to a master disc, to the pressed disc you buy, looses quality.

Records are also a good example of changes being brought about by digital technology. In early 1980 several companies were marketing long-playing records originally recorded in digital (rather than tape) form, then reproduced on conventional discs. Because one of the analog duplication steps is skipped, the records are perceptibly clearer than their traditional counterparts. The next and critical step, however, is to prepare such recordings for digital *playback*, which requires a different recording medium for the record as well as new digital playback equipment. The digital record of the future could well be a small plastic card with no grooves to wear out.

The shrinking size and cost of microprocessors make "going digital" a very attractive alternative for all types of communication.

Look for evidence everywhere of the growth of digital communications. Expect also that the microprocessor business will become increasingly competive worldwide as demand grows for chips to be used in everything ranging from your car's fuel injector, video games, programmable door chimes, videodisc players to the watch on your wrist. Look for combinations of communications and computing to bring us a variety of new services, eventually probably including a home-to-home electronic, packet switched, mail service. Anticipate that the distribution of computing power via networks will grow. (Anthony Oettinger of M.I.T. calls this "compucation.") Digital music should replace traditional systems sometime in the 1980s. This change will have a profound effect on the home entertainment market as the shift to LP records did over 30 years ago. There is already a company forming which will offer you digital recordings "on order" over your telephone line. (If you have just made a big investment in a traditional stereo system, you'll be sorry.) The Sony Corporation has already stunned the photographic world with their announcement of a filmless camera that stores images with digital electronics. Whether they are hand-held calculators, electronic games, or tiny radios, digital electronics are a part of the communications revolution that you have in the palm of your hand.

Computing Around the House

The Micro Invasion

A few years back *Spectrum* magazine ran a story about a computerized golf game developed by a man named Bob Wilson in Salt Lake City. He calls it "Par-T-Golf." You use your own clubs and regulation golf balls. The decision whether to play Pebble Beach or West Palm Beach is easy because you can do both right in your own living room. No worry about getting to the course on time or a noisy gallery. And no lost balls. You select your course, tee up, and drive into a screen on which there is a projected image of what you would see on the real fairway. Optical scanning beams "measure" the ball on the way to the screen and a microcomputer calculates where your ball would land on the real thing. Then up pops another slide showing your approach shot. You take this shot, then the computer calculates what number of putts would be required. It scores you for the hole then tees you up for number two. If you are an old hand at the course, you can program in a wind factor. The word is that Mr. Wilson plans to work the system up to handle 12 different golf courses.

Although most of us probably won't be playing computerized golf in our living room in the near future — the system costs about $17,000 — we are daily coming into contact with new gadgets, services, and even simulated experiences brought about by what is at the heart of Mr. Wilson's system — *the microprocessor.*

Microprocessors, as we said in Chapter 9, are all of the essential electronic ingredients of the central part of a computer reduced to fit on a chip of silicone the size of your little fingernail. Remember the transistor we discussed in the last chapter. Imagine positioning up to a half *million* of them on a chip about this size: ☐ . That's where we are heading with miniaturization.

These advances in miniaturization are the main reason that the computer has invaded so many aspects of our everyday life — our watches, telephones, cars, microwave ovens, pocket calculators, and those buzz-beep electronic games. All of these, as well as Mr. Wilson's bizarre home entertainment device, have been made possible by the rapid evolution of the microprocessor. The design and manufacture of microprocessors is a booming business in this country. Demand was so great in the early 1980s that oftentimes manufacturers could not keep up.

While microprocessors have entered our daily lives in the types of devices mentioned above, we have also seen, beginning in around 1977, the marketing of what has been variously called "personal" or "home" computers. Unlike the devices above, these microprocessors are programmable by their users. You can get them to do different things by feeding them previously prepared programs or you can compose your own program and enter it via a keyboard if you know how.

Most programs are purchased off the shelf on audio cassette tapes, small magnetic discs, or little cartridges where circuits are already programmed. Because loading and running such programs is usually very simple, it brings the use of programmable computers to the majority of the population who otherwise would never touch computers except perhaps for calculators or TV games. Doing your own programming of a home computer is not overly difficult; however, the practice will probably be restricted to home computer enthusiasts or students who will gain some direct benefits from it. This includes developing programs otherwise unobtainable, modifying existing programs, learning about computers, or simply the enjoyment of figuring out program strategies.

In the early 1980s many of the half dozen or so of the least expensive personal computers could be bought for between $750 and $1500 for the basic machine. If you wanted a better display device than your home TV set, a monitor would be another $300 to $500. A small disk unit for storing and loading programs was another $600 and a printer around $800. The price of a complete system quickly added up. If you were to invest in a system that was truly useful in a small business for bookkeeping, inventory control, and word processing, you could easily work your way into the $10,000 to $15,000 range. This would still be much less expensive than the $25,000 on up systems, for small businesses sold by the larger computer manufacturers.

The three most popular machines in this period were the TRS-80 (Radio Shack), the Apple-II, and the Commodore "PET." These were in the price ranges mentioned above and could all be expanded for small business use. As of about 1980, the forecasts for sales of such machines were highly optimistic. It was thought that personal computers would be bought by people who were beyond the group of electronics and computer hobbyists who bought, but mostly built, small machines in the 1970s. Total sales of small machines was about 25,000 in 1977 and 250,000 by late 1978, a tenfold increase. By the early 1980s there were well over one million personal computers in use.

By late 1981, however, it was becoming clear that the "home" market was not growing as much as forecast. Although people other than hobbyists had bought personal computers, the average person was not rushing off to newly opened "computer stores" to buy these small, readily expandable machines. Instead, they were being bought by people who usually had some definite use for them in mind, such as stock market analysis, home educational tutoring, or for expanding them for small business use. More people were buying *function* — that is, a specific task that could be accomplished — than a flexibly programmable small computer per se.

Buyers who were looking for game and simple educational functions were drawn more to less flexible machines, which were generally marketed as more sophisticated versions of electronic games. These machines, like the Atari, and Mattel's "Intellivision," typically took cartridge-type programs which loaded much more easily and reliably than small tape units. The companies which marketed these machines also took the lead in marketing a large number of programs ("software") for them.

Although the more flexible personal computers mentioned earlier have had great amounts of software written for them, some of the "off the shelf" games, educational tutoring, or financial analysis programs in the late 1970s and early 1980s were less than satisfactory. Many programs had been developed by small entrepreneurs and quality control was lacking. Cartridge programs, by contrast, require complex manufacturing equipment, so they are more under the control of larger companies doing business in the home computer market. By late 1981 it was clear that the somewhat less expensive cartridge-loading home machines were growing in their share of the market with the so-called "average" consumer who otherwise might not have any special interest in computers. As such, their marketing was substantially expanded by discount stores and record and video shops, as well as chain-operated electronics and computer stores. Although the figures are still coming in, it seems probable that more of the broad public in America will purchase their first "computer" as a mass marketed, discount item and they will buy it for the specific "functions" it can perform.

On the other hand, most of the manufacturers of the cartridge-loading small computers either already, or have plans to, offer "add-on" units for their machines. In this way, once customers have been "hooked" on their game computer, they can expand it into a more flexible machine. Or else they might buy a more expensive machine from that same manufacturer.

Look for continued growth in the home computer market but not especially with the same multipurpose types of machines which launched the revolution in the late 1970s. Although sales of increasingly powerful home computers will certainly grow, the mass market will probably be taken over by simpler machines for which high quality cartridge type programs are readily available and which are priced well below $500. Expect to see these mass marketed machines in discount stores by the dozens, along with "rack-sales" displays of programs. Meanwhile, look for manufacturers of the more flexible and programmable computers to come out with less expensive "home lines," which among other features can be cartridge loaded as well as loaded by tape or small disc. Expect, too, that the memory limitations of small computers may soon be strikingly overcome, with capacities on better machines reaching into the billions of "bits." The business will also continue to boom as giants like IBM and Xerox vie for the small computer market. Researcher Jack Nilles (in press) estimates that small computers alone could account for $3.5 billion in revenues by the 1990s. Why not buy one today and answer your electric company's computerized letter with one of your own!

Spreading the Power Around

The greatest growth in microcomputers in the $1500 and up range has been in the small business market. In the 1960s it was unimaginable that a small business might be able to gain its own "computing power." At that time such power was confined to large installations, and the only way to distribute it was through "timesharing." (As mentioned in Chapter 9, this is where many users are simultaneously wired into a large computer.) Timesharing has always been costly; not only is there the fee for use of your share of the computing charges, but telephone charges get to be expensive also. Perhaps even a more major problem is that the computer services — such as accounting, payroll, inventory — available over timeshared services don't always exactly fit your needs. Too often you have to make costly and inefficient adaptations to the capabilities of the large machine to make it worthwhile. Moreover, even as timeshared services became more adaptable and came down in cost, most small businesses could not afford them.

Small computers allow the "distribution" of computing power which, of course, does not depend upon a tie-in with a central system. As such, programs can be adapted to local use. There are no telephone charges. The computer is available full time (as long as it is working!). And, finally, since the cost of computer manufacturing has decreased so greatly, the power of computing has come well within the price range of the small businessperson.

Because the small business market has grown sufficiently better than the home market for the $1500 and over microcomputer, many of the computer stores which began opening in the early 1980s have shifted their concentration to serving these customers rather than the individual who wants a simple machine with prepackaged games. There is more profit in the former and the latter are now being taken over for sales by discount stores and other mass merchandizers. This is a contrast between a $10,000 to $25,000 sale and a $149 one. However, when businesspersons shop for a $20,000 machine, they may also find themselves talking to Xerox, IBM, Hewlett-Packard, and other manufacturers which formerly only carried expensive machines.

One of the most intriguing but as yet unrealized growth areas for microcomputers is in education. Although there are many instructional computer programs now on the market, the adoption of this type of technology by schools remains miniscule. As discussed later in Chapter 17, the computer has an almost unlimited capacity as an instructional device. Just as small computers have allowed for the distribution of computing power to small businesses, they can bring many instructional innovations into the classroom. "Computer-assisted instruction" need not be the ponderous "rote" type of programmed learning experimented with in the 1960s. It can be exciting and creative. The twist is to put the student in charge of the computer rather than vice versa.

There is only a fine line between really intriguing computer games and use of the computer for instructional purposes. When the challenge, suspense, and interactive qualities of superior computer games are used as a context for instruction, learning can become truly exciting. The problem is that we lack sophisticated programming of this type that incorporates sound educational practices. Too many prepackaged computer instructional programs are written by game programmers and lack a basic instructional strategy (giving encouragement rather than saying "Wrong dummy!") or are poor examples of that which they claim to teach (for example, misspelling in a spelling program).

On the other hand, microcomputers have so much potential for instructional purposes that only a miracle could prevent them from becoming one of the most revolutionary educational devices in history. Remember, too, that as children learn math or spelling on a small computer, they are also being introduced to the communications technology that will probably do more to shape their lives in the twenty-first century than any other popularly available device.

Look for the microcomputer to be the great *popularizer* of computing power. Expect continued growth of small computers and excellent programming for small business applications. In fact, this majority share of the market may continue for some time to come. Expect the manufacturers and suppliers of formerly large-scale systems to move more aggressively into the small business market, perhaps with foreign-built machines. Increasingly, your local "computer store" may cater to the small businessperson rather than the home computing novice. Look for computing power to be distributed down to the smallest business in terms of compact, inexpensive, desk top, multipurpose (typing, calculating, telex hook-ups) machines. How would you like to mail computerized bills rather than receive them? Watch for the instructional capabilities of the microcomputer to become widely acknowledged. Off the shelf programs should steadily improve as they are written by educators rather than game programmers. Because public schools are so slow in adopting new technologies, look for more growth of microcomputer instruction in private instructional organizations and in the home. Realize also that using a small computer to tutor a child in spelling also introduces them to the world of computers. Next time your school complains that they cannot live within their budget, ask them why they haven't entered the technological age.

Growing Together

As more and more home appliances have microprocessors and home entertainment-information systems take on personal computing components, it is anticipated that these units will become interconnected. It is also expected that different units could be simultaneously operated by a central computer in the home. If the investment in multiple microprocessors were combined in a central one, still more services might become available. Planners are now envisaging home "command and control" units to monitor and regulate heating and cooling, turn lawn sprinklers on and off on schedule, monitor door and window openings as a security measure, turn lights on and off on whatever program you schedule, monitor smoke alarm units, and even provide a basis for programming whatever tune you want this week on your door chimes. All of this would be in addition to providing you with the earlier described services of a personal computer — that is, games, instruction, files, problem solving, financial records, and word processing.

Several other changes in personal computers should make them increasingly useful to the average person as we approach the twenty-first century. Programming a personal computer is relatively easy but probably not worth your time unless you enjoy it as a leisure time activity. Experts in the computer science field tell us to expect some substantial advances in programming languages. Among these are languages which are not only very close to natural language (such as English) but the program structure may adapt in a specialized way to the type of uses you contemplate (word processing, tax records, instruction). Ideally you should be able to turn on your personal computer and *discover* very easily and pleasantly how to get it to do the job. Advances in "automatic programming" may bring us to a point where everyone is computer literate so long as they can turn on the machine.

That still leaves the problem of typing. Will computers ever talk and listen? Getting a computer to turn text into speech is much simpler than getting computers to understand the very complex and variable speech wave. But if human and machine agree upon a limited vocabulary, then computers are much better off in recognizing the spoken commands of their human users. Already, there are calculators which can respond to carefully articulated spoken numbers and commands. Surely at some point in the next 20 years there will be some breakthroughs in using speech to get your computer moving. Already keyboards can be by-passed by "tablets" or a "light pen" which works on the screen, or by the use of knobs or "joysticks" such as with computer games.

Imagine stepping into the living room of your twentieth-story condominium, telling your central computer to turn the heat up, to inform security that you have reached your home safely, then using it to select a TV show on your wall size screen — all by *voice*.

Look for more and more computer applications in the home and the emergence of centralized computer systems installed right along with the heating and plumbing. Look for programming languages which are increasingly like the natural languages. Speech synthesis by small computers is now available, although recognition will for a long time be limited to a specific vocabulary. Perhaps your home computer in the twenty-first century will tell you a bedtime story before it turns off the lights!

Neither Snow, Nor Rain, Nor ...

CHAPTER 11

In 1970 the Republican administration, with the approval of Congress, tried to extricate the U.S. Post Office Department from political patronage by setting up the government-owned corporation known as the U.S. Postal Service. This was supposed to be an important turning point for mail service in the United States, one operated by a management more attuned to modern, efficient business methods. The problem is, things turned the wrong way. Government subsidies have grown. The mail is delivered less frequently and service often takes longer now. By 1981 the cost of mailing the first-class letter was 33 percent greater than in 1971. Lines in big city post offices are longer than ever. New postal horror stories abound at business luncheons.

Yet within about a decade we will probably not have the same old postal service to kick around anymore. It's not that those red-white-and-blue boxes will entirely disappear nor mail carriers cease their rounds, but that those types of point-to-point one-way messages which can tolerate a few hours or even overnight delay, and which are often sent in batches, will not be transported entirely in paper form. It seems increasingly the case that wherever practicable and economical, electron movement will replace paper movement.

The Coming of Electronic Mail

Forms of electronic mail have been familiar to us for many years. The well known "telegram" or even the contemporary "mailgram" fit into this category because for most of their movement they are transmitted electronically. But they also represent very specialized types of messages and a small percentage of our point-to-point messages. Compared with what you can send in a first class letter, telegrams are vastly more expensive. Even as "night letters' (sent at nonpeak times, delivered more slowly), or "mailgrams" (transmitted to the nearest post office, then sent to you by regular mail), these forms of electronic message services compete more with long distance telephoning than with mail. When some type of written document is desired, when immediate or interactive feedback is not critical, or when batches of messages are to be sent, are all instances when the telegram is used instead of the telephone.

Large users of such electronic message services are usually on "Telex" networks where they can enter and receive messages directly. Most casual users of telegraphic services, however, still dictate their messages over the telephone to a nearby office, a procedure costly to the service and prone to error. In many cases it is simply easier and less expensive to place a long distance call. As long distance tolls have dropped, so has the number of telegrams sent.

The largest current growth area of electronic mail, however, is not telegraph services but a process known as *facsimile* transmission or what users call simply "fax." Using fax is like using a copying machine. Fax can accommodate printed or typed documents, graphs and tables, and some will even do a usable job with photographs. As with a copying machine, the materials are simply inserted and the image is scanned. Only in this case, the scanned image, now in the form of electronic signals, can be transmitted as sounds over regular telephone lines to anyone who has a similar machine at the other end. The received copy looks much like you pull off from an everyday copier. Machines of this type can now be leased inexpensively and will operate with any telephone receiver.

Unlike what you might imagine from their advertising on television, fax machines do take several minutes to transmit a page of information. What happens when you want to send copy to an individual who does not have a machine? The partial solution is a growing number of small business which offer electronic "mail drop" services. They will receive messages for a fee, then have them available for pickup by the fax address. Many of these businesses will also transmit fax messages for you. These types of fax transmission equipment and services, unlike telegrams, compete more directly with traditional mail service than with long distance telephone calls. It is likely that this competitiveness will increase as fax machines become more widely available and prices decline. Because of microprocesser technology such machines will still reduce somewhat in price, or for the price will offer better service. Costs of electronic transmission, particularly in the age of satellites, will continue to decline for some time. Compare these factors with the labor costs of hand delivering letters as well as the rising costs of petroleum-using trucks, trains, and air transportation systems.

One major trend is for corporations to market entire electronic mail systems. One example is "Faxpak," a service introduced by International Telephone and Telegraph Company. Faxpak will receive facsimile messages in a computer storable form, then the messages can be forwarded largely automatically to any number of designated recipients. The cost, according to ITT, is less than if a user were to send the same facsimile message over conventional long distance telephone circuits. Such services are not only in competition with AT&T's Bell System but with other fax networks, for example Southern Pacific Communications Conpany's "Speedfax" or Graphnet System's "Faxgram."

Because of the equipment required, the fax business will grow much faster in business and institutional uses than in the home. Facsimile should be the leading form of electronic mail by 1990. Growth in use of the machines is predicted to be 17 percent annually, with some 200,000 units in use by then.

Look for continued expansion of facsimile services, including advances in the quality of reproductions. Higher transmission speeds will reduce the cost of long distance telephone line times. Competition in transmission services is already resulting in reduced rates. Several new machines have transmission delay features which allow for automatic dialing and transmission during night periods when rates are less. Advances are being made in getting different brands and models of fax machines to link with one another. Fax in the home will still be a long time in coming, so don't throw away your first class stamps yet.

Telephone Your Mail?

Several fortunate coincidences in communications technologies are speeding the growth of electronic mail systems.

Take, for example, the traffic loads on telephone systems. A remarkable fact is that traffic is at a minimum about *two-thirds* of the 24-hour day. When you use the telephone, it requires that you, whomever you are calling, and the telephone link are all simultaneously tied up for the same amount of time. The peak traffic loads in the day come right before and after the noon hour. At night, transmission drops to a minimum. Mail transmission, by contrast, does not require that you, the receiver, or transmission system be tied up at the same time. Mail is usually sent at the convenience of the sender and read at the convenience of the receiver. If sent in electronic form, it makes good sense to transmit it at the convenience of the system, which is in the nonpeak hours of telephone usage. In this respect, electronic mail has a multibillion dollar transmission network waiting to be used more efficiently.

Another fortunate development is that transmission and switching technologies, even for voice, are evolving toward digital design (see Chapter 9), or in simple terms, the same form as data transmission. If we are to accomplish efficient mixes of telephone and electronic mail transmissions on the same system, there are great advantages if the system is primarily designed for digital communications. And this seems to be increasingly the case. As telephone systems are modernized, they are all the more compatible with transmission of electronic mail.

But even with the foregoing coincidences, how are we to get the mail in *electronic* form originally? We have already seen one way which is growing in popularity: the *fax* machine. More important than this is the curious fact that much of first class mail is already in electronic form before we convert it into paper form and to transport it. How many of your personal or business bills are in a computer generated format? Receipts? Invoices? Form letters? Checks? Credit card statements? Obviously we are rapidly reaching a point where instead of converting messages from an electronic form inside a computer to a paper form for old fashioned mailing, the "mail" will be fed directly into an electronic transmission system. Why transport paper?

Estimates are that by the mid-1960s more correspondence was prepared on electric than manual typewriters. This is still another fortituous circumstance for electronic mail, since the operation of the electric typewriter does in fact convert text into an electronic form. With minor alterations the pulses from the typewriter can go into the transmission network instead of, or in addition to, going on paper. In business and government environments, the splicing of the electronic typewriter and electronic communications system has been developing for a decade. Yet most electronically typed mail still ends up on paper.

Look for growth of electronic mail in forms beyond facsimile transmission systems. Most immediate growth is in business and government environments, especially where telex usage is already commonplace. Watch the several large data-oriented corporations market electronic mail services for business usages. Ask your congressperson to find out what the U.S. Postal Service is doing about electronic mail, and why we should continue to subsidize the Post Office for sending mail the old way.

New Twists

Given that a multibillion dollar transmission system is available and that many messages are in electronic form before they are committed to paper, what slows the development of electronic mail, especially in the home? As you might expect, electronic mail in other than facsimile form has developed first among organizations already dealing in computation, telecommunications, or both. Mainly this is because they have a part of the system in place. For example, the computer network sponsored by the U.S. Advanced Research Projects Agency was set up to experiment with pooling the power of a number of large computers here and abroad, where the unique capabilities of different installations could be shared over a network. In requiring considerable coordination, it was necessary to develop a message system for the network, one giving priority to messages of different levels of urgency, having format standardization and efficient ways for individuals or units to address one another. Member individuals can dial into this network from any telephone temporarily linked with a computer terminal, and can then check designated files for messages; that is, they can check their "mail."

Digitally coded and computer assisted electronic mail systems, while more complex than fax systems, have a major advantage in that message handling — that is, encoding, decoding, storage, retrieval — can be largely automated. Paper may in many or all steps be bypassed completely. Although facsimile systems, due to their smaller initial investment and simplicity, are growing rapidly in business applications, the larger scale, automated digital communications systems will probably be the ultimate mail technology for the long term future.

And in the home? Because of the investment required to change, and long ingrained habits of using, traditional mail, a full service electronic mail from home to home will probably be a much more long term development. Partial variations of it do exist now. For example, telephone text services (Chapter 8) such as England's *Prestel,* have an electronic mail capability. You could switch your television set to the telephone line, dial up your identification number or "mail box," then display on your videoscreen any messages found in the files. Similarly, you could send messages to other files if your home information system had some type of input device, perhaps your electric typewriter linked to a home computer and TV.

While we already have service in some parts of the United States where you can pay your bills by telephone, including systems where you signal transactions by pushing the buttons of the telephone, planners are working on methods so that you receive the bills electronically. By one method available in today's technology, the sender's message comes electronically to a local post office and a facsimile or decoded printed bill is created for mailing to you. Most of the distance that paper would have had to travel is bypassed electronically. But suppose, for example, that you could receive the bills directly via your television text system. Once a month, you could check your bill file, see the charges displayed on your living room or office television, then order payment electronically. In this way, all paper transport would be alleviated, including the paper for the checks. Your transactions for the month could be recorded for you on a small electronic disk which you could file for a few years, then reuse. The system (as some prototypes now do) could allow you to retrieve entries easily from the disk, classify them, do household budget analyses, and probably even develop a special record to be submitted with your income tax return (which you could probably send electronically too!).

Pollsters, market researchers, and government data gatherers are especially interested in mail systems that can "interview" large numbers of people automatically. This could be done in either computer generated voice or text methods. Your telephone number (or mail address) would be randomly selected and the message system engaged. If you chose to respond to the survey, you could speak your answers (or type them) directly into a computer file. The results of the survey could be automatically analyzed as fast as interviews were completed. The same system could easily serve for public "hearings." A list of ongoing hearings would be disseminated via the electronic mail system or international television, then if you wished to have your views registered on the question, you would dial into an interactive file and give your responses. Such systems could certainly give an electronic boost to democratic government.

There are many reasons for speculating that as increasingly sophisticated entertainment centers are found in homes, the same technology will serve telephone and mail needs. Voice or text options should be easily available as well as the opportunity to generate a received message in vocal, text, or graphic forms, with the latter options displayed either on paper or TV screen. Such systems may operate, depending upon the priority and type of service, through links with advanced types or telephone lines, cable TV lines, or some combined form of the two, and perhaps under some circumstances through broadcasting.

As computers become better able to recognize carefully spoken words from a designated vocabulary, it should be possible to initiate text messages or "voicegrams" directly. Here you would simply speak into the telephone and the message would be translated to text by a computer, then stored. According to its priority the message would then be forwarded to your addressee for receipt as text on a TV screen, a printed form, or as speech regenerated by the computer.

Look for electronic mail services in the home to first evolve around use of the push-button phones, such as in current services for bill paying. Later as TV text services become available, assume that electronic mail may be received via your TV screen and perhaps originated through your electronic typewriter or home computer. Eventually, the integration of the telephone, television, small computer, and electric typewriter into home entertainment/communications systems will bring advanced electronic mail services, no doubt eventually involving small home printers or facsimile components. What a way to send your Christmas cards!

**LIVING IN THE
COMMUNICATIONS
FUTURE**

CHAPTER 12

Leisure: Life in Electronic Space

FOR SALE BY OWNER. 4 bedrooms,
3 baths, living, dining and communications room. Utilities, fire and police
alarms computer-controlled.

Moving Toward Electronic Leisure

Mention *leisure* to someone and you are apt to find yourself in a discussion of one of the least understood social
psychological concepts of the twentieth century. For a type
of activity we all like to spend some time in each day and
which business sees as one of the largest growth areas in our
post-industrial economy, it is paradoxical that we know so
little about the basics of it.

Leisure is depicted as freedom to pursue personal interests in the hieroglyphic inscription in Egyptian temple and
tomb walls of nearly 4000 years ago. The ancient Greeks
pondered the values of pursuing leisure behaviors for their
own ends, such as in contemplation or music. The Romans
fixed social values on rest, recreation, celebration. Even
Christians of the Middle Ages saw a valued leisure in religious contemplation. But the industrial revolution reduced
Western concepts of leisure to the narrow definition of that
which is *not* work. Often leisure has only been considered as
behavior engaged in by the very wealthy because they did
not have to work, or by laggards who refused to work.

Even in these last decades of the twentieth century there are many of us in so-called advanced societies who feel a little guilty if we are away from work too long, and even worse, a little uneasy if our work seems to have a touch of leisure in it. Some of that puritan ethic still survives. Our challenge is to broaden concepts of leisure, to see it as a necessary and fulfilling part of life, and most of all, to learn how to use it. Leisure is not just nonwork. It is recovery from fatigue, deliverance from boredom, personal growth. Joffre Dumazedier (1967: 16-17), French sociologist and authority on leisure, holds that

> leisure is activity apart from the obligations of work, family, and society, to which the individual turns at will, for either relaxation, diversion, or broadening his knowledge and his spontaneous social participation, the free expression of his creative capacity.

Some theorists argue that in the future an individual's success with leisure may become more important than success in work. The general trend of work in a highly technological society may be one of standardization and conformity rather than individual expression. Moreover, we will have more time and demands for leisure. Automation of industry and the trend toward a post-industrial economy will result in shorter work weeks. The average life span is steadily increasing. Also, more highly educated populations will demand that more national priority be given to the physical and personal well-being of the individual.

How do we Americans spend our leisure time? Although going to sports events, pursuing hobbies, or exercising might come to mind, studies show that watching television is our number one leisure time activity. We spend roughly 40 percent of our free time with television and all indications are that this figure will increase as the work week reduces and as the new communications technologies transform our environment. Most television sets in this country are now on over six hours per day, tuned in to what adds up to about five million hours of programming annually from over 700 stations.

Among the most enthusiastic consumers of television in America are our children, who, depending upon their age, may average up to four or five hours of television viewing daily. In fact, it has become almost commonplace to point out that children by the age of 12 will have spent more hours watching television than they will have spent in school. Perhaps you have heard of the study several years ago in which children aged four through six were asked: "Which do you like better, TV or Daddy?" Almost half of them (46 percent said: "television."

Most social scientists who write about television still make the mistake of considering it as only one of our many *media* of communication, along with radio, movies, or the newspaper. Perhaps this was true in the 1950s when television was growing up. But now television is much more to us than just one of the media.

Television constitutes an increasing and significant share of our environment. More and more of our leisure time will likely be pursued in this electronic environment.

Look for use of television for leisure activity to increase as energy shortages discourage recreation away from home. Expect massive competition for your leisure time dollar in the form of cable and pay-TV systems, disc, videocassette, and direct broadcast satellite. Assume that big money interests will continue to get into the home entertainment business. (Chances are that your home entertainment system, rather than your car, will be your most major purchase, second only to your dwelling.)

What You See May Not Be What You Get

What kind of leisure is TV viewing? What do we get out of what we see? One generalization that has emerged in 25 years of social research is that most people watch TV simply as a means to relax. Although program tastes and the resulting TV rating systems are evidence of the importance of particular programs or types of programs to viewers, there is good evidence that as often as not the decision is one of simply *watching* TV rather than planning for a detailed schedule of shows. This thought was captured in a cartoon that appeared a decade or so ago where a family sat happily and comfortably in their living room watching a TV set on which was the notice:

Program delayed due
to technical problems

Although researchers disagree about it, evidence has been offered that individuals sometimes view TV in a mesmerized state (see, for example, Krugman, 1971). This is deduced from the presence of a brain wave pattern termed the "alpha state." It occurs during periods of inattention, daydreaming, or falling asleep. You cannot be in an alpha state and actively concentrating on anything in your environment or your thoughts. Studies of this type have generally indicated that a viewing alpha state is often maintained even when the researcher changes the program.

How many times have you turned the TV on at 7 p.m. then been surprised to find yourself suddenly watching the *Tonight* show sign off at 1 a.m.? (Did the sign-off music wake you up?) Perhaps a properly scheduled evening of TV intentionally mesmerizes us in stages until we doze off as movie stars are explaining world politics to us. Perhaps the secret of the *Tonight* show's success is that it strikes the right chord of alpha waves just at the time we are ready for them. This is at least one good reason why some have claimed that the television of today has replaced the hearth of yesteryear as our *electronic fireplace.* Accordingly, we will not usually seek information or entertainment from it, but simply distraction, much the way staring into a campfire is relaxing to us.

This mode of television leisure aptly fits the "chewing gum for the eyeballs" description of American commercial programs: Strictly relaxation.

But then there is also television which, for lack of a better term, titillates. Our senses are aroused by colors, actions, juxtaposition of sounds, interesting faces, sexual images, violence, or the unusual. Obviously this is not an alpha state type of leisure. It fits the type of content that researchers have used to snap viewers out of such states, for example, a scene from *That's Hollywood* where Marilyn Monroe is being hugged while Jane Russell sings in the bathtub. The so-called "T&A" or "jiggling teeshirts" shows of the 1978-1979 season tried to capitalize on this mode of television. (Can you remember *any* plot from *Charlie's Angels?)*

Several studies of children's use of television are as clear as our sophomore psychology lab experiments were in demonstrating uses of the laws of attention. Children tend to watch the television screen most consistently when high attention editing techniques have been used. Researcher Robert Krull claims that he can predict with 80 percent accuracy when children will pay attention to a TV program. He does this based upon analyses of fast cuts from scene to scene, zooms, and camera angles.

In one of my own published studies, Williams, 1969, children were found to talk most about detached scenes with high action content when describing the contents of favorite television shows. Often the plot was of less interest to them, if they understood it at all.

This second type of TV leisure is a momentary and detached arousal. It has been referred to as "junk food TV" by a former corporate television president. It gives an immediate satisfaction. It has no long range value. From the TV business side of things, it gets big prime-time ratings, and that is why there is so much of it.

Television does not have to be all relaxation or momentary arousal, it can also be intellectually and culturally rewarding. We have seen most such examples of this in the form of imports from the British Broadcasting Corporation (BBC) shown on our Public Broadcasting System. *Civilisation, America,* and *Ascent of Man,* along with occasional breakthroughs in American programs, such as *Cosmos,* are persuasive evidence that leisure hours spent with television can be enlightening, if not instructive, in a pleasant sort of way.

We have also had some strong commercial successes in America with programs every bit as rewarding as the aforementioned BBC series. The late 1970s brought a phenomenon in television fare that reached an audience of incredible size (50 million). Neither a war nor the Olympics, it was the historical dramatization of Alex Haley's novel *Roots*. This was the most watched series of television programs in history. This program, later miniseries such as *Holocaust*, *Roots: The Next Generations,* and some since then have demonstrated that there is a viable market for commercial television which is intellectually as well as emotionally re-warding. As David Wolper, producer of the two *Roots* series, has said:

> If somebody has an idea that if the audience is large, the material is less intellectual, that's not true. The audience can be large and the material can be intellectual [*Emmy*, Summer 1979: D-25].

Programs such as *Roots*, which David Wolper calls "docudramas," along with the well known BBC series, might aptly be taken as examples of television as a *literary* form. Such programs are interpretative, creative, humane, have an excellence of form, and contribute ideas of a lasting value. Not all television leisure need be simple relaxation or arousal. Instructional programs, such as *Sesame Street*, are yet another example of a function which television can be used to accomplish. (More thoughts on this use are dis-cussed in Chapter 17.)

Finally, news programming should not be overlooked. Network news in America has a major informational func-tion. It brought the Vietnam War and Watergate directly into our living rooms. The drama of our space shots became near personal experiences for most of us through national televi-sion. National mood has been massively influenced by such television news events as the Kennedy assassination and funeral, the first moon landing, the Sadat-Begin meetings, coverage of the Iranian crisis, and our unfolding challenges of the 1980s.

Americans depend upon television for their information. Since 1963, according to the Roper organization, television has been cited by individuals as their main source of knowing "about what's going on in the world today." Figures from their 1978 survey showed 34 percent saying TV was their main source, 27 percent both TV and newspapers, and 19 percent newspapers only. Roper surveys have also found television to be the most believable news medium, and this since 1961. In 1978 TV had a two to one margin over newspapers in terms of believability (TV 47%, newspapers 23%, radio 9%, magazines 9%).

The overall generalization is not so much exactly what television can be used for or that all programming should look like *Civilisation*. It is that television can offer us many different forms of leisure. Our use need not be all light entertainment nor even literary fare, but whatever mix of uses is most beneficial if not pleasant to us.

Our problem has been that commercial television has not given us the alternatives for that mix. Its programming has tended toward a sameness centered around content that will deliver the largest number of viewers to the commercial period. If these individuals are in the 18-45 age bracket, the segment of our population that does the most buying, such programs will be all the more likely to prevail. It is a marketing pattern which does not cater to alternative tastes.

Nor can we expect noncommercial television to provide the alternatives as was the promise of Public Broadcasting in this country. The Corporation for Public Broadcasting and the Public Broadcasting Service, other than being known for not getting along with each other, are most identified with successful British imports and *Sesame Street* (which was another group's idea). Bill Moyers is a former assistant to President Lyndon Johnson, and himself a public broadcasting figure. A member of a commission to overhaul the system, he says:

> I don't really believe public broadcasting matters very much right now . . . It is a welcome respite from time to time. But as a force in its own right, it has 'miles to go, and promises to keep' [Associated Press, October 23, 1979]

Despite the current conditions of commercial and public television in this country, the communications revolution is positioning us for massive change. The technologies of cable, disc, cassette, and direct broadcast satellite, as discussed in earlier chapters, will create relatively small and specialized markets for television programing. A program will not need to support the overhead of the current network television distribution system. But any successful program will have to carve out its share of market, and this should be a driving force for specialized programming.

Mass television may soon go the way of mass market magazines, and like them (or radio) be replaced by many more alternatives, each catering to specialized markets. Network officials are now often found making public statements that the new technologies will not affect them to any serious degree. But a glance at the financial pages will show you where they are putting their money.

> *Look for* television, because of programming alternatives provided by new communication technologies, to be a far more rich source of leisure activity than it now provides with mass marketed programs. Expect increased opportunities for improving the quality of television offerings. This does not mean just more cultural programming but more alternatives to cater to individual needs and tastes. For this scenario to succeed, viewers will have to use the alternatives and even be willing to pay for them. Otherwise, look for mass marketed mediocrity to move into cable, tape, disc, and pay TV. Either way, your television watching will increasingly be not of what's on but of what you *put* on.

"Waiting for Kojak"

Although we hear many warnings about the quality of television in this country — "coalitions" for this or that, the "moral majority" — American programming has been a constant source of complaint from most foreign countries, particularly those in the developing or "Third" world. We have been accused of cultural imperialism because our prime-time reruns are so cheaply and widely available around the world. The problem is that once a national television is established in a developing country, the population develops a near insatiatible appetite for programs. "Used" U.S. programs are by far the least expensive way to fill the airtime. It is also clear that the general population likes to watch them. Sociologist Elihu Katz once threatened to title his book on Third World broadcasting "Waiting for Kojak."

When television comes to a family or even a nation, it preempts some activities and those which it does not cut into, it may change subtly or even drastically. Television affects lives and cultures.

American Samoa has been of interest to many TV researchers because television only came to this society in the mid 1960s, first as a basis for mass teaching of English, but soon thereafter as an entertainment medium. According to reports from Barry Siegel in the Los Angeles *Times*, life in Samoa has changed appreciably with the invasion of television. Buying habits now include demands for many items intensively advertised in television commercials which, incidentally, were not produced for this broadcast market but imported along with the programs. Breakfast cereals, Tang, Scope mouthwash, Pringles, and Shout are popular items, as is shampoo, which Samoans had no tradition of using before TV. Even Pepto Bismol sells briskly. The local general store which was much the same for 57 years is being replaced by a five-story supermarket.

So too are many traditions changing. There is the *lotu*, the village evening meeting, announced by conch shell blows, where people gather, pray, and discuss the day's happenings. Sunday's lotu is now at a different time so as not to interfere with *All Star Wrestling*, a favorite of the tribal chiefs. The traditional communal meal, consumed by men sitting crosslegged on the floor of an open hut and served by the women of the village, is the same as it has been for generations, except that the NBC *Game of the Week* between the Pittsburgh Pirates and St. Louis Cardinals beams from a television set off in a corner.

> The Pirates score two runs in the first inning. The scene cuts to commercials, taped off KRON-TV in San Francisco, for Pentax cameras, Delco shock absorbers, Ortho Lawn fertilizer, State Farm Insurance and Gillette Foamy shaving lather [The Los Angeles *Times*, June 14, 1979].

Tradition also took a beating when television came to Essex, California in December 1977. For years the residents of the 15 homes in the little desert community got together for Thursday night movies in the one-room schoolhouse, had square dances on Wednesdays, and spent their leisure time with games, books, and visits with neighbors. Now most of the leisure time is spent watching television, even on Thursday nights now that the movies aren't shown anymore. Buying habits have changed too.

> "I think the commercials make more of a difference than the programs," says Mary Howard, who teaches the town's 16 elementary school children. "They have a bigger selling impact than radio or magazines. After watching the commercials, I just had to see if the Ball Park franks really popped and the Imperial margarine really tasted like butter, and I'm trying to think of an excuse to go to Phoenix so I can eat at one of those restaurants I see on television with the sizzling steaks" [*Wall Street Journal*, October 2, 1979].

A lot of life in Essex is scheduled around favorite television shows. Football on TV is now a more popular sport than baseball which was heard on the radio. Children's heroes now include rock and television stars. They express dissatisfaction that there is no nearby roller rink or disco. Television sets are on most of the time, even when reception is bad. They say the noise keeps them from getting lonely. In July 1979 most of the community worried about Skylab falling. Even the kids now tend to pay more attention to the news, claims the local teacher. "It's like being part of the world."

Numerous anecdotal accounts and a few studies reveal consistent effects when television is *turned off* in a home or viewing is otherwise drastically curtailed. The effect is like withdrawal from a habit-forming drug, says Marie Winn in *The Plug in Drug* (1977). There is a period of disorientation lasting anywhere from a few days to a week. Family members are restless and irritable at first, particularly until other leisure time activities begin to substitute for time formerly spent with television. Eventually, family members become more actively interested in what one another are doing. Group meals reappear with conversation again becoming important. Children began to seek out creative activities again (crafts, playing musical instruments, playing outside). Just sitting around and talking becomes important. Some of these effects are obtained when families have substantially reduced time spent in television viewing, say from 25 to 5 hours per week. But there are cases where families have taken the ultimate step of putting away their TV set altogether.

The consequences of reduced television viewing are similar to the observations just described. When television first comes to a community, viewing time is taken away mainly from leisure time activities. These have included movie attendance, social gatherings outside the home, reading, listening to radio, walking for pleasure, conversation, and time spent with hobbies. Contrary to the image of the late-late show addict, most studies have not shown great amounts of sleeping time preempted by TV, usually not more than 15 minutes or less on a daily average.

What can be summarized about television for leisure? First, the status quo, as described from the comprehensive review of research literature by George Comstock and his associates (1978):

(1) We use television mainly to serve our entertainment motives.

(2) We usually *think* of TV as entertainment although it can be used for many ends.

(3) Viewing is more often a decision to turn on the set than to watch a certain show.

(4) The expectation of a type of pleasing program rather than a certain episode is more often our reason for turning to specific programs.

(5) Despite differences in attitudes expressed by people of varying educational levels about TV, most use it for entertainment.

Can we blame American mass marketing of entertainment programs for our shortsighted use of this powerful medium? Probably not totally, for it is our selection of programs, and hence the ratings, which drive the program market in the current system. Although we have long demanded more programming alternatives, they have seldom achieved the viewership necessary for commercial survival in a mass marketed system. As long ago as 1959, in the book *Television in the Lives of Our Children*, we were warned that it's not what television does to us that counts, but what *we do with television*. The communications revolution is transforming the television marketplace. We may well have the alternatives so long sought. Their existence may not have to depend upon mass audience acceptance. If we take advantage of this opportunity, by the next century we might hopefully say that:

(1) We use television to serve many of our information, educational, entertainment, and cultural needs.

(2) Television can be a positive and pleasing source of leisure time activities.

(3) Viewing is most often a decision to see or participate in a particular program.

(4) The expectation of filling our specific needs is the main reason for seeking out a specific program.

(5) Most people's use of television fits their valued personal needs rather than reflecting their being drawn to one type of programming as a mass audience.

Look for an increased concern of the effects of television viewing as the new technologies increase tenfold the programming available to us. Will we view more television or will we view more selectively? Will we use it as "popcorn for the mind" or as a basis for fulfilling a wide range of our personal needs? If it is changing our culture, will we know about it before it is too late to do something about it?

CHAPTER 13

Transportation:
Communicate to Work

Chicago, 1990. Fran and David Lopez have lived two years now in Hartswood, the new greenbelt area about 55 miles northwest of Chicago. In that time they have seen the final installation of the telecommunications services that make it possible for David, an insurance executive, and Fran, an accountant, to live the rural life that this inner city Chicago couple had always dreamed about. The key to the Lopezes' rural existence is that they live within a modern communications network that has replaced many of the functions of the old transportation one. Even the paper carrier has been replaced by electron movement.

Communications/Transportation Tradeoffs

For almost all of the first three-quarters of the twentieth century, transportation in this country was one of the largest growth areas of the American economy and a topic seldom treated in crisis terms. All of this came to an abrupt end in 1973 with the Arab embargo on petroleum exports to this country, the shortages six years later and the rise of crude oil prices over a decade in 1000 percent terms. Not only have we faced visible consequences in terms of long waits at gas stations and an inflationary economy, but we are about to witness many changes in our petroleum-based transportation systems, including their replacement in some cases with communications systems. In research circles these are called *communications-transportation tradeoffs.*

Communication and transportation have a number of interesting relationships. Until the advent of the telegraph in the nineteenth century, all long-range communication was limited to the speed of the transportation system. From the first civilizations of around 4000 B.C. until the implementation of the steam locomotive, messages could not be sent faster than the fastest runners, horses, or sailing vessels, at best around 20 miles per hour. The nineteenth-century locomotive brought this speed up to 30 or 40 miles per hour, but soon thereafter the telegraph freed us from the speed limits of transportation and allowed us to send messages at the speed of light.

Even as we approach the twenty-first century, much communication still moves at the speed of the transportation system, as in the delivery of mail, shipping of books, or distribution of newspapers. This is done at considerable expense of energy, resources (such as paper), and if we carry the argument far enough, most transportation contributes to environmental pollution. But when communication is freed from the bonds of transportation, as with telephone, radio, television, or facsimile, energy use is miniscule, resource needs are negligible, and pollution is almost nonexistent.

The trick is to substitute electron movement for paper or people movement. This is done when the daily news is disseminated by radio, television, or videotext to the home, when educational materials are transmitted to the student rather than having the student travel to them, or when we watch a first-run movie in our home rather than a downtown theatre.

Our homes are inviting environments for communication transportation tradeoffs. Many activities for which we must use transportation, as in education, banking, recreation, or even our jobs, can be carried out partially or totally by communications. We have been "letting our fingers do the walking" for some years now. But our move to adopt these substitutes will probably come about more as a function of the rising costs of transportation than from our eagerness to try out new communications innovations. For example during the fuel crunches in the 1970s, market analysts were busy predicting winners and losers. Any business that depended upon auto travel, for example, was a loser. These included vacation resorts, highway restaurants (notice how many are closed now?), remote amusement parks or shopping centers. Among the biggest winners were "stay at home" items or services — for example, swimming pools, home video equipment, cable and pay TV, and electronic games.

Fuel prices or possible fuel shortages are the basis for many forecasts of growth in communications devices and services. The telephone, for example, will increasingly be used not only for the usual social purposes but to substitute for transportation wherever possible. It is expected that shoppers will do more checking by phone before driving around to stores looking for what they need. Salespersons will use the telephone as a substitute for personal visits to some customers; in fact, the telephone company can show you how to make such substitutions effectively. Even the U.S. government has actively lobbied for use of the telephone as a gas saver; supposedly an average call only uses an amount of energy equivalent to a half tablespoon of gasoline.

It is also expected that mail order and telephone shopping will increase as fuel prices rise. There are already several experiments in this country where shoppers can browse through electronic catalogues via displays on their television sets. They can then place orders via two-way communications links, usually as a part of a cable television system. Banking services are becoming widely available by telephone (see Chapter 16) and in some experimental versions via two-way cable television.

Home entertainment is already known to be one of the most major growth areas of the current U.S. economy. Whereas two parents and their two children would have to pay up to $10 to $20 for movie tickets and another $2 to $5 for auto transportation (gas, parking, maintenance average), they can now have a pay-TV, first-run movie in their home for well under $5. If the current climate of deregulation of cable and satellite broadcasting continues, pay TV may well become one of the biggest growth areas within the already burgeoning entertainment area. Transportation costs, according to analysts, have already influenced this growth. Similarly, the market forecast for all types of home communications devices, including games and computers, is up. Large companies such as Warner Communications and Music Corporation of America which deal in multiple facets of home entertainment such as pay TV, movies, records, books, and video packages are experiencing major growth.

Almost all the services which are deliverable to homes via a communications network to consumers involve some degree of substitute for transportation. Experts on such networks, as reported in a study by Herbert Dordick and his associates (1981), expect that banking and entertainment services will be used in roughly 50 percent of all households in this country by 1995. Other projections of adoption of new services by that year include:

45% — information such as addresses, numbers, calendar of events

40% — home security such as fire and police alarms

30% — shopping by catalog

30% — directory of goods and services

30% — personal message system

30% — games

25% — public information such as zoning regulations, elections, laws

20% — library services

Education is a natural for a communications-transportation substitution if lessons can be transmitted to the home rather than transporting the student to the school. We already have some experience with this in the form of telephone tutorial services set up for homebound students, educational television programs, and the usual "corre-spondence" courses. But as discussed in Chapter 17, educa-tion in this country has little tradition in the use of tech-nology. We will probably see more educational "services" brought into the home by consumers of electronic games, home computers, or educational TV viewers than as a conse-quence of any concerted effort by school systems.

Communication substitutes for transportation have even been introduced from time to time in arguments over school racial integration by busing. Here it has been suggested that classes of racially different schools be linked by video and audio systems rather than transporting pupils across a city so they can experience one another.

Look for increasing uses of communication substitutes for transportation associated with home life. Expect petroleum shortages and skyrocketing costs to accelerate the trends for such substitutions. Look for innovations in patterns of work, leisure, and eventually education so as to reduce needs for transportation. Get ready to put your summer auto trip money into a new home communications system.

Are You Ready to "Teleconference?"

Business is another environment in which rising trans-portation costs and the efficiences of communications tradeoffs are bringing new substitutions. Take, for example, business travels, which accounts for approximately half of the airline travel in this country. Many such trips are for purposes of brief conferences involving exchange of infor-mation, planning, scheduling, and the like. Except for the communication and social advantages of face-to-face con-versation, most of the communications at such conferences could be exchanged electronically — thus avoiding the time and costs of travel. The costs savings of this tradeoff are inviting.

In a study reported by Jack Nilles and his associates (1976), costs of traveling versus communicating from Los Angeles to

New York, Chicago, or San Francisco were compared. In 1976 prices, travel costs (air ticket, taxi, hotel meals) for a one-day trip to New York were $473 per person as compared with $225 if that person were equipped for a full day with a computer terminal, audio line, use of a facsimile machine, plus the cost of the communications circuits. By 1980 the cost of travel increased an estimated 30 percent while the communications costs were about 20 percent reduced. Several additional interesting generalizations were developed from comparisons of different distances and durations. If the New York conference were stretched into three days, then costs of communications would begin to exceed those of transportation and lodging. Also, the distance factor is much more relevant to transportation than communications costs. For example, relative to travelling from Los Angeles, communications substitution saves more money in New York than Chicago, and the latter more than in San Francisco. This substitution, usually called *teleconferencing*, should replace some, but probably never the bulk of, business travel.

A number of large companies, including the U.S. Department of Defense, regularly use teleconferencing in place of travel. Some of the Bell Telephone companies now have teleconferencing installations available for business use. Public television stations, through use of their new satellite interconnection, have begun to teleconference on topics of current interest — for example, women's jobs in broadcasting. Experience increasingly shows that teleconferencing can replace transportation, thus saving energy costs, not adding to pollution, and reducing travel congestion. Message movement replaces people movement.

Another intriguing target for communication-transportation tradeoffs are those of us who have to travel 50 or so miles round trip each day to our jobs. If we work in an information occupation — such as accounting, education, banking, government, certain planning and monitoring sectors of manufacturing — why not use communications to bring some or all of our "work" to us rather than transporting ourselves to the work? This proposition underlies a number of studies into possible ways to decentralize information-based businesses or services. For example, in the Nilles study, one further focus of the research was to consider all of the factors — savings, costs, problems — in decentralizing a large insurance company. Rather than continuing to expand in expensive central city offices, where operating costs are at a premium and to which workers must commute many miles, why not expand instead into smaller, multiple facilities, each located within communities or near workers? For personnel working in an electronic information network, it is not all that important that they be housed under the same roof.

The business environment can also be transformed into an educational one by use of communication-transportation substitutions. In both the Los Angeles and the Palo Alto areas of California, a number of university level courses are broadcast directly into remote classrooms in business and manufacturing organizations. The system, called "instructional television fixed service," is operated in those areas by stations located at the University of Southern California (USC) and Stanford University, respectively. There are also installations in several other parts of the United States. The campus component of the installation includes master classrooms similar to other lecture facilities but with several important additions. They are equipped with remotely controlled television cameras which can follow the lecturers, or focus on the chalkboard and even small hand-held charts or tables. Also, for every two seats in the classroom there is a small television receiver equipped with a "talk-back" microphone and a buzzer device.

Students in the campus classroom follow the lecture as they would any other, except when they have a question they "raise their hand" electronically by pressing the buzzer, then ask their question via the microphone system. Similarly, students in the remote classrooms follow the class on their TV sets and can also "raise their hands" and ask questions via the electronic feedback system.

Student papers and materials provided by the instructor are transported by a regular courier service between the university installations and the remote classrooms. One instructor even worked up a routine whereby students were asked to mail in photographs of themselves which were displayed for the television camera when it was their turn to give oral reports.

The Stanford and USC systems, which serve mainly engineering and computer business employees in nearby corporations, have been well accepted by the students. Many students have reported that the courses were equal to regular classroom experiences on campus. Also, there were savings in time and money because commuting to class was unnecessary. An additional finding of the studies was that many students reported that they probably would not have continued their studies had the classes not been so readily available.

There is no particular reason why educational institutions could not extend their services to a much wider range of potential students using two-way telecommunications. One study on the planning boards several years ago was to extend university classes to a remote classroom in a retirement community. Other ideas have been to offer beginning university classes in high schools, military bases and even prisons.

Look for communications-transportation substitutions to move rapidly into business uses. There is also some growth of distributed work, where an individual does "information" work from home. Expect to find these innovations made earliest by organizations with prior experience in telecommunications, such as research and development groups, oil companies, telephone and communications companies, and "information" industries. Expect aggressive marketing of such services by telephone companies. Also anticipate that these substitutions well occur even more rapidly if we have further fuel shortages or sharp increases in costs. Look for educational and leisure services to be made available by telecommunications in what were originally only work settings. Expect increased opportunities to do certain types of work in the home. Are you ready to *communicate* to work?

The Possibility of New Rural Societies

Communication factors, like geographic and transportation factors, are a basis for designing the boundaries of a "community." Most cities of ancient times evolved because they were convenient to a river or a natural seaport, were situated at the juncture of major trade routes, or were protected from plunder by geographic barriers. Communication in those times was highly tied to those same factors. Message travel was limited to human travel. Public meetings were limited to the range of the human voice.

From the Middle Ages to the industrial revolution, advances in human systems of transportation, and thus communication, began to break free of the geographic barriers which since the beginning of civilization had defined much of what we call "community" or "society." By the time of the Industrial Revolution, community patterns grew largely around transportation systems. Transportation included not only the importation of raw materials and exportation of manufactured goods, but was used for movement of workers between dwellings and factory. We reached the extreme of this in the twentieth century with the evolution of "suburbs," possible only through large-scale transportation systems. American cities maturing early in this period grew around rail systems, as in Chicago. The later ones were patterned by the automobile, as in Houston or Los Angeles. Transportation was the dominant factor.

As we approach the twenty-first century, the concept of a human community is becoming increasingly independent of geographic and transportation factors. Communications-transportation substitutions allow the formation of "communities" through communications networks. These free us from the two forces which have shaped our communities since the beginning of civilization. We are apt to see some major changes in the configuration of human communities, or the new "people networks."

One major consequence is that our choice of dwelling places — that is, the physical environment which is most desired by us — can be increasingly independent of where we must be in order to earn a living, or in a more modern sense, to pursue a career. Some of the most enlightened thinking on this topic came from the late Peter C. Goldmark (1972) in his concept of the "new rural society."

The problems of the city, among other things, stem from the consequences of high density living, a situation which imposes undue stresses not only on the individual but upon now overburdened systems of urban government. The industrial age moved economic opportunity, and thus populations, from the farms to the cities. Mass industrialization requires population concentrations. The trend has been for cities to continue to grow into advanced states of unmanageability. Many of our largest cities are growing into one another so as to form megalopolises such as with the Boston-Washington areas or Los Angeles-San Diego. Meanwhile, many of our rural areas have become economically depressed. One solution studied extensively by Goldmark was to decentralize cities by use of telecommunications technologies. He envisaged a powerful communications network which would distribute work and necessary services to rural communities each limited to a size which would optimize quality of life. Just as the industrial age and transportation advances spawned the growth of cities, the post-industrial age and communications may encourage new configurations of housing patterns.

In describing his strategies for developing the rural society, Goldmark (1972) drew upon results of British research which indicated that the greatest single problem in urban decentralization was likely to be "reduction in operating efficiency due to the stretching of communication links." The key then would be to devise ways of "stretching," and for this Goldmark proposed a system of new community communications networks. The main network would be a substantial expansion of the telephone system so as to include videophone and computer linkages for data transmission. The objective would be to interconnect as fully as possible everybody in the community. This would be just as critical as the streets, electricity, and other utilities are to a modern city. "Stretching" was to be accomplished by having all homes just as connected as if they were in physical proximity, perhaps even more so.

The second network would be similar to current radio and television broadcasting, but insuring that all citizens had full access to it. This would be complemented with a third network in the form of a powerful two-way cable communications system. Using this system, citizens should have access to a variety of information sources pertinent to their "community," allowing monitoring of local municipal events such as budget hearings, community council meetings, school board proceedings. Participation in these meetings could be accomplished remotely by using the two-way capability of the cable system. Additionally, the two-way system would provide a basis for instant polling of public opinion on local issues. Videotext services would provide information on shopping, travel, weather, entertainment, civic meetings, and any item of potential importance to the community members. As with many modern cable installations, additional commercial and public television stations would be made available, as would pay entertainment services and instructional materials.

A fourth major network would interconnect the operating components of the community government — city office, fire and police, airport, train stations, schools, libraries, and hospitals. Smooth operation of city government, which itself may be physically decentralized, is a vital requirement of the system, which would make desired interconnections between the city government components and dwelling units. These interconnections would likely involve all of the first three dwelling unit networks as appropriate. For example, emergency weather conditions might be announced via regular television or radio broadcasts, but further information could be obtained by telephone or interactive cable TV.

It is important to emphasize that the great array of services just described are intended to fulfill internal communications services of the decentralized community. They were Goldmark's strategy for "stretching the links" so to speak. The community would additionally have all of the traditional external communications links, plus special links for such services as electronic mail, pay TV for sports and cultural events, and interconnection with several colleges or universities.

Look for a steady growth of interest in city decentralization through communication networks as urban problems mount, transportation becomes prohibitively expensive, and population concentrations overburden the pollution tolerance of our environment. At the same time expect marketing of communication network services to home and business to promote growth in the direction of infrastructures necessary for urban decentralization. But due to the massive investments involved and the necessary overriding of protective and outdated legislation, do not expect significant progress toward urban decentralization until it becomes our government's policy. It's still too early to give up your New York apartment.

Switched On Communities

Too often we think of "community" in physical terms but for us humans it can just as well refer to community of interests. The freedom from geographic and transportation factors that communications provides is the basis for new types of communities, ones assembled via communications networks. The ad hoc or "birds of a feather" community formed when individuals use the same communication-based service or services might be as transient as the audience of a prime-time television special or as permanent as the international communications network of a multinational conglomerate.

When considered in more abstract terms, the development of communications infrastructures in education, health, leisure, politics, or for decentralized employment are ad hoc communities ordered around the interconnection of specialists engaged in the services or activities. When outsiders partake of the services, they are momentarily visitors to those communities. The specialists who compose these communities and their customers or visitors, because they are linked by communications networks, are theoretically free of geographical and transportation restraints. The probability of a viewer tuning into a network TV special in Seattle is no different in geographic or transportation terms from a person tuning in from Orlando. Members of the American Medical Association in those two cities are *almost* unhampered by transportation factors in their professional linkage save for the fact that the mail still goes by land and air transportation.

As we said in Chapter 6, once a satellite communication system is in place, message distance among communicating units is irrelevant. When we reach that point of a "wired world" or "global village," the communications networks of the future will not only allow us to dwell independently from the physical source of services or activities we desire, but will increase the probability of any one of us joining a mixture of *ad hoc* community networks.

If you have ever experienced both life in a small town and life in a large city, or can imagine the contrast, you will sense the freedom of alternatives that communications-based communities will bring. In a small town your educational, occupational, and recreational activities often have a substantial overlap of the same individuals, the same social grouping. Information overlaps also. People in your recreational activities can be influenced in their attitudes toward you from a knowledge of your occupational or educational doings or background. Your various communities tend to be superimposed by geographic factors. By contrast, life in a city, due to transportation, allows substantial independence among the "communities" where you work, play, learn, or engage in politics. Geographic factors are less relevant. You may not know who lives next door, let alone who lives in the neighborhood. You can change your leisure community simply by driving to a different part of the city. The choice is yours whether you wish to generate overlap in the people who populate your different communities.

Look for your "community" options to increase far beyond the options brought to you by the transportation networks as the new large communications networks become personally available to us. Just as the talented and the creative have always sought out great cities as the environment offering the widest choices, so will they be drawn to network communities. The communications-based communities of tomorrow will play host to the brightest and most energetic of our society. But the networks alone will not guarantee this optimistic future. The full human potential of the network communities will only be reached if we plan positively for it. The same network could also be a suffocating tool of an oppressive government. Just as great cities become oppressive under negative conditions, the new network communities could also become very lonely places. Even if transportation crises are met with communications solutions, expect to ask the question: Is life any better?

Health: What To Do Until the Computer Comes

Cape Kennedy, FL, 2001. The Satellite Health Service of North America (SHSNA) launched the first of its "A" series medical network satellites today. SHSNA-A will provide two-way medical telecommunications services to 1500 remote diagnostic units located in sparsely populated regions of the North American continent. This will bring primary medical services and preventative health programs to nearly three million remotely located individuals, about 50 percent of whom have no other means of modern medical care. The launch team affectionately calls the new bird "Kildare I."

Prescription for Change

Medical services are among the most changed — and highest changing — institutions in the modern world. Physicians are high adopters of technology, both the soft technology of "know-how" and the hard technology of instrumentation. The sum of all this is that the quality of medical care has improved immeasurably in our century, although there are inequities in the availability of it. Just how communications technologies will blend into health care can best be seen

AUTHOR'S NOTE: I am indebted to Dr. Charles Lewis, Chairman of the Department of Medicine at the University of California, Los Angeles — a colleague of mine for a sabbatical year at the Annenberg School — for reinforcing my thoughts on the concept of using the media for the advancement of a positive public image of health, which is explored in this chapter. Dr. Lewis is a coauthor of *A Right to Health* (1976).

against the broad context of change in medical practices. What is this context?

Most physicians are now specialists. Granted some of us, especially in small towns, may know our doctor as we know our banker or lawyer. But the majority of physicians and their patients will increasingly come into contact with one another for specialized rather than general medical consultation. This presents the problem of the distribution of specialists. A town may have its "doctor," but it is unlikely this will involve in every case a substitution by a team of specialists. There is the problem of how specialists are distributed for the best access by the population.

We already know that specialist medical practices promote institutional settings. Most of us visit our doctors in clinics, hospitals, or office medical complexes. The doctor practicing out of a home or the "house call" exist mainly in memories or TV shows. Specialists require settings which can also house their increasingly complicated diagnostic equipment and the personnel to operate it. Consultation and referral among specialists is greatly enhanced when the experts, the technology, and the administrative personnel are under one roof. Although this configuration benefits the physician and the patient who has easy access to the facility, it increases the distance between the average patient and physician, especially in rural areas. Centralization raises problems of patient transportation, and for some of these communication might offer a solution.

We are also likely to see more personnel substituting for the physician on certain routine tasks. The physician's time can be more efficiently spent in the interpretation of diagnostic information rather than in the "hands on" procedures of X-ray, blood tests, urine tests, and the like. Even increasing amounts of the verbal consultations with patients are carried out by paramedical professionals as in gathering medical history, handling medical administrative matters, or hearing the initial health complaints. Just as these personnel have replaced the doctor for many routine tasks, so now is technology assisting and in some cases replacing the paramedic. This is seen, for example, in automated analysis of blood samples, or the use of small computers to "take" medical histories. The centralization of specialists in large medical complexes increases the likelihood that investments can be made in such technologies.

Most of us have access to far superior medical care than was available in the past, even in the absence of house calls. But probably even more visible to the average citizen has been the spiraling cost of health care, which has increased to the point where without insurance or some type of medical coverage, treatment of any significant illness is likely to be accompanied by traumatic financial effects. Between 1960 and 1980, personal expenditure for health care rose nearly 600 percent, and one estimate for the period from 1980 to 1990 is a further increase of 300 percent. Inflation is one factor in these increases, but more significant ones are high costs of new technologies, the involvement of more and highly trained specialized personnel, the use of more diagnostic testing techniques, the increasing necessity and cost of malpractice insurance, and the costs of administering health insurance plans.

The cost of medical care is not likely to recede to prior levels. As a society we have chosen to commit a greater share of our wealth to health care. It is one of those major growth areas of a post-industrial society. Somehow, like increased investments we have made in transportation, education or government, the financing of health care will no doubt have to evolve with as radical changes as the practice of medicine itself. Perhaps greatly improved practices will promote a shift toward less costly preventative medical care.

Advances in biomedical technology are forcing upon us far more profound value judgments than simply the delivery of services. These are the weighty issues of birth control, abortion, genetic counseling, fetus diagnosis, patient's right to treatment, medical research on human subjects, *in vitro* conception ("test tube babies"), genetic manipulation, mood control, euthanasia, organ transplant "rights," and the legal, biomedical, and theological definitions of life and death itself. By the nature of their existence these issues are due to advances in biomedical technologies, but public awareness of them is almost exclusively a function of far reaching and dramatic treatment by the mass media of communications.

Medical controversies make exciting and salable news. Even the practice of medicine itself is a natural for television plots (*Dr. Kildare, Ben Casey, Marcus Welby, Medical Center, Emergency, General Hospital, M*A*S*H*). Much of the public attitude regarding medical issues is conditioned by sensational news coverage or "show business" treatments in the media rather than careful dissemination of facts or by personal experiences.

Biomedical technologies continue to advance rapidly — more rapidly than we have public consensus or laws to guide vanguard medical practices or experimentation. Yet public knowledge and consideration of medical issues which reach to the very foundations of our attitudes about life and death are mostly reactive, and unfortunately often a response to superficial and sensational news reporting. We seldom use our national media as a basis for anticipating biomedical issues, and even less often as a forum in which to deliberate rationally on the values of alternatives.

Meanwhile, implicit values slowly reveal themselves as we witness the effects of the biomedical revolution upon our society. We are having fewer children. The traditional family is accompanied by a variety of single and group lifestyles. We actively seek mood control. The mean age of our society is steadily advancing. The growth of health care as a component of our economy is exceeded only by our expectations of its services.

Look for the continued implementation of communications technologies to alleviate problems in the delivery of medical services. Clerical automation — medical recordkeeping, accounting, word processing, appointments — can reduce administrative overhead in large clinical settings. New generations of smaller and less expensive computers, combined with improved programming, will distribute these services to smaller clinical units. Expect to see continued growth in medical information networks which allow for the rapid dissemination of medical research information. As in the "SHSNA" example, assume that two-way diagnostic services will expand on communications networks. Note that the medical profession is already looking to the new communications technologies for their "career-long" education needs.

"The Computer Will See You Now"

Jerrod Maxmen, in his *Post-Physician Era (1976)*, predicts that in 50 years the computer will replace the physician as the primary agent of health care. A few highly skilled physician-researchers could monitor and constantly improve the automated medical decision systems. The necessary "human" link between the computer and the patient would be a health care professional selected for talents in interpersonal communication and sensitivity toward the ill. Simple medical advice could be dispensed directly by the computer to the patient.

Computers and physicians share a number of characteristics. Both depend upon memory, or a "knowledge base," for many types of problem solving. Both have strategies for evaluating new problems against the knowledge base. Physicians have their medical history forms, their routines, and questions which by process of elimination narrow down to identification and analysis of the specific problem. Computers have "branching" program procedures which take input data and attempt to assess them in successive steps. Both physician and computer use procedures whereby data can be evaluated in alternative ways for comparative purposes. Both attempt by the most objective manner possible to derive a rational solution, or more often, probabilities of alternative solutions. Physician and computer can repeatedly reassess these probabilities. Finally, both can take experience gained from one case of problem solving and add it to the knowledge base to facilitate future solutions. In theory, there isn't much that a physician can do that a computer cannot, including development of a good bedside manner. This is a challenge for computer programmers.

Whether Maxmen's prediction of physician obsolescence will hold is not as important as the fact that computers do have especially valuable capabilities for diagnostic procedures. No human processing and storage of large bodies of medical information, even by teams of specialists, will ever match even obsolete computers. To the extent that medical practices do not take advantage of this information processing power, they are themselves obsolete.

Yet to solve problems, or, for example, to determine from diagnostic information the nature of an illness, a computer must have an accurate program. Although the science of automatic programming (that is, where a computer develops its own program rather than being programmed) is growing rapidly, there is scant research into medical applications. To solve a complex diagnostic problem a computer must have a decision and evaluation pattern much the same as the physician follows as a matter of experience. There may be disagreement on these patterns or "logical pathways" for certain types of serious illness, so it is not just a matter of converting them to computer form. Also as anyone who has had some experience in computer programming will understand, a formal undertaking to develop diagnostic programs will have the extra benefit of clarifying thinking on the nature of the diagnostic patterns themselves. Put into simpler terms, the computer modeling of complex problem solving often lends fresh insights into the topic of study. It is hoped, then, that research in this area will not only result in the automation of diagnostic procecures but will contribute to our understanding of the process of diagnosis itself.

Another advantage of large computer systems is that they can be used to assemble the collective experiences of a great variety of diagnostic instances. These assemblages, by including rare and exceptional cases, could increase the diagnostic power of the system. Not only would such systems provide a basis for pooling the collective experiences of experts, but could continually add ongoing diagnostic experiences as well. If this system were a network of computers and remote diagnostic stations, we would have a system of almost unlimited growth and coverage.

What about the bedside manner of computers? There are numerous examples where computers are being used successfully to gather patient background or administrative information. The Veterans Administrative Hospital in Salt Lake City has used computer-conducted interviews extensively for mental health diagnoses. The amount of time expended as compared with traditional three to five day routines was reduced to five hours. Costs averaged about $120 rather than $500 per patient. But it is hard to imagine computer terminals as we know them being used in a great variety of medical communication situations. Perhaps this is why Jerrod Maxmen has predicted the emergence of the new medical professional to serve as a link between the patient and medical computing system.

Because great amounts of a physician's time are devoted to diagnostic procedures that can be conducted by a single human mind with access to reference books, it is not likely that physicians as we know them will pass soon from the scene, let alone be replaced totally by computers. Nonetheless, we are already experiencing the growth of computer applications in medicine. A more conservative prediction is that just as the computer has not replaced the designer or manager, it will not replace the physician. However, we may expect computer-assisted medicine to evolve in ways not dissimilar to computer-assisted design or computer-assisted management.

Look for steady growth of computer application in medical settings. Already widely used for administrative purposes, computers will grow in use for the storage, manipulation, and retrieval of health information. Eventually we should see regular application in the automation of diagnostic processes, both in research and practice. Ultimately, public access to medical computer systems could handle many routine health needs and could serve in health education (. . . and the million dollar computer said "take two aspirin and go to bed").

From Manuals to MEDLARS

The output of medical research literature is too overwhelming for any one scholar or practitioner to assimilate or even to monitor effectively. It exceeds a quarter of a million articles in over 20,000 journals. The National Library of Medicine in Bethesda, Maryland houses our nation's best, if not the world's foremost, collection of these materials. How can the information in these journals and several million books be best managed? A partial solution was achieved in 1964 with the introduction of the Medical Literature Analysis and Retrieval System ("MEDLARS" for short). This computerized system allowed for automation of many of the procedures involved in indexing, filing, and retrieving information on specific topics. Its *Index Medicus,* an annual publication in the neighborhood of 1000 pages, can be retrieved and compiled by the computer in a single morning. The index is circulated to some 8000 medical facilities and libraries around the world. MEDLARS is one of the foremost examples of a computerized management information system in practical use.

As with most advanced information systems, the next step is to make the files directly available to system users through their own computer terminals. Rather than forwarding a request to the library staff for a literature search, clients can do the search from their own office. This "on-line" version, known as "MEDLINE," began operating in 1971. Clients make inquiries via their own computer terminal keyboards, most terminals being linked via regular telephone circuits to a library computer. Materials are designated under any one of a combination of up to 13,000 different subject labels, by author, title of the original article, or publication reference. Given the request, MEDLINE then provides a full bibliography of entries in the designated categories, and in some cases article abstracts. Clients include major medical schools, research centers, and hospitals. About a half a million searches are made per year, each one taking only a few minutes. MEDLINE files cover journal articles for the most recent three years with older materials available through special files. Specialized bibliographies are available in subject matter areas such as toxic chemicals, cancer, and identifications of chemical substances.

Given the continuing decrease in the costs of computers and associated data transmission systems, it is only a matter of time until medical information management systems become available in most medical settings. Not all users need be connected to the National Library of Medicine or its affiliates. It is quite possible for smaller information retrieval systems to be installed in medical school libraries or major medical complexes. Clinics or individual physicians could then subscribe locally for information services. Computer and videodisc storage systems make it feasible also to consider compact computerized "libraries" in small clinics or office suites of physicians. (Remember that a videodisc can hold 55,000 "pages.") These systems, coupled with programs for assessing diagnostic information, medical recordkeeping, or continuing education for medical personnel, make the cost-benefit arguments even more attractive for the spread of small computerized information systems in the medical field. Already, there are examples where small computers, often costing under $10,000, are used to automate routine tasks such as the audit of medical records, scheduling of nurses and other personnel, monitoring certain physiological information, as well as managing data files of small, specialized units in a hospital (such as medical supplies).

Look for the spread of information management services throughout the medical profession, the automation of record keeping, and, perhaps most important, facilitation of the flow of medical research information to the practicing physician. Because of speed, cost, and power of information management, expect medical publishing to go increasingly "electronic." The next logical step is to bring the patient "on line" with the medical information system. Certain medical files can logically be shared by physician and patient. Don't be surprised if within this decade a computer, rather than a nurse, will collect the details of your medical history during a visit to your physician.

The Coming of "Telemedicine"

Directly contrary to centralization of medical facilities is the need to deliver medical services to remote areas. Perhaps you have read of small communities in the United States advertising for a town doctor, even offering financial guarantees. Physicians have always tended to prefer urban areas. Now the attractiveness of clinical environments and advanced technologies are increasing this trend. There is also a correlation between per capita income and the ratio of physicians to inhabitants. How can medical expertise be widely distributed when the trend is for centralization? One answer is the use of telecommunications technologies, including communication satellites.

There has already been successful experimentation with use of satellite communications to link remote areas with centralized medical facilities. One involved the ATS-6 satellite launched by the U.S. National Aeronautics and Space Administration for research purposes, including the delivery of social services. In 1974, after a research phase which included dissemination of public educational material to the population of India, ATS-6 was repositioned for experiments in Alaska and our Rocky Mountain states. Among these was the linkage of five remote sites in Alaska so that television, voice, and medical data transmission could be exchanged. Also linked in Alaska were examining rooms in Galena and Fort Yukon with a Public Health Service facility in Tanana.

Another linkage was possible with the National Library of Medicine in Bethesda, Maryland mentioned earlier.

Medical personnel, patients, and researchers were generally satisfied with the results of the experiments which included regular diagnoses and treatment of individuals in the remote locations. The communications network was extended easily to other locations in the northern hemisphere so that extra specialists could be consulted. Patients' records were successfully maintained in an experimental link with a unit in Tuscon, Arizona. Researchers concluded that medical care in the experimental areas was significantly improved, including acknowledgment that several lives were saved. Human adaptation to the telecommunication systems was demonstrated as feasible and practical. Costs, as in any experimental project, were high. But there was promise that the investment could be amortized over a reasonable period of service. It might be possible, too, that other services simultaneously provided by the satellite (TV broadcasting, education, navigation, business data links) would significantly reduce the cost for medical (or *telemedical*) applications.

There are also examples of linkages of remote medical facilities that are well beyond the experimental stage. Boston's Logan airport has a health station linked by two-way television and audio with Massachusetts General Hospital. The station is supervised by a staff nurse who, when necessary, can contact the hospital for the services of a physician over the video system. Physician and patient can interact directly. Certain data obtainable from X-ray, EKG, or even a stethoscope can be transmitted over the link to the physician. Experience with this unit has been judged most satisfactory, both from doctor and patient standpoints.

The University of Alabama Hospital operates a 24-hour medical information service for physicians in the state. Called "Medical Information via Telephone." the service handles 300 to 400 calls daily.

Current barriers to the use of telecommunications for delivery of medical information or health services are not necessarily technological ones. There is far more communications technology in place than is being used for health-related communications. The barriers are more ones of initiative, attitudes, and, of course, costs. Most applications of telecommunications in this area have been stimulated by agencies other than the health service units and personnel directly involved. The initiative for trial use of telecommunications technologies has come from researchers and planners rather than health care practitioners, and have mostly been in the form of grants from the federal government for demonstration projects.

Often there are attitudinal barriers such as found by Herbert Dordick and his colleagues (1981) in their study of telecommunications uses in vocational rehabilitation. Potential users of communications technologies often had quite fixed attitudes from prior experiences with them in everyday life. Television, for example, was thought of as solely an entertainment medium, as were video cassette or video disc. Clients rarely considered how television might be used for educational or two-way communications purposes. Radio was often considered as simply "background noise" for home, car, or office rather than a potentially useful communications medium for dissemination of rehabilitation information. Many potential users of sophisticated applications of telephone service such as in conferencing or fascimile transmission were unaware of such services. And computers were typically considered excessively "complex and uncontrollable." The researchers took the position that existing attitudes about communications technologies were one of the most complex barriers to surmount in getting people to use the new telecommunications techniques.

Look for steady growth in the use of telecommunications in the conduct and delivery of health services. Expect increased centralization of medical facilities to promote the need for telecommunications services for the delivery of health care to remote or unique sites. A desirable long-range goal is to provide services and information as directly and interactively as possible to the patient. Presumably this will be via telephone, cable, or satellite medical communications networks. Maybe "home calls" will return again, but in electronic form.

A Mass Communication Rx for Health?

Lewis Thomas, in his *Lives of a Cell* (1975), makes the point that technology in medicine, unlike in space, defense, or industry, goes largely unevaluated. We assume its existence and development. Yet upon closer evaluation, technology enters into medicine on some remarkably different levels. One level is the many hours that physicians devote to supportive therapy — being with a patient when there is not much else that can be done; for example, with polio victims when that disease existed widely and treatments were unsure. This is an almost *non*technology level. Great amounts of costly professional time are involved, but there are no technological substitutes.

A second level is a kind of "halfway" technology where compensations are sought for the debilitating effects of disease. This includes heart and other organ transplants, major therapies for cancer, or the high technology of coronary care units. This is an extremely expensive application of technology and it is only a compensation for what we cannot otherwise prevent or cure.

Finally there is a level of technology so effective, according to Lewis, that we rarely appreciate it. This mainly involves immunization and antibiotics. Here we understand and thus prevent or control disease, if not eradicate it. The cost of this technology is low, especially when compared to former costs of treatment when the disease went largely unchecked. Imagine, for example, the cost of a polio shot compared with a lifetime of recuperation and therapy. If we were to have more control over our investments in medical technologies, Lewis would opt for far more research into the basic biological mechanisms of disease. Such research is the basis for the third and most efficient level of medical technology.

If we conduct a similar analysis of communication technologies as applied in medicine, the results offer an interesting counterpoint. In this chapter we have mainly concentrated on communication technologies as involved in medical information and services. The focus has been on use of technologies to manipulate large bodies of medical research information, long distance communications links, and the use of computers to automate the diagnostic process. Only occasionally have we alluded to the citizen's direct benefit from communication technologies in any health-related sense.

If we were given the hypothetical opportunity to guide investments in the use of communications technologies in health care, where might the most significant gain be made? The applications of communications technologies in medical settings are growing as fast as the health profession can assimilate them, so massive extra investment would probably not be warranted there. Relative to its potential, we do have one great failure in the use of communications technology in health areas. This is the use of the nation's mass communications system not only for public education on health matters but for deliberation over the value decisions thrust upon us by biomedical advances. Consider, for example, some of the medical dramas of the last half of this century:

- Controversies over fluoridation of city water supplies.
- National immunization campaigns and the rare but tragic mistakes. (Did you receive one of the "swine flu" shots a few years ago?)
- The side effects of Thalidomide; limbless children; the case of Sherry Finkbine, who had used Thalidomide and sought an "illegal" abortion.
- The right to have abortions; the rights of the fetus; government sponsorship of abortions.

- Chemical or physical barriers to conception; the ethics of promotion of birth control among given groups. Is it genocide?)

- Availability of vital organs for transplant; currently the decision lies solely with a donor, yet there are many more needs for organs than there are organs available.

- When is death? Who has the right to "pull the plug" on patients with irreversible brain damage whose life processes are supported by machine?

- Do patients (or parents of same) have the right to "last chance" experimental drugs (such as "laetrile") when medical authorities declare them worthless or even dangerous?

- The first "test tube" baby is growing up. *In vitro* conception paves the way for genetic manipulation of the fetus, not to mention its effects upon traditional premises of human gestation.

If these problems have not already had their toll in challenges to individuals, they pose a monumental challenge to the ability of our society to generate value-based judgments. Unfortunately, most public knowledge has come after the fact, has been played up in sensationalist newspapers, or has been the occasional topic of a dramatic television show. We have not used our national media to alert society to these issues, nor to provide a forum for full and balanced deliberation. Somehow we must use the new technologies, especially their interactive potential, to facilitate social awareness of, and reaction to, biomedical techniques which may soon have the power to alter human life itself.

But perhaps there is an even more basic use of our communications technologies. This is to promote a positive public attitude about health itself. Too often we consider "health" as only the opposite of "disease" rather than a positive goal to be sought in everyday living. If we were to invest as much in our national media for a campaign to build highly positive attitudes toward physical and psychological health as we do for patent medicines, sugar cereals, and deodorants, we might accomplish as much toward the prevention of disease as we do with all other communications technologies used in the institution of medicine.

Look for the image of health and disease as portrayed in the media — even how physicians and their practices are portrayed — to receive more attention. Note that attempts to promote health by media are not typically successful, including the television series developed by the makers of *Sesame Street*. Despite the remarkable advances in uses of communications technologies in medicine, look for perhaps the greatest challenge to be in the advancement of a positive public image of health itself.

CHAPTER 15

Politics: Push-Button Government

NEWSTEXT FLASH, April 16, 1994. At 18:30 E.S.T. this channel will carry the national pro and con report on the President's proposed network of fusion power plants. Following the program at 20:00, you are invited to participate by sending in your opinions. Your interactive channel "B" will be linked to the National Polling Corp. computers . . . Press "5" if you wish more information on this now.

1984?

Communications systems can be a basis for widespread participation in government by an informed citizenry, or at the other extreme they can be one of the technologies by which an elite can enslave a population. Surely the current great advances in communications technologies could be used for either. It is the hand of the controller which counts.

Political systems and communications systems are two sides of the same coin. For most of history we can see how the limits of political influence were defined by the limits of the communication system, which itself was configured by geographic and transportation factors. That the great civilizations of antiquity were configured by rivers such as the Tigris and Euphrates, the Nile, or by natural sea ports on the Mediterranean is as much a communications phenomenon as a geographic one. Artifacts of Egyptian hieroglyphic writing reveal to us how the political order of the pharaohs was carried by written and spoken symbols to the limits of their transportation system (which included the land of the after-life). The spread of the Roman Empire can be studied in terms of great investments in a transportation and communication system.

It was not until the nineteenth century and the invention of the telegraph that communication networks of nations were able to transcend transportation ones. Messages now could move at the speed of light rather than the speed of humans or transportation machines. Further advances in communications, the telephone, and radio in the late nineteenth and early twentieth centuries made possible changes in political orders heretofore restricted by geographic and transportation limits. The ascendance to world power in the mid-twentieth century of such geographically dispersed nations as the United States and the Soviet Union would have been improbable under a political system where the communications and transportation infrastructures were synonymous.

In the age of mass communications it is also easy to see how the operation of a national communications system reflects the political philosophy of a country. Well before the USSR was founded, Lenin wrote in the revolutionary paper *Iskra* ("Spark") about the importance of using communications to raise political consciousness and to promote the socialist political order. When the revolutionary government came into power, radio was used as an important instrument of political communications in a country spanning two continents. An extensive system of loud speakers carried the radio message to virtually every public gathering place in the nation.

The mass communications system is an important branch of government in socialist countries. It is a tightly managed, centralized system of political and cultural orientation. Although we in the West freely criticize socialist press and broadcasting for its characteristics, most notably lack of "free speech," it would be illogical for them to operate in any other way. (As I was reminded by an Eastern European colleague: "It is *your* First Amendment!")

Government control of communications in this country has a tradition of being weak, the application being mainly upon regulating the *carriers* of electronic communications rather than the content of what is transmitted. Limits of the broadcast spectrum and the advantages of a certain degree of monopoly in wired communications services have necessitated a minimal level of government regulation.

Regulations about content have been mostly in regard to our First Amendment, the guarantee of free speech, the legal interpretations of which extend far beyond any communications medium possibly imagined by our founding fathers. We have the tradition of journalism being a "fourth estate" (after government, church, and so forth) in the operation of our society. If there were any doubts about its power in recent times, they were dispelled by Watergate.

Socialist theorists of communications criticize our communications system as being exploitive and disorienting, not only to ourselves but to other nations when our programming is exported. It is declared exploitive because advertising creates false markets. Presumably it encourages the public to buy goods and services they do not need. Disorientation is said to stem not only from the effects of advertising but from the argument that our media do not expose the social injustices of a capitalistic society, the so-called "objective reality." As the world's largest exporter of movies and television programs, we are often accused by socialist and Third World countries as "media imperialists," a new form of colonialism.

Although we are not ourselves uncritical of the media in our country, its survival (if not flourishing growth) in a free marketplace is evidence of its wide public acceptance among Americans. It is questionable whether any other type of system would be compatible with our political orientation. This is perhaps why public broadcasting has had such limited growth as a major medium in this country. We simply have no tradition for any other system than a commercially based one.

Third World countries often characterize socialist and U.S. media systems as opposites on a political continuum. Many of these countries have established systems that have sufficient government control to advance national political goals, but which also allow some opening to the commercial marketplace. The public corporation of a BBC type is attractive to Third World countries, but it is usually coupled with the opportunity to accommodate limited amounts of advertising. The latter stimulates the economy and provides revenue to offer entertainment programming.

How might the communications revolution affect the communications infrastructure of political orders? Will it make centrally controlled systems all the more powerful for political orientation of a nation? In a free enterprise system will it expand the marketplace for commercial sales of program material as well as for advertising? The answers are not simple, but as communications systems play an increasingly key role in post-industrial economies, we can expect changes in the communications infrastructures of nations to have consequences upon the political ones.

Since the mid-1970s we have seen an increased international interest in the flow of communications, particularly news. In the United Nations Educational Scientific and Cultural Organization (UNESCO) we have had frequent debates on the need for a "new world information order." Debate is fueled in part by the imbalance in Western (or northern) media flow into the Third World relative to national production in those countries. It is also based upon the biases imposed by the free world's news services which often fail to do in-depth reporting in developing countries, instead emphasizing crisis, disasters, and incompetence.

On these counts it is difficult to deny the arguments. On the other hand, the socialist countries have joined Third World countries in proposing international communications agreements which, among other things, would license journalists. Promoted under the guise of "protecting" journalists, such agreements could effectively control international news flow. In the majority of the countries of the world, internal news flow is regulated to various degrees by governmental agencies, usually the "ministry of information." This is a direct reflection of using national communications to advance political stability and power. As we have already said, it is a logical extension of a political system. There are, however, two inevitable challenges coming to the fore and they are brought by the communications technology revolution.

One is reflected in the debates over the "new world information order." New technologies make it increasingly difficult to control international news flow. Some of the same foreign governments who so vehemently complain about Western journalists reporting about their country freely monitor international news feeds via satellite broadcasts and use these as a major basis for their own interpretations of world events. The feeds are not retransmitted to their populations, nor do the countries legally subscribe to the services.

The second challenge is that it is becoming increasingly impossible to halt the flow of electronic communications into a country. Censorship is becoming prohibitively expensive. It is not unusual in many Third World countries to see peasants carrying powerful portable radio receivers, capable of pulling in a great variety of foreign stations. The image of the peasant with the tiny, weak transistor radio is fading fast. Satellite broadcasting will vastly expand the signals available in many parts of the world. (This is why, among other reasons, some countries want control of the satellite airspace above them as was noted in Chapter 6.) Television signals spill over the borders of unfriendly countries. West Berliners watch TV from East Berlin. And the wealthy in Pakistan watch forbidden Indian movies on videotape.

Look for politics, both nationally and internationally, to be increasingly played out in the new communications networks born of the communications revolution. An Orwellian *1984* version of a totally controlled society will be difficult to achieve when there are more channels of communications than could ever be effectively controlled. Control of the majority of channels, however, will still be a basis for political power. Expect that more than ever before in history, political orders will be communication orders.

Voting for Images

Modern communications, especially television, may be changing the nature of how the public responds to political candidates. Research by Elihu Katz into the first "great" TV presidential debates (Nixon-Kennedy) concluded that the public chose the winner upon the basis of their performance of a debater, not upon their credentials for the presidency (Katz and Feldman, 1962).

Since the late 1930s researchers have tried to delineate the role of public communications media in the election process. Opposing theories have been offered for "strong" as against "weak" roles of mass communications — that media can control voter behavior, or that it is simply a reflection of many other happenings and is only a minor factor in voter decisions. As television began to enter the political process during the Eisenhower campaigns, it was treated as just another medium like newspapers, radio, or magazines. Eisenhower was such an immensely well known candidate that it was difficult to detect if television — or any other medium for that matter — played any special role in his being elected.

But the presidential campaign of 1960 was another matter. The medium of television, now in most U.S. households, was the basis of a new experiment in campaign communications: a series of nationally broadcast debates. Here the candidates were to be pitted against one another so that verbal exchanges would work down to the basic campaign issues in the election, perhaps even as dramatically as the debates a century earlier between Abraham Lincoln and

Stephen Douglas. Another opportunity presented itself: the field of communications research had matured to a point where the televised debates would be the most studied political communications event to date. The results were surprising to most who held the opinion that direct debate was a way of reducing campaign communications to important issues. They were also an unpleasant surprise to the candidate who had been in the public eye as Vice President for eight years and who lost the election to the relative newcomer, John Kennedy.

Contrary to expectations, many studies revealed that candidate personality, or more generally, "image," turned out to be the major factor in the minds of the viewing public. Concern with issues, even recognition of them in the exchanges, was less salient than reaction to candidates' personalities. Moreover, many audience members seemed to attach more importance to personality as a factor in the television performance than to expectations of a presidential leader. Kennedy looked dynamic and robust, Nixon tired and unshaven, mostly due to contrasts associated with television lighting, make-up, and looking into the camera.

Careful analysis of transcribed texts of the exchanges revealed that Nixon had presented a greater number of facts and, in the opinion of several experts on debate, had constructed the better arguments of the two candidates. There was one report that persons who had heard the first debate on radio had assumed Nixon the clear winner, whereas TV viewers felt Kennedy the stronger. On a more general level of communications analysis it was also said that Nixon did indeed address Kennedy, but Kennedy mainly addressed the viewing audience. Across the duration of the series of debates, surveys indicated that public preference differences between Kennedy and Nixon narrowed primarily in favor of Kennedy, who came from a position of being relatively unknown. Ratings of Nixon changed little.

Richard Nixon, however, may have learned an important political lesson from the debates. His use of television in the

1968 election had all the characteristics of a perfectly orchestrated Madison Avenue product campaign, all documented by Joe McGinniss in *The Selling of the President* (1969). There were no real debates in 1968 nor 1972.

Although the 1976 campaign debates between Gerald Ford and Jimmy Carter lacked the milestone quality of the Nixon-Kennedy debates, studies of them also indicate a public concern more with image and television performance than with positions on, or command of, the issues. In the conclusions of one study, the public "learned little" about positions of the candidates. But these debates plus extensive television coverage of the primaries and campaign made it possible for a virtually unknown one-term governer of Georgia to move from the position of a campaign curiosity to becoming President of the United States.

As we entered the 1980s even greater amounts of campaign funds were earmarked for television promotion, particularly in the form of short, high pressure commercials. Republicans openly raised over $5 million to defeat Democratic candidates for Congress and the results were astounding.

Television production is typically in the hands of one of the nation's dozen or so firms specializing in political promotion. Typical of such producers is Bob Goodman, who produced commercials for Republican George Bush in the 1980 presidential primaries. According to a *Wall Street Journal* report, Goodman's career dated back through 64 campaigns in 31 states to the election of Spiro Agnew as governor of Maryland.

A classic media campaign was Goodman's image manipulation of Malcolm Wallop, a former Easterner running for a Senate seat from Wyoming. In one ad Wallop rode at the head of 75 horses and riders hired by Goodman, while the voiceover proclaimed "Come join the Wallop Senate drive" . . . "Ride with us, Wyoming!"

In his unsuccessful campaign for George Bush ("a President we won't have to train"), Goodman was unconcerned with facts and issues.

"This tube is a very emotional thing," he says. "We measure passion, not fact. What I'm trying to do is show this man the best way I can, to capture his essence. Feelings win elections. What I strive for is an emotion, not a position" [*Wall Street Journal*, July 24, 1979].

Look for increasing use of "media blitz" techniques, especially via television commercials, in major U.S. election campaigns. Expect more criticism of these practices, not only because they allow finances to have additional influence through media purchase ability, but also because of superficial orientation they bring to the election process. Assume that if media blitzes do not taper off of their own accord, legislation will eventually set media guidelines for campaign practices. (Before we knew it, the "Selling of the President" took over from the "Making of the President.")

"Dial-in" Voting?

The democratic process has always been hampered by the one-way nature of mass communications. By its traditional pattern of being communication from "one to many," mass communication favors central authority as it exists in government, opinion leadership, or even the political candidate. Letters to the editor or guest appearances in TV editorial spots are a miniscule feedback channel for public expression of political thoughts. Public opinion polling also is a narrow and biased channel; the topics are selected under control of the pollster rather than the polled. Riots and demonstrations are a form of public input in the mass communications system but they too are at the mercy of what media wish to report, and are an expensive form of communication to society. The referendum or "proposition" (as in California) is a form of citizen feedback, yet it requires a nearly full scale public campaign to become formally implemented. Our democratic system has only allowed citizens one true communications channel that is theirs exclusively. This is the ballot box.

Communications technologies now may make that box "electronic" and in your home. Already we have technology that with a few modifications would allow nationwide polling via telephone networks and almost totally automated polling if push-button telephones are employed. We have had several successful experiments where two-way cable television systems (as with Qube in Columbus) have been used to solicit public opinion on government issues. There have been detailed experiments proposed but not implemented to conduct regional public hearings by linking meeting sites via interactive television networks. (Interactive television text systems such as Prestel in Great Britain can be directly used for public polling, as noted in Chapter 8.) There has also been considerable success in the last decade in the design and implementation of electronic systems for automating group decision processes.

Interactive cable TV services (as discussed in Chapter 7) allow a viewer's message, usually originated by pressing keys, to be sent to the broadcast facility. The "two-way" capability is not so much a challenge as is what to do with viewer inputs when they arrive at the central facility. Return signals require only some type of originating device (such as the keypad) and a more complex coaxial cable within which some circuits carry signals to the station rather than only from it. If only a few subscribers were sending messages to a station, they might be handled much the way telephone calls are — each one individually answered or put on "hold" if the lines get too busy. But what happens if literally thousands of people send in messages at once? This is where the computer can take over.

In the Qube system in Columbus, a central computer is capable of polling any or all of up to 100,000 incoming signals within a period of 10 seconds. It retains these signals and can calculate summary figures almost simultaneously which can be examined in numerical or graphic forms. In the fall of 1978 the Qube system was used by the Commissioner of the U.S. Food and Drug Administration to solicit public attitudes about food labeling practices. The Commissioner laid out the major issues in a usual television show format. This was followed by questions which viewers could answer by pressing one of five buttons on the keypad in their homes. Incoming responses were polled by the central computer and results displayed on home television screens within seconds of posing the questions. The Commissioner and a portion of Qube's 20,000 subscribers at the time were able to interact on an important public issue.

Similar but more patchwork versions of the Qube experiment could be carried on nationwide this very day and not require installing one item beyond the television set and telephone already in most homes. The main requirement would be a central computer to receive and collate incoming signals sent over the telephone network. (Push-button phones are preferable because they can originate computer-sensed signals). Questions could be presented in any type of multiple choice or yes-no format and audience responses given by pressing desired numbers on the phone keypad (or by some simple encoding device over conventional dial telephones). Such a system need not be tied to television presentations. For example, a computer-aided automatic dialing system could draw a random sample of telephone subscribers in the nation, and relay a brief spoken version of the questions to which responses could be given and recorded.

Videotext services such as Prestel in England already have a two-way capability where subscribers can enter information into the master computer file.

Various types of computer aided response systems have been available since the mid-1960s but mainly as designed for installation in classrooms or auditoriums for use in instruction. Usually commercially developed for educational purposes (where, for example, an instructor can get instant tabulations of answers to questions during presentation), these systems have also been adopted to facilitate group *decision* procedures. Only recently has the computer capability of such units been sufficiently powerful to accommodate large numbers of simultaneous inputs and to present nearly simultaneous results.

> *Look for* increased availability and technological advances in interactive communications systems ranging from units to assist group deliberations to nationwide electronic polling. Expect that if interactive TV cable systems become financially viable through shopping, information, and banking services, they will evolve into a critical component of the political communications infrastructure. As citizen and government become more directly linked through interactive communications, assume that political theorists will question the roles of deliberative governmental bodies originally designed to facilitate citizen-central government communications. (Should interactive telecommunications eventually replace members of Congress?)

Prime-Time Diplomacy

It is becoming much less unusual to see the affairs of states played out in prime-time television interviews, on the evening news, or even by international satellite hook-ups on morning talk shows.

As we approach the twenty-first century, virtually every spot on earth can be reached instantaneously by electronic communications media. Proliferation of international communications presents both advantages and disadvantages for political systems. Above all, it promotes change.

In a highly centralized political system, obviously the more communications capabilities a government can control, the more political influence it could wield. Increases in communication power are increases in political power. On the other hand, the increasing pervasiveness of world communications systems makes it difficult to keep a society closed to outside communications.

One of the largest investments in a national communications system was made in the 1970s by the government of Shah Reza Palavi in Iran. National Iranian Radio and Television was considered a key component in the modernism campaign in that country and it exercised the political orientation one would expect in an absolute monarchy. At the same time, however, there had developed an extensive underground distribution system of tape-recorded political messages from the exiled Ayatollah Khomeini. The Muslim leadership had developed their own revolutionary communications network. Also, it has become well known that Iranian listenership to BBC and Voice of America radio increased drastically during the final months of the Shah's government when there was near total censorship of the Ayatollah's actions on the country's regular broadcast system.

Although international radio broadcasting for political purposes has gone on for some time, nations have been surprisingly conservative in the use of television for similar purposes. One reason, of course, is that unlike short wave radio, the television signal does not have long-range capabilities unless assisted by wire, microwave relay systems, or satellite. The former two systems are not only costly but require often impossible international agreements for installation. Until recently, satellites have not had the channel capacity to carry many television programs, nor have agreements in use of broadcast frequencies encouraged growth of international television. Exceptions are news and sports networks among cooperating countries and occasional special arrangements, as in the live broadcasts of President Nixon's China visit. For the time being, prospects for new cooperation do not look encouraging. Third World nations have accused the industrialized countries of monopolizing broadcast frequencies as expressed in proceedings of the World Administrative Radio Conference of 1979. Potentially controversial arguments about satellite frequencies were postponed for deliberation until the 1980s when the charges of "communications colonialism" will be probably even louder.

As has been mentioned several times earlier, Third World countries have become increasingly sensitive about importation of foreign television programming, particularly reruns of prime-time commercial series from the United States. There is an expressed fear of cultural erosion and especially of values important for maintenance of political order. As a consequence we are witnessing many examples of nationalistic regulation over the percentage of imported television fare that can be used. Socialist countries have virtually barred nearly all foreign television programs save for those consonant with their political goals.

But as very powerful communications satellites are put into space over the next decade, it will be difficult to halt the growth of international television. Earth receiving stations which once cost millions could become as widely available as television sets. (The more powerful the satellite the smaller and less expensive the receiving station.) Video recording technology, especially the disc, allows program material to be disseminated without regard to broadcast transmission. In the coming years it may be as difficult for countries to close their borders to recorded television materials as it is now to confiscate traditional phonograph records and cassette or eight-track tapes. Hardly anything imaginable, save nuclear devastation, will hold back the growth of international telecommunications. Even limited wars or economic depressions have aspects encouraging to the growth of communications technologies.

The speed of modern electronic communications also raises political concerns around the world, including in the United States. In this country and many others, citizens followed World War II in terms of morning headlines (adjacent to maps of the battle fronts), radio newscasts, occasional newsreels, and magazine reports. There was a technically imposed communications lag between the event and public perception of it. This lag often made it possible for presidential commentary to accompany the news of an event, thus shaping public interpretation of it. International negotiations were reported mostly in terms of what diplomats wanted the public to think, coupled with whatever scraps of additional news reporters could uncover.

Certainly for the United States, television coverage of the Vietnam war marked a turning point in all of this. On-the-spot coverage was delivered so directly and quickly to the nation's living rooms each evening that it was difficult to interpret Lyndon Johnson's pronouncements of our policy. The direct message was already digested; the pronouncements came after our personal opinions were formed. Then hardly a decade later, the President of the United States was reduced to being a TV bystander like the public during the hostage crisis in Iran. Iranian officials, hoping to sway U.S. public opinion, bypassed diplomatic channels altogether. They refused communication with government officials but freely granted interviews with network reporters, and even appeared on "Issues and Answers" type programs. On several occasions, when Jimmy Carter was asked his opinions of the latest Iranian position, he was forced to preface his remarks with "Well, I watched that program too . . ."

The Iranian crisis, the direct negotiation by TV news commentators with Prime Minister Begin of Israel and President Sadat of Egypt, and the earlier mentioned coverage of the Vietnam war are profound evidence of how international communications is affecting both our nation's and the world political order. Just as the international political order up to the nineteenth century was highly influenced by control of sea lanes, and in the twentieth century by airplane and missile capabilities, so too may we expect international politics to be tied to control of the powerful new worldwide communications networks. Those who control the networks could control the world.

Look for rapid growth of international communications networks, not only for data and telephones, but eventually for television broadcasting. The satellite will play the key roll in expansion in the form of new communications platforms serviceable by space shuttles. Expect international conflict in control over these networks, not only in broadcast frequencies and "slots" for satellites, but in authority over content (in which we in the United States have little experience). World communication conferences in the 1980s may be as important to our future as are past international accords on the oceans and airspace. (Will you want 20 international channels available in your 100-channel cable TV system?)

Is Democracy Obsolete?

Not only is the communications revolution changing the way of traditional political processes, it is beginning to force us to recognize that new political theories need to be devised. A system of government which is based on the rights and intelligent participation of the individual may be especially realizable in an era in which virtually every citizen is linked into a national communications infrastructure. It should also be particularly effective in a post-industrial society where the knowledge class is influential and where the national resource is intellectual technology.

Yet we have no assurance that our current political practices will naturally evolve so as to take advantage of the communications revolution. Communications networks can be equally advanced for dictatorial as democratic ends, depending upon who controls and who has access to the technological future. Just as new communication infrastructures could bring a greater portion of a national population into governmental participation, it could equally as well be used to control them. So too could access to new communications powers be denied to citizens. New technologies are expensive and tend to favor intellectual and economic elites in a society. We could easily fall into the trap of perpetuating the economic gaps between classes in our society by substituting information ones.

The world of the eighteenth century in which the U.S. Constitution was written differs far more from the world of the impending twenty-first century than from the birthplace of democratic theory in the Athenian world of the fourth century B.C. A citizen of ancient Athens would be less challenged to understand the workings of democracy in revolutionary meetings in Boston's Faneuil Hall in the 1770s than would an American patriot plopped two-and-a-quarter centuries later in the midst of Washington, D.C.

In the time since the American Revolution, we have transformed the speed of human communications from the speed of transportation to the speed of light. Through computers we are automating the storage, manipulation, and retrieval of potentially infinite amounts of information. With the merger of telecommunications and computer technologies, our power over information makes possible a communications infrastructure instantaneously and totally incorporating all citizens. No longer is a political event limited by the distance voices can be heard nor a political unit limited to the distance that we can travel in one day. No longer are political perceptions delayed by the times necessary for transportation systems to deliver the news. No longer does governmental perception of public reaction depend upon flow from citizens via elected representatives to central government.

The political order of nations is being rapidly transformed from the written document and spoken word to an electronic communications network enveloping everybody. The new political order *is* the communications infrastructure. Such a transformation would probably be incomprehensible to a citizen of eighteenth-century Boston, including the writers of the U.S. Constitution, under which we are daily governed.

Look for the communications technology revolution to place new strains on how we operate our government. The eighteenth-century constraints of transportation and communication which were the basis for organizing the operation of our democracy are long removed. The new communications technologies offer opportunity for citizen information and participation undreamed of by our Founding Fathers. Anticipate that we may have to adjust our democracy away from the constraints of the eighteenth century and toward the advantages of the twenty-first. Democracy is not dead but some of our ways of practicing it are obsolete.

CHAPTER 16

Work: Making a Living with Knowledge

New York, 1985. A few years ago you would have called Franklin Smith, an executive in a large medical insurance firm a "paperpusher." Now he's definitely a button pusher. A pop-up screen on Mr. Smith's desk gives him his day's schedule, office memos, the budget report, correspondence file, and a fiscal analysis program so he can simulate the consequences of his likely upcoming transactions. Smith knows that he won't always be a button pusher because the next model of his communications unit will be voice actuated.

Enter the "Knowledge Worker"

As discussed briefly in earlier chapters and in more detail in Chapter 18, our country seems to be entering into an age of post-industrialism. Business is growing more in information, knowledge, and service areas than in manufacturing ones. This transition is changing the nature of work in this country. Workers are growing in numbers in information-handling occupations. Managers are dealing with intellectual technologies. Knowledge, particularly theoretical knowledge, is the basic resource in this new economy, according to Daniel Bell (1973). The manipulation and communication of information by professional and technical workers is the premium occupation in this type of society. Advancement within occupational ranks will be due to education and skills rather than wealth or cultural advantage. Professional careers in the post-industrial society will be played out in an occupational environment akin to a meritocracy. This is the era of the "knowledge worker."

Not only do we have a shift in the types of occupations which are experiencing growth, the characteristics of the U.S. work force are changing too.

- The average age of the worker is increasing both with the advancing average of the population as a whole and with the extension of mandatory retirement ages.

- Accelerated by equal opportunity legislation, there are more interest groups seeking employment rights. This has included minorities in the 1960s, women in the early 1970s, and homosexuals in the late 1970s and early 1980s. In each case, legislation has been enacted to further employment of the groups.

- The average educational level of the work force is steadily increasing, spurred particularly by the growth of community college programs as well as the more advanced technological skill requirements of the occupational marketplace.

- The educated worker is demanding more control over the work place, as can be seen by trends of increased incidence of participatory management, "upward" vertical communication programs in industry, and worker representation on corporation boards.

- New values are being revealed in worker preferences about job conditions, educational opportunities, flexible hours, time off versus overtime, and the importance of job satisfaction.

The transition of our economy into more emphasis upon the service sector, coupled with a more mature and independently oriented workforce, is likely to change the nature of work more in our society than at any time since the rise of the industrial economy out of an agricultural one. Theorists are speculating about the consequences of these factors upon possible changes over the traditional life pattern of education-work-leisure into patterns of multiple careers, each segmented by periods of education and leisure.

Look for changes in the U.S. workforce, with jobs increasing in the information, knowledge, and service sector and declining in traditional manufacturing (except high technology components). "Know-how" with computer and telecommunications technology is a major occupational growth area, as can be seen by glancing at the job opportunities listed in any metropolitan newspaper. Expect that the knowledge worker will be more educated, more professionally oriented, and require less supervision than his manufacturing counterpart. In *Managing in Turbulent Times* (1980), for instance, Peter Drucker predicts the demise of the foreman.

The Office of the Future Is Now

The fastest growing area for the knowledge worker is business occupations. Automation based upon communications technologies is bringing many clerical assists to the office. Management is now played out more and more in conjunction with computer-based information systems.

Although we have had electronic aids for accounting and inventory control since the 1950s, and manufacturing control in the 1960s, the introduction of "word processing" in the mid-1960s has had major effects upon the organization of the office clerical environment. Part of the appeal of word processing was the promise that text preparation, the costs of which were skyrocketing, could be made more efficient through partial automation as had been the case with "data" processing. The new technology was the "memory" typewriter, which by magnetic or punch tape recording could store text for repeated use in letters or reports. It allows for the revision of draft materials without the necessity of retyping entire documents. In some cases where further typesetting is involved, the typewriter memory record provides a basis for avoiding costly linotype services. Word processing also typically involves reorganization of typists into a central clerical pool where all office typing jobs are submitted, and dictation either from tape or via telephone is recorded in a master unit.

Although word processing has steadily grown, some of its problems typify the challenge of introducing new technology into information occupations. Word processing has not been without serious criticism, especially from clerical personnel who feel their work depersonalized when working more in conjunction with machines than people. The personal commitment to an executive, including the ability to fill in the little oversights which are often a characteristic of dictation, are lost in the "pool" concept. On the other hand, the acquisition of the originally expensive memory typewriters could not be justified save for the centralization of typing facilities.

The availability of well designed word processing programs for central as well as stand-alone computers is currently changing the clerical environment even more. The replacement of typewriters with computer terminals allows for a network of typists to be connected to a single computer equipped for word processing. It is also a step in the direction of having the equipment necessary for an entirely electronic message system for communication within the organization. Another trend is the development of the "intelligent" typewriter, a much more compact and powerful version of the original memory typewriters, and a unit that in many cases will also serve as a terminal for text processing by remote computer.

Many automated information services have been widely available to managers since the late 1960s, including the availability of interactive telecommunications links with large computers. Such services were especially enhanced by the Carterphone decision of 1968 (mentioned in Chapter 5) which dropped restrictions on linking remote terminals to computers via regular telephone connections. The availability of practical portable terminals shortly thereafter made it possible for a manager to tie into the system wherever there was a telephone available. Usually called "management information systems," these units were designed around a computerized filing and retrieval procedure with some capability for data analysis.

Take, for a simplified example, the management of a government-sponsored research project involving the coordination of a dozen field teams located in different parts of the country. One very useful file in the management information system is the detailed schedule of steps for accomplishing the project, including designation of:

- what steps are to be accomplished
- what prerequisites must be accomplished for each step
- who is responsible for accomplishment
- deadlines for each step
- orts required
- costs, planned and actual
- directory of field personnel
- directories of supervisory personnel.

Key central office and field personnel all have access to the same file by linking their terminal via telephone connection to the central computer. Regular interrogation of the file can provide a schedule of upcoming responsibilities. Necessary modifications can be actively entered into the files so that other staff personnel may see and make adjustments. Interrogations can be ordered in any of a variety of formats by "sorting" on designated entries or their combinations. For example, the responsibilities of an individual staff member can be itemized, as can be current budget expenditures on a step by step basis. Even ongoing reports can be entered directly into appropriate locations of the information system, thus allowing for successive reports to be aggregated into progress reports at important milestones in the project.

Put into more functional terms, such a system can be (1) shared easily by all users, (2) constantly updated, (3) interrogated in any useful output format, (4) the basis for calculation of budget, deadlines, or task figures, and (5) an aid for preparation of required reports. In more abstract terms it is a technology which greatly facilitates the development and use of an information infrastructure.

Goals in the development of the above system, or what is more generally regarded currently as "computer-assisted management," have been more challenged by barriers to adoption than by limits of the technology. For one thing, the operation of the system, even its language, must be as tailored as possible to the practices, the management style, of the user. Computer programmers have been notorious over the years for adapting their "software" to fit with system architecture rather than user styles.

Another problem is that many executives have not had direct experience with computers and feel that "hands on" use of "clerical" equipment would be demeaning to them. The counter-strategy here, according to one computer systems marketing executive, is to design terminals which do not look like terminals, then to try to make a status symbol out of them (like the executive washroom key). It is not usual to see a "pop up" screen on an executive-style desk, some with keypads purposely not configured like typewriter keyboards, or systems where commands can be entered on touch-sensitive screens. There are also fashionable lightweight portable terminals, all far removed from the arm-stretching ones of ten years ago.

Sometimes the problem is one of an executive not wishing to share management power with the computer, perhaps for fear that it will lessen the importance associated with traditional executive decision-making capability. Another concern is that others will gain the basis for equally powerful decision-making via the computer. These attitudinal barriers are the most difficult to surmount, and in the experience of an oil company personnel officer were cited as one of the reasons for the rapid advancement of young executives over older ones.

Until the mid-1970s most of the expectations about the growth of computer-assisted management were in the form of large and powerful systems. This trend is continuing but is joined by the increasing use of small computers, or microprocessors, as an aid to management. For the next few years, small computers are limited mostly by memory and processing speed which does not make them practicable for the manipulation of the large bodies of data which are often the heart of management information systems. They are most useful, however, for certain calculations or simulations which do not require great amounts of input data but may have relatively complicated analysis procedures (*algorithm*).

For example, some small computers — mostly under $10,000 in the early 1980s, some even around $5,000 — have commercially available programs for stock portfolio analysis, a general ledger system, tax analysis, certain medical diagnoses, mortgage amortization tables, depreciation, home purchase and income property cashflow analysis. These systems, which are decreasing annually in price yet increasing in computing power, bring the advantages of computer-assisted management to the small business owner and independent consultant who otherwise could not afford such services.

Nipping on the heels of small computer systems are increasingly powerful hand-held calculators, some specifically designed to assist in certain types of decision algorithms, others which are programmable. Some of these currently have plug-in program modules to assist in securities analyses, surveying, marine navigation, electrical engineering calculators, and investment analyses.

Look for widespread utilization of computer assists in management, ranging from large management information networks to hand-held calculators. Expect increasing user adaptation in the design of system software, so that such systems are employed with a minimum of training or adaptation by the user. Assume that prices will continue to drop as the price of digital circuitry continues to drop. Expect that breakthroughs in memory capacities and central processor capabilities will greatly increase the advantages of microcomputers in management, especially in small businesses, and eventually the home. As is happening now, the successful managers of the future will be those who can command the information infrastructure, if not aid in creating it. The information infrastructure rather than the office is the new management environment.

Working with Electronic Money

"The more I learn about electronic funds transfer, the more I realize that communication is three-fourths of what the banking business is all about," interjected a bank vice president giving a briefing on management decisions involving computer systems.

Paper communication in the form of checks, some 35 billion per year, accounts for the transfer for something more than 95 percent of the financial value of annual total transactions in the United States. At a cost ranging up to 75 cents each, this is an expensive form of communication, especially when we realize that a great share of these transactions could be done electronically.

Over the last decade banks have slowly but steadily adopted new communications technologies. For example, 33 "Automated Clearing Houses" were established in 1978 as a national network to permit electronic distribution of payrolls. The system provides the basis for crediting an employee's account wherever it exists in any of some 12,000 financial institutions. Other types of technology more visible to the public are funds transfer systems which are accessed via telephone. Here the customer directs the payment of bills by a coding system and the bank credits the accounts electronically. Some of these systems allow use of home push-button telephones for directing the transfers, using the keypad as a "terminal." There are also experiments in using two-way TV cable systems for funds transfers.

Acceptance of these systems, both by bankers and customers, has been slower than anticipated. "People like to see and feel their money," as one bank manager put it. Equipment for such transfer systems, especially if it requires anything special for the home, is expensive. There is also the fact that electronic systems because of their speed cut into "float," the few days most of us have depended upon at one time or another before our check is actually charged to our account. Other types of new services involve "automatic tellers," including ones which dispense traveler's checks at the airport.

For some years now, banks have had a variety of network options for electronic funds transfers among themselves, including "Fedwire" and "Bankwire."

Look for occupational changes in banking and financial institutions as a consequence of adoption of electronic funds transfer systems, automated tellers, and remote shopping services where payment is credited electronically. Expect continuing resistance to new systems but also substantial career advantages to individuals who can promote the acceptance of electronic banking practices. Anticipate continuing problems with computer-based embezzlement schemes. Are you ready for a cashless and checkless society?

More Jobs and Lost Jobs

Telecommunications and computer businesses in themselves are growth areas for jobs in the new economy. Some of these are due to advances in technologies, where there is a rush to replace old systems so as to remain competitive or become so.

Wired communications is challenged by inexpensive and highly efficient fiber optic systems. Analog communications systems (see Chapter 9) are being replaced by digital ones. Land based communications networks will be increasingly integrated with, and sometimes replaced by, satellite communications systems. Computer hardware technology is advancing faster than we can supply it with softward (programs, applications). Digital recordings will make current long playing records obsolete. Videodisc is already a challenge to videocassette systems, and now quite different disc systems challenge each other.

Even the configuration of communications businesses is shifting annually as old-timers such as telephone companies find themselves challenged on all fronts with competing transmission networks, message services, and other companies selling telephones. Theater owners are challenged by cable operators. The traditional broadcast networks are challenged by pay TV and direct broadcast satellite. Newspapers have had to adopt new typesetting methods, and then turn around and figure how they are to remain competitive with cable TV and videotext services. Smaller computer companies, unhampered by large corporate structures and traditions, challenge giant IBM from all sides. American Telephone and Telegraph, long denied entrance into the computer market, may finally be let loose, as may be Western Union from artificial barriers to using all available satellite transmission services.

The computer-telecommunications profession shows all indications of being the most opportune occupation for the next several decades. In the late 1970s and early 1980s all type of inducements — paid vacations, automobiles, extra time off, bonuses — have been advertised for recruiting professionals to computer industries. Many economic forecasts reflect the assumption that growth in the computer industry will be so strong as to be unaffected by the temporary dips in the economy. The epitome in job opportunities are in the concentration of computer industries in the Boston-Cambridge area, and south of San Francisco (now called "Silicon Valley").

One of the most pressing current questions is the degree to which growth in communications related occupations in the post-industrial economy will replace occupations lost due to widespread automation in clerical work environments, banking, and other service industries. Even manufacturing is losing many jobs due to automation. Several studies suggest 30 percent to 50 percent reductions in the need for clerical workers due to new technologies. Countering these are estimates that there will be 10,000 new jobs per year in selling and servicing new communications and computing technologies. Unfortunately, we lack in-depth studies of job transfers likely to accompany the communications revolution. However, there is widespread agreement that the lower skilled of the clerical occupations will be hardest hit by communications and computing automation. A study by Siemens, a West German company, estimated that automation could eliminate up to 2 million of the 5 million secretarial jobs in that country.

Patterns of communications-transportation substitutions (Chapter 13) should also affect the job market. Sales and service for home entertainment devices should generate jobs lost in the decline of transportation-dependent recreational activities. Remote shopping and banking services should create some new jobs but probably not as many as lost in the reduction of sales and clerical staffs. Sales staffs may be further reduced in numbers and required level of sophistication as automated cashier devices (as in the computer-readable codes now found on most packages) are installed. If use of the automobile eventually declines due to petroleum prices and shortages as well as communications substitutions, then we should expect a decline in occupations related to sales and service of the family car.

Look for continued rapid growth of employment in the communications business — design, manufacture of equipment, sales, service, and the offering of computer or communications services. Expect change brought about by technological shifts (such as copper wire to optical fiber). Assume that many clerical occupations, especially the lower skilled ones, will go the way of the farm worker as automation takes over. Worry that some predictions say there may not be enough jobs to go around. What kind of job do you want in the post-industrial economy?

Productivity, Participation and Promises

There are many good reasons to anticipate that the communications revolution will have as significant a qualitative as quantitative impact upon occupations. Mostly this focuses upon characteristics of the "knowledge worker," the person "making a living with knowledge," the "intellectual technology" of our evolving society. It is ticklish (if not tedious) business to argue over details of who is or is not a knowledge worker. Everyone uses a degree of knowledge on the job, but not all occupations deal with the acquisition of knowledge as a business. Engineers and physicians are in the knowledge business since they apply it. Teachers are in the knowledge business since it is their task to transfer it. Managers of data banks or data flow are in the business of knowledge acquisition, storage, and retrieval. Many additional occupations fit wholly or partially into these categories, but classifying them becomes more of an academic matter. An important point is that the number of knowledge-based occupations is increasing rapidly in our society. An even more important point is that they are qualitatively different from other occupations in several important characteristics.

Productivity is difficult to gauge in knowledge work. In agriculture, productivity is easily defined as how much one person, or family, plus a horse or mule, could grow and harvest in one season. That is, what was achieved (output) relative to what was invested (input)? The productivity of a sixteenth-century candlemaker was not difficult to gauge either. Nor was the productivity of a nineteenth-century ironworks, provided one had an accurate record of plant, employment, and product. But even in manufacturing, there begins to be a problem in calculating productivity of management, plant investment, and product research and development components. We usually treat them as "indirect costs" which when added to "direct" costs (such as material, labor, distribution) to become the *input* side in the productivity calculation. But as individual components it is difficult to consider their productivity. The success of one component of management (sales) may be so inextricably tied to another (advertising) that productivity evaluations relative to ultimate goals (profit) become impossible or impractical. Or take research, for example. Impacts may take five to ten years before they are visible. How then is productivity calculated in the first ten? Further, as is often pointed out, we must develop innovative methods for determining how the costs of information automation actually affect our labor costs. The answers are complex.

The knowledge worker is especially motivated by knowledge, interest and work satisfaction, according to Peter Drucker. Even if knowledge workers, like all of us, get concerned about their paychecks, there is still abundant evidence that interest and challenge are strong occupational motivators. Knowledge workers are usually attracted to their specialities because of the specific subject matter involved. A professor is always a specialist in some type of subject matter, most physicians in a type of practice, engineers in a certain applied area, and so on. Whereas professional managers could be equally at home in a factory making light bulbs or one making underwear, knowledge workers will only be at home with their knowledge specialty. A professor of chemistry wouldn't last long in a history class.

Drucker's thesis that knowledge workers prefer to be guided by priorities emanating from their knowledge areas rather than by the dictates of administrators seems to be increasingly true these days. It has always been evident that doctors and professors are indifferent as regards their administrators. New breeds of knowledge workers such as found in large service organizations or research and development centers tend to be organized more in terms of project teams than traditional administrative hierarchies. Among research workers, administration is often looked upon more as a "support service" than as a level of authority. "Participatory management" is a predictable topic in the job interview of a candidate for administration in a knowledge worker organization. Even the Roman Catholic church, the world's oldest and largest administrative hierarchy, has been slowly instituting participatory reforms since the important mandate of Vatican II in 1962. Congregations now participate actively in the mass. Lay "councils" are now organized to advise in the operation of local churches.

One further consequence of being motivated by specialized knowledge interest is that the knowledge workers may want to change jobs if their interests change. In fact, we might expect that such changes would take place several times in a lifetime. Scientists and engineers in information technology areas, especially where pay is high already, are often recruited by the nature of the problems on which they will be working. Very practical evidence of this is easily found in the classified ads in major newspapers and technical magazines. Professors in topical areas of high demand (computer science, high; history, low), have a high mobility rate and tend to seek environments most conducive to the problems *they* wish to work on.

Look for some of the basic characteristics of work as we have understood them to change as much as we shift from a manufacturing to a post-industrial economy as they did when many of our ancestors left their farms to go to work in cities. Anticipate that "knowledge workers" will have a different set of attitudes toward their job and that this will require new management strategies. Look for the productive integration of human and communications technology to be a management challenge. Workers will wish to participate in decisions about the technologies with which they are to interact. Get ready to manage intellectual machines and help them get along with people!

Education: School at the Flick of a Switch

CHAPTER 17

Atlanta, 1986. Alice Frost, age 65, has decided to finish a college degree that was interrupted by marriage 45 years ago. No need for her to pack her bags and head off to campus, for a rich mix of the greatest living teachers is being brought into her living room via enrollment in the United States Tele-university. Patterned after the successful British Open University, the curriculum is available 24 hours daily over a television channel distributed nationally by a direct satellite broadcast system. A small $100 unit fixed to Ms. Frost's TV set allows her to switch to the text mode of the university channel, where among 1000 electronic "pages" are assignments for her courses, self-administered quizzes, as well as a bulletin board where she can post a message "long distance."

A Natural for Technology

Education abounds with opportunities for the use of technologies — not just technologies in the "hard" or equipment sense, such as computers, television, or telecommunications networks — but also in the "soft" or instructional strategy and management sense. Ironically, when any of us goes to a typical "back-to-school" night with our child, there is little that is substantively different in a technological sense from our own days in school. Compare this with 20 to 30 years ago in a health clinic, an accounting firm, or in the contrast between flying in a DC-3 and a Boeing 747. Our schools, with their assembly line instruction and even their bells, are a holdover from the industrial age of our

215

country, as Alvin Toffler described so vividly in *Future Shock* (1970). Yet we are depending on them to train our youngsters for life in a clearly developing post-industrial era of high technologies.

Why can't we use more technology in education?

Take the computer for example. It's a natural for managing drills in the so-called "basics" — reading, writing, and mathematics. When used to assist teachers, computers are highly effective instructional tools in areas requiring extensive drills for skill building, an activity that is dreadfully boring for teachers. Why should a human be forced to correct spelling errors over and over again when a machine can do it so well? We are not necessarily talking about gigantic computers which take hundreds of thousands of dollars to install and to maintain. Have you seen Texas Instrument's "Speak and Spell"? Its retail price is a little over $50 and it can teach more spelling in half an hour than most teachers could in a day. And it's more fun too.

Computers of a little larger size, but still in the under $5000 range, can be especially valuable in all phases of instruction, including special education where even more drill than usual is required. Such computers came on the market in the late 1970s; some could be purchased for a little over $1000 by 1978. By the mid-1980s, sophisticated school computer units could be down to the $500 level. It may be that more children will experience computer-assisted instruction in the form of electronic game-type units in the home than they will any type of computer aids to instruction in their schools. This is not what the experts originally thought when during the 1960s there were dreams of how all of the mundane aspects of instruction — drill, correcting spelling and math texts, grade keeping — would be turned over to large computers.

Although still not widely used, computer-assisted instruction has come a long way from the simple "programmed" learning of the early large demonstration projects. There is much more creative use of the computer now, even in addition to the "gaming" formats so popular on computers found in the home. Consider the following:

- *Intellectual zoo:* Lay out bits and pieces of a subject matter so that the student can browse among them in no particular order other than what their own interests dictate.

- *Grab bag:* The computer makes available a great variety of images of familiar things (people, candy bars, cars, space ships) which can be manipulated as a basis for instruction.

- *Friendly expert:* Use the computer as an electronic encyclopedia, atlas or as a file of aids for problem solving.

- *Simulator:* How many different shapes can you construct with these five lines? What happens when you add oxygen to hydrogen? How well can you drive in traffic?

Added to these is the more general proposition that learning and using a simple computer programming language is good mental discipline in itself. Basic notions of conjunction, orders, or hierarchies become very concrete with a child's experience with programming. A child who is learning to read, age five or six, can be taught to do simple programming. Eventually there will be major languages developed specially for children. We can expect even greater variety in how computers can be used in instruction, the key being advances in programs ("software") rather than the design of the machines. Inexpensive electronic home games will increasingly have instructional applications as will such home entertainment devices as television, video cassette and disc.

Another exciting communications technology for the schools, which even came earlier than computers, is television. Beginning in the 1950s research funds supported many experimental projects to assess the instructional potential of the television medium. These studies were mostly comparisons of "TV vs. live" lectures. Students liked the flexibility of being able to attend the TV lectures, usually at several optional viewing periods during the day, and they liked being able to repeat a program. They did not, however, like the lack of opportunity for feedback — that is, the chance to ask questions, to seek clarifications, or to render different opinions. Identical examinations given to TV and non-TV groups of students in the same courses usually revealed the same overall learning.

Even though television showed no advantages in the learning that resulted, its use might be favored for convenience's sake by administrators — especially at faculty payroll time. And this is one of the key reasons why educational television of this type never caught on. Teachers and professors have not been enthusiastic about making themselves obsolete. The most successful use of television in education has been more as a component to facilitate the teacher's instructional activities. Home use has grown remarkably. A decade ago *Sesame Street* demonstrated that the high-attention production techniques used in television commercials had a great potential for use in teaching children basic mathematical and verbal concepts. *The Electric Company* was successful use of television in helping children to read. *Villa Alegre* and *Carrascolendas* brought inviting and positive images of what it is like to be bilingual in an English-speaking country. *Mister Rogers Neighborhood* proved that a warm and attractive personality to children could be captured in the electronic medium.

Social science research over the last decade credits television with many effective instructional uses, for example:

- Television is a powerful medium for illustrating social concepts.
- By identifying with personalities in television drama, children interpret such materials very personally.
- Television is excellent for prompting class discussion, especially of social concepts interpreted personally by a child.
- Television can be useful in prompting a life futures orientation in children.
- Instructional TV productions can be especially cost-efficient if they can also be seen at home.

Nevertheless children still spend most of their time viewing commercial programs originally produced for prime-time, adult audiences. In the 1970s several groups of researchers and educators began to take a unique approach to this problem. They tried to devise ways by which children could gain some advantages from watching prime-time programs. Or as psychologists Jerome and Dorothy Singer put it, "to watch TV with more than a blank stare." Several such projects have involved developing units of school curriculum devoted to increasing "visual literacy." This includes raising children's awareness of what they may or may not get out of time spent viewing TV, fallacies of commercials, prevalence of social stereotypes, overemphasis upon violence and dramatic action, fact as compared with fiction. In all, the training is intended to make children more critical in their viewing. In some projects, children learn some of the tricks of production technology, such as canned laughter, lighting, editing, or musical scoring. In the late 1970s the U.S. Office of Education launched a $1 million plus project to develop curriculum materials from kindergarten through college to enhance critical TV viewing skills in children and young adults.

But why not try to improve the TV program alternatives for children? This may now be easier than you think. New communications technologies make possible many more television channels than the current market supports. We already know what types of television are attractive to preschoolers and we know what is best for their development psychologically. So what would it take to develop a positive television environment for our children ages one through five?

Once the process is well organized, an hour of high production quality television for children can be realized for about $50,000 on the average, including costs of top writers, directors, and editors — but not highly paid stars, who are unnecessary. One year's worth of this high quality programming, three hours per day, seven days per week would cost approximately $55 million, which we could round down to $50 million because some segments would be repeatable.

We could have separate programming for children up to 18 months, 18-36, 36-48, 48-60, and 60-72 months respectively for a total of $250 million. Given very high capacity cable TV systems or direct broadcast satellite, a separate channel could be assigned for each of the five age groups and programming broadcast continuously throughout the day.

This would be more than showing a program. It would be the establishment and maintenance of an electronic learning environment. As appropriate, this environment could be modified by parents who would change channels as the child grew through each age range. In fact, a child's set could be locked on the appropriate channel for each year.

There would be no need to replace the original programming immediately since children would be moving on to new channels each year. Improvements and updates might be done on 10 percent of the programs annually at a cost of around $2.5 million. Expenses for distribution could be subsidized by commercial operators of the new transmission systems, a small fee paid by users, or from federal revenues allocated to education.

For a quarter of a billion dollars, we could solve our worries over very young children watching television. At the same time we could create a learning environment carefully calculated to promote positive social concepts, reading and math readiness, and perhaps even try to teach these children how to watch television successfully. The cost is less than one-fourth of a naval warship.

Look for pressure brought on schools to become better adopters of communications technologies. Uses of computers for educational applications need not dehumanize instruction. They can bring entirely new experiences to the classroom and also relieve teachers of the drudgery of rote drill and the tediousness of correcting papers. Assume, too, that these uses of technologies, if done effectively, will further introduce students to our technological age. Computers and educational TV systems are not hard on school budgets. And they don't ask for tenure!

Why Not Bring School to You?

The network information services concept discussed in Chapter 16 is as relevant to our educational institutions as it is to business. For example, we can begin by linking our schools into powerful communications networks. Since the development of public education in the nineteenth century, we have already organized our schools into network type patterns. Today with our many consolidated school districts and with state and federal influence, our country's public education system is a national network in many respects. Yet in as many ways this network is configured by geographic and transportation factors which communications technologies now allow us to transcend.

Suppose, for illustration, that the schools in any given district were linked into an electronic network capable of accommodating voice, television, and data transmissions. One immediate advantage is that many administrative tasks would be greatly simplified, including attendance polling (children could "punch in"); coordination of pupil assignment to classrooms; supplies ordering and inventory; central storage of administrative records in electronic form; registration of new students; fire and police alarms; playground and night surveillance via TV camera; automatic control of lights, bells, and doors; and a centralized word processing and message system.

So much administration might be automated or handled in a distributed manner that there would be a much reduced need for a central administrative staff for the school district. Administrators themselves might be housed in one or several of the schools and serve part-time as teachers.

Each school in the network could be equipped with what already exists now as a two-way "instructional television fixed service" (usually called ITFS) facility; some will seat up to 100 individuals. A small television monitor with buzzer and microphone for "talk back" would be mounted for each two or three seats. One facility or the school district headquarters would be equipped with the necessary television cameras and sound equipment. The television and "talk-back" network could serve many purposes:

- Lecture-discussions by outstanding teachers in a subject; videotapes could be made and reused
- Lecture discussions by teachers of highly specialized subjects who cannot be in every school
- Broadcasts of outstanding films or tapes to be followed by discussion via the system
- Administrative meetings of teachers
- PTA meetings
- In-service orientation of teachers
- Teacher union or professional organization meetings
- School board meetings
- Specialized adult classes taught from a central facility but attended in neighborhood schools
- Public meetings or hearings where representatives from neighborhoods can participate electronically

The local school communications network would also incorporate a computer system which in addition to administrative uses mentioned above would support programs for computer-assisted instruction. The computer network could support the school district's diagnostic and achievement testing programs. Each school building might have a central information facility, perhaps a twenty-first-century version of the traditional library. Most of the remote computer terminals would be in this facility, where they could be supervised by professional staff members. Students could engage in a great variety of computer activities, including instruction in use of the computer itself.

Also housed in this facility would be TV playback units and a library of frequently used discs and tapes. In one school or a central facility, a master library of video materials could be housed. Delivery of needed materials to a school could be done via the communication network rather than by physical transportation.

In some circumstances it will be advantageous for school districts to interlink their communication networks. This provides for resource sharing, as, for example, a highly talented teacher or a specialist. Interconnection would also allow students from different schools to communicate with one another. One of the most intriguing early satellite experiments brought children from a French-speaking school together with those from an English-speaking one. And the course? The French language for one, English for the other.

When it becomes impossible to desegregate our schools further through busing, attractive programs, or other physical means, extra communications linkages can be used to reduce racial isolation.

Eventually, state and federal education agencies could form networks tying in administratively to local schools, not for purposes of control we hope but for data gathering, information, and instructional materials services. Currently, one of the greatest barriers to the implementation of educational television is getting it disseminated. There is no one effective organization that can completely coordinate delivery of a new educational television program to our nation's schools. This would become a simple matter if there were a national educational communications network. One moderately sized satellite and a large number of inexpensive earth stations could do the job.

Secondary schools might draw upon the same facilities as just described, but with some additional services. In the final two years of high school, some students are ready for college-level courses. The usual physical separation of the two facilities prevents students from moving ahead in these subject areas. Through use of instructional fixed service, certain college courses could be offered in high school environments at the same time they are given in the university. Also, the highly motivated high school students might be encouraged to pursue more of their studies independently, taking advantage of computer-assisted instruction linkages, instructional television, and other types of remote instructional resources. Such independence from the high school physical environment would allow more time to explore and learn directly in business and university environments.

Given a little imagination there is literally no limit to the advantages of linking schools in modern communications networks. Yet we must not overlook another obvious use of educational networks. Why not link our homes directly into these services, and thus save transportation costs, valuable time, and adherence to rigid schedules? Why not bring school to us?

The delivery of educational services via communications networks becomes especially attractive on the college and university level. We are still a nation where only a minority of high school graduates complete a four-year college program. And no one can argue against the observation that the price of getting a higher education is soaring. The university, as much as any other unit in our educational system, could and should undergo transformation with the communications revolution.

Although much has been said about the success of the British Open University and the anticipated success of the University of Mid-America, or the project planned by publisher Walter Annenberg and the Corporation for Public Broadcasting, we still have not tapped the major potential for using telecommunications — especially interactive technologies — in higher education. Perhaps when the opportunity comes for a university-level communications infrastructure, we should not be so tied to existing institutions. But neither should we expect to translate all of higher education into a grand TV series.

Additionally, the nation would benefit from a college preparation curriculum which would be taught remotely. This would allow universities to get out of the remedial education business. Finally, the market should increase for individuals who are already well trained in one field to pursue work of interest to them in another. Most of this would not be for degree credit but simply for the learning experience. An engineer may wish to take work in the humanities, a salesperson to study computers, or international travellers to learn conversational skills in another language.

A national telecommunications university service could tie in with many existing facilities, not only with institutions of higher education but with libraries, research institutes, and high schools. With such networks in place, it will hardly be justified for people to spend the time and money to travel to the central location for instruction.

Look for slow but definite growth of network distribution services in education. It is a too valuable use of communications technology to go undeveloped. Expect that if public schools continue to lag in the adoption of technologies, parents will turn to private alternatives, including the delivery of some educational services directly to the home. Expect university level "telecourses" to grow in popularity for "lifelong" learning, the now largest growth area in higher education. These will be used not only for people to continue degree programs in later periods of life, but special programs will also be provided for professional education in fields which are always rapidly changing (medicine, engineering, law). Look for uses of such technologies as small instructional computers, tape and disc machines to complement over-the-air (or wire) instruction in the home. Expect also that these educational services could be delivered to your workplace (see Chapter 16). Get ready for classes at the flick of a switch!

Why the Hold-Up?

As compared with the adoption of technology in business and manufacturing over the past 20 years, public schools have implemented only a smattering of technological innovations. In fact, as mentioned earlier, as a parent visiting your child's classroom, the equipment, materials, and procedures will not look all that different from your own days in school. Why?

Public school administration in the United States is markedly traditionalistic. Change has always been very difficult to bring about. In the mid-1960s, most of the educational programs in the War on Poverty, including "Head Start," were organized largely outside of existing educational institutions. Administration even at the federal level was through the Office of Economic Opportunity and not the Office of Education.

A number of contemporary critics fault our educational institutions with too much of a preoccupation with the past, both in operating style and in curriculum. Our schools are locked into an early twentieth-century version of an industrial society that is already taking on the characteristics of a new age. We are not using the one best institution we have for adapting to rapid change. As businessman-scientist Simon Ramo (the "R" in TRW) argues (1970), education is the only way that society can try to catch up in changes imposed by modern technology. How can we expect voters to make intelligent decisions on scientific questions of public importance (such as nuclear power) unless they have some basic level of understanding of what the problem is about? If we are to survive, we must have much more of an orientation toward change, particularly technological change, according to Dr. Ramo. Perhaps, as Dr. Ramo puts it, we need to put a premium on "education of, by, and for technology."

Look for pressure to be put on our public schools to better prepare our youngsters for the technological age. This pressure may come in the form of referenda for "voucher" system financing of education, where parents take their child to the school of their choice. Payment is made by the distribution of public education funds in the form of vouchers. The parents, rather than the government, distribute the funds. Expect to see also the growth of private educational programs specializing in technological education, including materials and devices for the home. Revolution of one kind or another may be necessary to sweep public education into the twenty-first century!

THE NEW SOCIETY

CHAPTER 18

On the Cusp

Change Is Nothing New

Despite the titillations we get from concepts like Alvin Toffler's "future shock," change and crisis are not so unique to our times. Take, for example, the fourteenth century as so vividly described by historian Barbara Tuchman in her *A Distant Mirror* (1978). The years from 1340 to 1360 were perhaps the most tumultous two decades in the development of Western civilization. Political power shifted uneasily among the church, powerful landowners, and royalty. England and France carried on a seemingly endless war not only for the usual motives of territory, influence, and honor, but also because it was good business for monarchs. Populations were becoming restless over loss of traditional values, especially as they experienced an increasingly corrupt and secular church. At the height of this period, nearly one-third of the population died of the black plague. Physicians sought the causes in their astrological charts. Jews were burned as well poisoners. Most people believed that an angry God was bringing the world to an end.

Yet the fourteenth century was also a most important period for the Western world. It gave birth to the Renaissance. From this eventually grew modern western civilization as we know it.

When historians in a distant future century look back on the twentieth century, there are compelling reasons to believe that this era will mark another great transition in the evolution of our civilization. It is a period marked not only by the expansion of war to global proportions, but that two such wars were actually waged, each of which shifted the global political order. This is also the century in which humanity developed weaponry capable of annihilating life on the planet. In the final third of this century, two nations could threaten each other and the world with these weapons, and up to five or six others could make uninhabitable large portions of the globe.

This is also the period in which we began to recognize that the earth had identifiable limits to growth in terms of population and unchecked industrial expansion. In the latter part of this century, we are witnessing an economic transition wherein advanced industrial nations are growing more in terms of the delivery of services than in the production of goods and where knowledge is becoming a valuable commodity. Further, as in the fourteenth century, there is an uneasiness over loss of traditional values. There is a questioning of the quality of life today, a questioning of things technological, a questioning of modernism itself. There is a raw, penetrating feeling of being swept up in change.

To all of this, the twentieth century marks the onset of the communications revolution. The human environment has been transformed by a panoply of electronic technologies. World satellite systems now make distance and time irrelevant. We witness and react to crises simultaneously with their happening. Networks of telephones, telex, radio, and television have exponentially increased the *density* of human contact. More people can be in touch with one another during any single day in the new communications environment than many did in a lifetime in the fourteenth century. The convergence of telecommunications and computing technologies distribute information automation to the limits of the world's communication networks. We are well past the point of having the capability to transform most of human knowledge into electronic form for access at any point on the earth's surface. Television, now advanced by satellite, has become so ubiquitous as to be more environment than communications medium.

There are advantages and disadvantages to our situation as compared with the fourteenth century. Twentieth-century problems are incredibly more complex. If we stave off nuclear war we still hazard the chance of death through pollution if our power plants are not better designed and operated. Perhaps synthetic fuels will replace petroleum but that will not lessen the growth of manufacturing. Pollution could be brought under control, but Third World birth rates continue to grow unchecked. We have a far larger and interdependent world than the Western world of the middle ages. Transportation and communication bring together in the global order nations of vastly differing political and religious philosophies. Nations are now economically interdependent. Our problems are their problems. Just as the fourteenth-century British and French could not settle their differences rationally (if indeed they really wished to), we have not yet after 600 years learned to do much better. It is doubtful if an historian looking back on our century would be at all surprised over the advent of a third world war. Like our medieval counterparts, we too live on the brink of disaster. After six centuries one would think we could do better.

Perhaps looming largest among our advantages over the fourteenth century is that we have become quite adept in our study of the physical world, including our physical selves. As compared with our ancestors, those of us who live in the modern societies of today are much less at the mercy of the raw powers of nature. Cases of plague today usually merit only brief and curious mention in the inside pages of our newspapers. Our infant mortality rate is much better than the one or two deaths for every three births in the Middle Ages. Transportation and communication have long broken the limits of the speed of human, horse, or carrier pigeon. We easily heat and cool our dwelling spaces. Heavy labor is done by machines. We have done well in taking positive advantage of nature. We have unravelled many of her secrets and have put them to work for ourselves. We are excellent inventors.

Yet our future is still challenged by nature in terms of limits to growth. We are reaching limits in natural resources, unchecked population growth, and pollution. The limits of industrial growth are becoming increasingly visible to us. Moreover, we are still not doing very well in getting along with one another and in planning ahead. We still have wars and they have gotten steadily more devastating.

Another advantage over the fourteenth century is that we have learned more about the processes of change. We know that the future, in part, will be made up of what we do about it. But we have failed as yet to become adept at managing change on a large scale. We know that world harmony will be necessary if we are to avoid nuclear holocaust. We know that we must somehow balance growth against conservation. We know that we must somehow keep our population's growth within the earth's ecological limits. We are steadily realizing that we have evolving in our times revolutionary new means for expanding our communications capabilities.

Perhaps we are in times where we can most capitalize on this newest revolution. Perhaps it can facilitate our need for managed change.

The Doomsday Theses

Arguments that the world has limits to its growth are certainly not new; however, the specific discussion of this thesis has grown markedly since the 1960s. One stimulus was Paul Ehrlich's popular book, *The Population Bomb*, (1968), a topic which has made the TV talk shows no few times. (Ehrlich's latest book, with Anne Ehrlich, *Extinction: The Causes and Consequences of the Disappearance of the Species* (1981), predicts the alarming rate of extinction of animal species.) Another was a small volume published in 1972 entitled *The Limits to Growth: A Report for The Club of Rome's Project on the Predicament of Mankind.* Although many researchers and even the Club of Rome have offered alternative views on whether we will indeed face an era of limits, and if so, what kind, the original analysis remains useful as an introduction to the concept.

The key conclusion of *The Limits to Growth* is that the basic pattern of exponential growth of industry and population will bring about an inevitable collapse. The argument is based upon computer simulation of interacting factors such as food production, pollution, population growth, industrial growth, and nonrenewable resources. Given that technology has allowed us to increase food production greatly over the last 100 years, to reduce the birth rate in the past two decades, and where we have seriously tried we have been able to curb pollution, *how much more can we put off the limits to growth?* The Club of Rome forecasts involved successive applications of a simulation model, each incorporating hypothetical strategies to allow for continued growth.

One analysis is summarized in Figure 18.1. Notice that the time frame is between 1900 and 2100. Various curves depict change in critical factors. Food production, population and industrial output continue to grow until the twenty-first century but soon thereafter they begin a rapid decline. In this analysis, the decline is a reaction to vast increases in pollution. The overall report includes different simulations, each one involving a solution of one or several disaster factors, such as assuming an unlimited form of energy or a breakthrough in pollution control. The discouraging results of all the simulations predict disaster in the twenty-first century.

A more recent but less well known report was the U.S. government's study of conditions "probable" for the year 2000. *The Global 2000 Report to the President,* released in 1980, is as gloomy as the Club of Rome simulations. It puts more emphasis, however, upon how the limits to growth will be encountered in different ways by people in various regions of the earth. Particularly bleak are the consequences of desertification, loss of soil fertility, and deforestation upon the now already abysmally poor regions of the earth. The decline of population growth in those areas may reflect to a

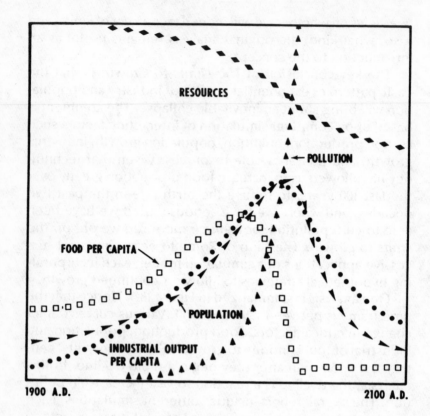

RESOURCES

POLLUTION

FOOD PER CAPITA

POPULATION

INDUSTRIAL OUTPUT
PER CAPITA

1900 A.D.   2100 A.D.

Figure 18.1   *The Limits to Growth*
NOTE: The Club of Rome projections predict industrial collapse at some point in the twenty-first century due to declining
resources, vast increases in pollution, and lack of adequate
food resources relative to population growth. The above simulation reflects the assumption that we have unlimited energy
available and that resources could be conserved to a reasonable
degree. (Adapted from Meadows et al., *The Limits to Growth*,
New York: Universe Books, 1972: 132. Used by permission.)

great extent the particularly unfortunate consequences of
infant mortality and child death from starvation. In essence,
the world's poor will suffer the first and possibly the most.

The U.S. report also puts some emphasis upon the inflationary consequences of world shortages or uneven dis-
tributions of vital minerals as well as petroleum. This report,
as have several others, placed the earth's ecological limits for

population at 10 billion, a figure they predict will be reached by around 2030.

Although nobody can deny the importance of studying limits and ways of adapting to them, the "doomsday" scenerios are not without their critics. Among these criticisms is the argument that political, social, and psychological factors may be as relevant, or more relevant, than purely economic and physical ones in modeling scenarios for growth. Also there is the fundamental weakness that the studies are solely the extrapolation of *trends*. As so succinctly stated by Rene Dubos in his criticism of the *Global 2000 Report* (Wall Street Journal, May 8, 1981), "wherever human beings are concerned, trend is never destiny."

Nonetheless in the year after publication of *The Limits to Growth*, Americans waited in gasoline lines and watched the price of fuels begin to climb. Six years later a fuel shortage hit again and by that time the price had doubled. Shortly thereafter the Three Mile Island nuclear plant breakdown galvanized us to the thought of environmental disaster. When the *Global 2000 Report* was released in 1980, drought and starvation had begun to take its toll, especially on children in the Horn of Africa.

None of the era of limits forecasts is meant to saddle us with an inescapable future. The Club of Rome report gives two alternatives for avoiding disaster: (1) Push for technological breakthroughs to solve problems of food production, pollution, and nonrenewable resources. (2) Recognize the limits to our industrial and population growth and scale back accordingly. The *Global 2000 Report* also stresses that its purpose is not to condemn our future but to alert us to planning alternatives. Although forecasters continue to argue about the validity of computerized simulations of our future, there is no disagreement that we are going to have to take better control of our own destinies in these matters.

Can *technology*, both "hard" and "soft," come to the rescue? Can the hard technology of equipment, devices, instrumentation and machines save us from pollution, enable us to grow and harvest better crops, and conserve our natural resources? Can the soft technology of "know-how" allow us to manage our resources in much superior ways over present practices?

There are theses, too, which assert that "manufacturing" based industrial growth is tapering off in advanced countries as their economies become more involved in high technologies and the delivery of services. This is called "post-industrialism."

Has "Post-Industrialism" Arrived?

Along with era of limits theses, we have also had our share of social and economic forecasting about the year 2000. Very visible among these has been the "post-industrial" theory proposed by Daniel Bell in his *The Coming of Post-Industrial Society* (1976).

Briefly, Bell sees us as in the transition into the last of a three-stage sequence of types of economies. First, there is *pre-industrialism,* an economy based mainly upon extractions from nature as in mining, fishing, or agriculture. There are many countries whose economies are totally pre-industrial, in fact the majority are. An advanced Western country such as the United States still engages in these types of activity, but they do not dominate the economy. *Industrialism* is based upon fabrication of nature, the production of goods, a manufacturing economy. *Post-industrialism* is an economy based upon intellectual technology and growth in the delivery of services. This is the economy of the knowledge worker. Whereas the pre-industrial economy is a game against nature, or the industrial a game against the fabrication of nature, the post-industrial economy is a game between persons where intellectual technology replaces machine technology. Bell's concept of post-industrial society has five dimensions:

(1) There is a shift from a goods producing economy to a service producing one. Although this includes personal services such as retail stores and beauty salons, the main growth is in transportation, communications, health, education, re-

search, and government. The majority of American workers are now in service occupations.

(2) There is an increase in size and influence of a class of professional and technical workers. In the United States, scientists and engineers form the key group in this new class. In this century, growth in their numbers has been much greater than that of other occupations.

(3) The post-industrial society is organized around knowledge, particularly theoretical knowledge. Innovation, social organization, and management draw upon the nation's intellectual technology. Computer technology has greatly added to our capability for managing knowledge. Research and development ("R & D"), or the joining of science, technology, and economics, is key to this society. Theoretical knowledge is the strategic resource.

(4) A critical aim is the management of technological growth. New methods of forecasting and of technology assessment make possible new levels of planning and control over change. This involves study of second and third order consequences, not just the main effects, of anticipated technological change.

(5) There is an emphasis upon the development of methods of intellectual technology. These are the algorithms of complex problem solving in games against nature, fabricated nature, or among people. The goal is the management of society, or "organized complexity." Intellectual technology could become as important to human affairs in a post-industrial society as machine technology is for an industrial one.

"Intellectual technologies," "information," and "knowledge" are popular terms in contemporary forecasts of social and economic change. "Knowledge" refers to the most abstract of the three. It is an understanding of the process of things, the theory, the model, or the algorithm. A "knowledge worker" applies this understanding as the basis for problem solving. Thus a physician draws upon medical knowledge for diagnostic and therapeutic applications. An engineer draws upon the physical sciences as a basis for optimum design of a structure. A manager plans the most efficient steps for processing financial records, based upon a knowledge of information processing. A social scientist evaluates the effect of television viewing upon children, based upon a theoretical knowledge of media and child development.

This ability to apply knowledge is a "technology" referred to by Bell as "intellectual technology." It is the basic resource of post-industrialism. Not only do we have the growth of a knowledge worker class, but within it are the new elite.

"Information" is something more transitory than knowledge. It has value to somebody — as in information of stock prices, the news headlines, your bank balance, where to buy good shoes — but it is momentary and not itself abstract or theoretical. Information may contribute to knowledge in the sense of facts being used to support or reject a theory. When we speak of the "information technologies" we are usually referring to ways of gathering, storing, manipulating, or retrieving information. This may be technology which refers to equipment such as computers or telecommunications links, or it may be our "know-how" in managing information flow. The latter is "knowledge" or "intellectual technology" as applied to "information" (to get them all in one sentence).

These concepts both serve to link and to contrast several contemporary forecasts about changes in the nature of our economy. Bell, for example, stresses "intellectual technology" as the primary tool of post-industrial society, the ability to manage complexity by application of theoretical knowledge. This is not only the basis of the economy but spills over into social attitudes. A population of knowledge workers would expect that social problems be managed through applications of intellectual technology. They would be impatient with traditional politics.

Similar concepts are found in the work of Marc Porat (1977), who acknowledges Bell's concept of post-industrialism. In particular, Porat stresses the growth of the numbers of "information workers." These are a larger group than Bell's since Porat includes virtually any individual whose occupation touches upon the manipulation of information. Porat's "information society" is not so much a stress upon intellectual technologies as it is a recognition that increasing numbers of people are employed in information related industries. His is more an economic than a social forecast.

Also, and much earlier, Peter Drucker wrote in his *Age of Discontinuity* (1969) about the growth of "knowledge work" as one of the major shifts in contemporary social change. His concept is particularly business-oriented, with knowledge seen as the new "central capital, the cost center, and the crucial resource of the economy." In the same decade, Fritz Machlup, in his *Production and Distribution of Knowledge in the United States* (1962), described "knowledge industries." Occupations in these areas include educators, physicians, governmental administrators, engineers, researchers, and jobs in the many areas of finance, communications, and the information sciences.

Bell, in his evaluations of trends in the U.S. occupations, noted that in a comparison of turn of the century and 1940 employment figures, the original ratio of three workers in service occupations and seven in production of goods had nearly equalized. By 1960 six of ten workers were in knowledge or service type occupations.

Marc Porat (1977) has drawn similar conclusions about what he calls an "information" based economy. He reported that in 1967 about one-fourth of the U.S. Gross National Product (GNP) reflected the production, processing, or distribution of information goods and services. An additional 21 percent was reflected in the purely informational demands of coordinating the remainder of the economy. Such activities engaged over 46 percent of the work force whose earnings were over 53 percent of the income from labor in the United States. Similar to Bell's statistical arguments, Porat further points out that the work force employed in agriculture dropped from nearly 50 percent in the 1860s to 4 percent in the 1970s and the industrial work force from nearly

40 percent in the early 1940s to 20 percent in the 1970s. By contrast, the number of persons in information-related occupations has grown from 10 percent at the turn of the century to 46 percent in the 1970s.

Not all observers agree with Bell's or Porat's figures because of differences of opinion on how to classify an "information," "knowledge," or what Bell calls "service" worker. But nobody raises any real issues about the reduction of the work force from occupations such as agriculture. There are disputes whether manufacturing occupations are really decreasing in relative numbers. There is definite agreement, however, that the knowledge industries are growing rapidly. As we entered the 1980s, the most profitable companies relative to capital investment were communications ones. As reported by *Forbes*[1] in the period of 1975-1979, media firms averaged 19.6 percent return on equity (amount of shareholder investment) as against 17 percent for energy companies. Oil companies had good return on shareholder investment in 1979 (for example, Standard of California, 20.6%; Exxon, 18.7%; Atlantic Richfield, 19%), but so did communications companies (Dow Jones, 32.1%; CBS, 20.7%; Washington Post, 27%; RCA, 18.5%). In fact, during the public uproar over oil company profits in the winter of 1979-1980 there was a minor flap over a television network's refusal to air a petroleum company advertisement which pointed out that the networks were more profitable than oil companies.

Remember, too, that the world's largest corporation, the American Telephone and Telegraph Company, whose annual revenues exceed the GNP of about three-fourths of the world's nations, is in the communications business.

Compare all of the above with the most serious decline in revenues in the history of American automobile manufacturers in 1980-1981. Surely we have signs of post-industrialism all around us. High technology, again both hard and soft, is becoming the basis of our economy.

Dream or Nightmare?

It is ironic that the same generation of men and women who will lead us into the twenty-first century were protesting in the streets in the late 1960s and early 1970s. On the surface, student unrest flared over such issues as "free speech" at Berkeley, the availability of student records for draft boards, jailing of black agitators (remember Angela Davis?), or the U.S. invasion of the borderlands of Cambodia. There were also the "drop outs," the Hippies, the Yippies, and the migration of young people to rural communal life. A common thread associating many of these happenings was a feeling among our young of the loss of individualism, that the person was subordinate to the system in an increasingly technological and corporate dominated society.

It is no coincidence that the best selling book on college campuses in those days was Herbert Marcuse's *One Dimensional Man* (1964). His thesis is one of the supression of the individual, of independence, of freedom of thought and especially the loss of the right to critical opinions as society becomes technologically advanced. As corporate and technological advances stress objectives and efficiency, according to Marcuse, there is a corresponding loss of intellectual and political freedom. Criticism or opposition is counterproductive to objectives. It is inefficient. How ironic, he stresses, that the very rights and liberties which marked the origins of industrial society are eventually bound to become its victims. As Marcuse (1964: 1) put it: "The achievement cancels the premises."

Although a technological system is by definition rational, Marcuse argues its irrationality as a social system because it denies the opportunity for self-criticism and alternatives. It is incapable of qualitative social change. Corporations or societies dominated by technological values are totalitarian. The inevitable consequence, in Marcuse's reasoning, is that such societies, and the United States in particular, must endure the tension between the forces which seek to contain social change and the forces which are aimed at breaking the containment. This is a situation which yields only alternatives of total oppression or revolution. Neither is particularly beneficial for the human condition.

French philosopher Jacques Ellul (1964) has offered an even more gloomy future for technological society. Modernization and technology have become synonymous. In the process we have *technologized* ourselves at the expense to traditional human values. Humanity has become subservient to the technological state. In Ellul's thinking there is no way that we can adopt technology without these social consequences. They are inherent. Moreso than even Marcuse, Ellul sees no way out of the dilemma.

Bell's concept of a post-industrial society includes a substantial value component and it runs directly contrary to the positions of Marcuse and Ellul and the many others who have written on the inherent evils of technology. In essence, he anticipates a shift in our society from an emphasis upon sheer productivity ("getting more with less") to more concern with social consequences and objectives. Bell contrasts these two ends as the *economizing* and *sociologizing* modes. In his words (1976: 42-43):

> it becomes less meaningful to talk about capitalism and socialism than about the "economizing" and "socializing" modes which are present in both systems. Each of these is a "logic" responsive to a different end. The "economizing" mode is oriented to functional efficiency and the management of things (and men are treated as things). The sociologizing mode establishes broader social criteria, but it necessarily involves the loss of efficiency, the reduction of production, and other costs that follow the introduction of noneconomic values.

The economizing mode reflects the traditional values of industrial society where goals are associated with costs-benefits, maximization or optimization. Less attention is paid to the social consequences of growth and productivity. Gains are measured in goods rather than in the quality of life. The sociologizing mode, on the other hand, represents an attempt to incorporate social factors in the implementation of technology. Here there is a formal attempt to assess social needs, to anticipate the social "costs" of innovations. Social ends become objectives of change.

Bell asserts that there is increasing public disenchantment over corporate values in our country as they are injected into the political system. There is a feeling that self-interest has too often replaced public interest in corporate policy. Environmental deterioration is believed to be one of the most visible consequences of the corporate bias. There is pressure for more social priorities to be recognized, more job satisfaction, more responsibility to communities, more equality in the distribution of wealth, and more desire to clean up the environment. Although it is recognized that corporations have been moving slowly in the direction of the sociologizing mode, perhaps it will take greater commitment to speed the transformation.

The result, to summarize Bell's picture of post-industrialism, would be a society where social goals are thoroughly researched and processes implemented to achieve them. Technologically driven change would be guided by research-based policy in which all of the social consequences would be considered. A new knowledge class would demand that intellectual technology be as much applied to quality of life as to any other ends in the society. The political process itself might be revised so as to be less haphazard relative to public decisions over complex technological problems. Bargaining and negotiation might well replace political debate. Decisions would be made against a context of well researched and futures-oriented alternatives rather than in the heat of a political election. Post-industrialism is eventually more than an economic order; it is a new social one.

Marcuse and Ellul, of course, would consider Bell's forecast a most improbable, if not impossible, future. At least one critic has accused Bell of painting a picture of what could be conceived only as a white, middle-aged, [then] liberal's political fantasy. Yet in the last two decades we have clearly vacillated between *economizing* and *sociologizing* modes in our society. In the late 1960s, we were in the sociologizing mode of Lyndon Johnson's "Great Society." In the subsequent Nixon and Ford administrations, we saw an emphasis upon the economizing mode (remember Spiro Agnew's comment about "benign neglect" in programs for Blacks?). Despite his promises of austerity, Jimmy Carter clearly emphasized sociologizing goals. Ronald Reagan was elected mainly upon the basis of a directly opposite platform.

We have seen "environmental impact reports" required but have also witnessed the squashing of the "Occupational Safety and Health Administration." The "Office of Technology Assessment" is an on-again, off-again entity. Nuclear power is a meeting ground for sociologizing-economizing debates, as in conservation of natural resources and offshore oil drilling.

Even if we have many of the characteristics of post-industrialism all about us, Bell's sociologizing bias has not been particularly as forecast. We are not clearly of one mind in where we want to go with our rapidly developing technological society.

Optimistic Change

Except for recognition of computers and telecommunications as important growth areas, we have not seen much theorizing as to how communications technologies fit into the grand design of change. They are often taken as symptoms of change but mainly in terms of their visible, razzle-dazzle details. As described in earlier chapters, it is clear also that communications technologies and services are a major component of our economic growth. We see this not only in terms of sales revenues but in the mainly economically (rather than socially) oriented debates over rewriting the Communications Act of 1934. Surely these technologies fit on a grander scale into the picture of change.

It might be tempting to see these new technologies as a key cause, effect, or panacea for our problems. But they are not. There is no immediate and simple way to cast communications technologies into a reason or result of contemporary change nor as a main cure for our problems.

But they are not irrelevant either. Indeed, communications technologies are very much embedded among the tangle of factors propelling us into a new era. They are mixed in thoroughly with change. *Communications technologies are a catalyst or intensifier of change.* They are a part of our problems but they are also part of the solutions. Communications technologies provide us with new alternatives for managing our future.

How ironic it is that our most rapidly advancing technology is also one which has a trivial appetite for energy. A home computer uses only a little more energy than an average light bulb. A large business-sized computer uses less than an average household. The orbiting communications platforms of the future will be able to operate efficiently on solar energy. Nor do communications technologies make undue demands upon our earth's natural resources for their fabrication. The main ingredient in microprocessors is silicon, the world's second most abundant substance. Copper, which is suffering from inflation and a forthcoming shortage, will become irrelevant as optical fibers replace wires. Moreover, the general trend toward miniaturization reduces the need proportionately for the physical resources for structural frameworks, housings, connectors, and packaging, not to overlook energy savings in operation and handling.

Shortages of natural resources, including those involved in the production of energy, have few direct consequences upon the manufacture and implementation of communications technologies. Nor are there necessarily economic limitations. As we progress through the 1980s, the costs of telecommunications and computer technologies still continue to decrease.

In a traditional sense, communications technologies, because they have no by-products, do not pollute the physical environment. We are forced to say "traditional" because some are beginning to argue that commercial broadcasting, particularly television, is polluting our social environment. By the same token, we could argue that this is not an inherent problem of communications technology, but rather a consequence of our careless use of it.

If the growth and applications of communications technologies were to be included in the complex Club of Rome computer-based forecasts such as described earlier in this chapter (see Figure 18.1), there could exist new positive patterns. For example, the low resource demands and the low pollution output of both communications technology manufacturing and the delivery of services could avert predicted problems in these areas. Social applications of large-scale public communications systems could also promote resource conservation, improved agricultural methods, and family planning. Pollution on all levels of society could be discouraged by public campaigns and in the long run by effective public education.

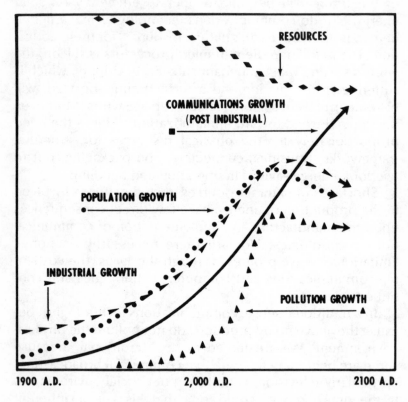

Figure 18.2   *The Ideal Interaction of Communications Growth and Era of Limits Factors*

NOTE: If the acceleration curve of communications growth were superimposed on era of limits factors, could we avert a "doomsday" based upon declining resources, rising pollution, and our problem of overpopulation? A communications economy would use few natural resources, be nonpolluting, and could give us the means to gain human cooperation on resource conservation and population growth.

Examine the idealized plot of Figure 18.2. It is meant to portray how a low resource demanding and nonpolluting communications-based economy might replace an industrial one. It represents the optimistic results of a "managed change" approach to the future. Would it avert doomsday forecasts or only delay them?

We can argue that communications have no limits to growth in an era of limits. Armed with our new technologies, perhaps we humans can bypass the doomsday predictions completely. To do so we are going to have to improve our capabilities for managing change, to use our communications growth for positive purposes including national and international cooperation, and to have a clearer understanding of what we want.

NOTE

1. I must acknowledge an article in the *Los Angeles Times* (January 13, 1980) for bringing this to my attention. It is noted too that the Times Mirror Corporation had a 15 percent return on equity that year.

CHAPTER 19

Scenarios to the 21st Century

Managed Change Vs. Muddling Through

Can we indeed manage change? Can we emphasize certain positive trends in our society while inhibiting others? Is post-industrialism a desirable future for us? How can we ride the crest of the communications technology revolution so as to maximize its benefits to us?

Nobody can predict the future. However with a careful examination of present circumstances, our resources, our challenges, and even our desires, we can derive some estimates on what a few of the alternatives might be. Of course it is important to bear in mind that there will no doubt be some alternatives which we cannot imagine at the present time, as well as some which could be so catastrophic as to make most any other detailed scenarios irrelevant.

We do know that our economy is changing and that this is likely to have many carryover social effects. It is likely too that inflation will persist as along as the industrialized world is dependent upon an energy source subject to cartel pricing. A more educated public, and particularly an older one, will require more public services, which will increase governmental expenditures. Despite the disagreement over era-of-limits scenarios, we are already facing some limits in terms of energy resources, limits reflected in malnutrition, and visible evidence of environmental pollution. We definitely have some adjustments to make.

Our social existence is growing more dense. There are more of us. As single family houses give way to condominiums and other multiple family dwellings, we will live closer together. Add to this the increase in the density of our social experiences promoted by the electronic networks of communication, particularly the telephone and television. We have fewer "buffers" to insulate us from one another and from our communications. Our privacy is additionally threatened by large-scale information networks. We regularly submit personal information to them in the forms of license applications, taxes, credit, job and educational applications, as well as the records of our business, health, and educational transactions.

Electronic media have cancelled time as a buffer also. We react to world events simultaneously with their occurrence. We are living in an increasingly tighter loop between happenings, our reactions, and reactions to our reactions. We are forced as a culture into the prospect of even more of a confining and simultaneous communal existence. The Adam Smith value system of what is good for the individual is good for the society is becoming questionable.

Service industries are growing as reflected in the expansion of health, educational, and governmental services since the early 1950s. Home entertainment, telecommunications, and computers are significant growth industries in today's economy and the pace is still increasing. Theoretically these areas should not be directly affected by an era of limits. Moreover, the climate for continued growth seems especially opportune in an era where knowledge and information take on increasing value. But there are challenges to profitability. How can proprietorship of information be protected in open broadcast communications systems? Once information is disclosed, it may have no further value. If the national political climate demands a sociologizing mode (that is, emphasis upon social goals) of business and industry, can profitability be sufficiently maintained? Productivity is a problem to gauge in a service economy. Will new insights be gained in the process for monitoring economic health?

New communications technologies are expensive, not only for consumers but to producers in preparing for their manufacture. Will we create a new "communications gap" social stratification as mainly middle and upper income classes purchase cable and satellite services or video disc and cassette machines? In a society where it is mainly the knowledge worker who is upwardly mobile, will we be creating new unemployable underclasses? Our educational institutions, which seem to be the last in our society to recognize these current forces of change, will probably be more of a liability than an asset in countering these potential social inequities.

Perhaps most challenged of all by the transition to post-industrialism, the era of limits, and the communications revolution is that institution upon which we may have to depend most of all, government. As communications and computer industries transform our social environment, government seems incapable of providing insights into either short- or long-range consequences. Communications regulation in the United States is based upon legislation enacted in 1934, before most of the technologies which bombard us today were on the drawing board. Technological change in communications is outstripping the government's ability to modernize communications legislation. This leaves us with an ineffective national communications policy and virtually no international one.

Yet it is these same technologies which could support an undreamed of level of democracy in terms of broad public deliberation and decision. In the last two decades of advertising we have made great strides in designing modern communications for purposes of promoting images and affecting attitudes. If just a portion of the resources which are invested in using these strategies to promote toothpastes, deodorants, breakfast cereals, and patent medicines were invested in public health information campaigns or in national education, we would see visible results.

Government itself is being challenged to slim down, to become more efficient, and to get out of service activities best done by others. Taxpayer revolts, a national anti-bureaucratic attitude, and the loss of confidence in politicians all raise challenges to the maintenance, if not the reform, of U.S. government. If we do move to a sociologizing mode of existence and all groups stake their claims, will the national political climate be so divisive as to paralyze change? Or will a more enlightened and educated leadership put the results of the communications revolution to work and create a new level of democracy in terms of public negotiation, decision, and implementation?

Let us consider three very general scenarios, one each for the business, social, and governmental dimensions of our future. The contrast in each will be between general extensions of our *status quo* (what I have called "muddling through) and "managed change," which tries to take advantage of our transition to post-industrialism, our advances in communications technologies, yet preserves the recognition that a major American strength is a free enterprise economy.

Business Scenarios

A Background of Inflation and Declining Opportunities

The economy of the United States faces changes greater than the rise of mass manufacturing early in the twentieth century and perhaps even the move from the land to the cities in the nineteenth century. The level of wages and benefits as well as the attitudes of the labor force lead to the demise in this country of labor-intensive industries (such as textiles). The same conditions plus the reluctance (or inability) to invest in plant modernization and automation in the late twentieth century contribute to the decline of heavy manufacturing industries such as automobiles. Without government subsidies and protectionist legislation, many large manufacturers of higher technology products cannot compete with countries which have modernized their factories (such as Japan); or for lower technology products, countries with inexpensive labor resources (China, India). The effect is to encourage national economies to become specialized.

An educated American public is distrustful of large corporations, especially those accused of profiteering (petroleum), bribery (weapons exporters), pollution (chemical), or a lack of public responsibility over safety standards (automobile manufacturers). This creates a regressive climate to growth as corporations are tied up with class action suits, product boycotts, and restrictive legislation from liberal minded reformers. However, the growth industries, primarily high technology and communications businesses, escape these problems for the time being. Except for the television networks, they are too young to be accused of profiteering or bribery. Their by-products are minimal and nonpolluting (by traditional standards). These same industries are less affected by "era of limits" problems. Physical raw materials for them are cheap and in abundance. Especially successful are the so-called "knowledge industries" which make low demands upon natural resources. Research is their fundamental resource. It is an employee's marketplace in the scientific and engineering professions.

Growth of national communications services is potentially hampered by powerful broadcast and theatre lobbies. Broadcasters, especially those who have not invested in the new technologies, see their monopoly threatened by cable and especially by direct broadcast satellite. Theatre owners see pay TV as putting them out of business. Giants in computing (for example, IBM) and telecommunications (AT&T) are bogged down in drawn out antitrust suits.

The public, coping with double digit inflation and the decline of employment opportunity in many manufacturing areas, is too preoccupied to be concerned with the lobbying of large interests trying to carve out their shares of the new communications and computing services.

If this is the status of business in the decade of the 1980s, where do we go from here? For one, we could try to preserve the status quo, even get back to the "good old days." I call this the "status quo" or "muddling through" alternative. Or we could attempt to capitalize on post-industrialism, our lead in telecommunications and computing technologies, and attempt a program of "managed change." A few projections of both are described below.

Muddling Through in Business

What if we try to protect the status quo? A scenario is presented here.

It is necessary to devote great amounts of governmental and public attention to the maintenance of a manufacturing economy in the United States. This is done through government subsidies to corporations and by protectionist tariff restrictions on imports. In contrast, communications businesses continue to experience rapid growth. The public goes on using media the way we have since entering the electronic age. There remains a strong mass market flavor in the content of entertainment media.

Lobbying to preserve share of profits remains so intense that it is unlikely that the Communications Act of 1934 will be revised in any substantial form. The AT&T and IBM antitrust suits are eventually settled on compromise and deregulated terms but after great time and expense. America's national and international communications policies follow rather than lead the communications revolution.

Satellite and cable continue to expand rapidly, especially as wealthy corporate money flows into them. The television networks try to move their money into the new technologies as their monopoly over program dissemination continues to collapse.

The result is an expansion of communication distribution systems probably in excess of owners' abilities to produce improved programs or services. There is a multiplication of the current TV mediocrity as profits are not realized in specialized high taste programming. Networks return to mass market programming but viewers now pay directly for it.

Technical design and interconnect capability of new distribution systems suffer from overextended growth. "Cream-skimming" continues as these services are brought first to those who can surely pay for them.

After the initial wave of growth, communications businesses slump because of overexpansion, the inability to deliver promised quality services, and the inefficiencies of single function facilities and incompatible equipment. Big investors pull back from further development but hold their franchises as equity on their investment.

Pressure groups rally public opinion over mediocre services and inactive franchise holders. The climate of antagonism develops between a public dissatisfied over services, large investors who have no opportunity for return on investment, and a seemingly powerless government.

The United States then faces lags in communications and computer research and development because of a poor investment climate and uncertainty about government regulation. Other countries, particularly the Japanese, take the lead.

Alternative Scenario: Managing Change for Profit as Well as People Goals

Rather than use our national resources to prop up aging industries, there is a national commitment to the development of a post-industrial economy. The United States asserts its world leadership in telecommunications and computing, recognizing this as the basis for our "reindustrialization" in the years to the twenty-first century. While aiming for maximization of growth and profit ("economizing" mode), care is taken to maximize the social uses of the new communications technologies. This includes stimulating the adoption of new technologies in the delivery of human services, as in health, education, and the operation of government. It is recognized that in a post-industrial economy there may be far less natural antagonism between economizing and sociologizing objectives. That is, a healthy and growing post-industrial economy can have concomitant social benefits.

The Communications Act of 1934 is revised in a comprehensive attempt to maximize the post-industrial growth of the United States. The preamble of the new act spells out the dual commitment of our national communications resources to new economic and social goals. New technologies are evaluated in terms of such criteria as: (1) potential for widespread delivery of services balanced against the potential for satisfactory return on investment; (2) multiple purpose uses (such as data, broadband, two-way); (3) compatibility with national and international standards; and (4) potential for growth as well as integration with other systems.

Investment in telecommunications and computing is encouraged by selective deregulation, tax write-offs, and low interest loans. Large-scale integration planning is particularly encouraged as, for example, local cable networks which offer a wide range of programs and services. Encouragement is given for state, county, and city cooperative investment in telecommunications systems.

Although the above policy initially shows development as standards are debated and the national policy is formulated, when growth is realized it is far more widespread and consistent than under a policy of muddling through. Social services increase as local telecommunications networks are interconnected to share in emergency warning systems, educational services, and health emergency and information networks.

The managed change approach is a growth policy with national objectives of revitalizing our economy. The international objective is to strengthen our leadership role in telecommunications and computing rather than to forefit it to others, which we are now doing.

The telecommunications networks — wire, microwave, satellite and open broadcasting — can be compared with the transportation routes which have brought prosperity and change to western civilization. As we have with the growth of the transportation systems, the growth of telecommunications networks requires such massive investment, that it requires public financial support. This is in the form of direct financing, low interest rates, or other forms of subsidy. It may include extensions of corporate monopolies. It definitely requires that government work with, rather than against, business.

By contrast, the development of services — banking, shopping, health, emergency, instructional, information, news, entertainment — is an opportune domain for corporate investment. Building the telecommunications networks of tomorrow, just as the highways and roads of yesteryear, will bring with it a revolution in new service and program marketplaces.

Managed change requires prompt settlement of long standing antitrust litigation with such corporate giants as IBM and AT&T. If we do not include the organizations which brought us to the brink of the communications revolution in a positive and productive fashion in our program of managed change, we will surely forfeit the world communications and computing leadership we now hold and possibly injure our growth potential as a post-industrial society.

We cannot afford to waste the advances we now have.

Social Scenarios

A Background of Deteriorating Social Environment

The decline of heavy industry and inflation, especially interest rates, is already having a profound effect upon the U.S. population. Economic opportunity is shifting from manufacturing to service industries. The shift, along with steadily increasing costs of energy, keep inflation at a double digit rate. This has particular impact upon low income and fixed income groups, especially those on welfare and retired persons living on pensions and savings. These groups, which are growing relative to the rest of the U.S. population, demand subsidies so as to maintain a minimum standard of living including income supplements for food, energy, housing, and health care. Tension increases between the subsidized classes and the middle and upper income classes who grow increasingly politically conservative in their attempts to restrain the growth of government and subsidies.

World tensions increase, particularly between superpowers over politically unstable Third World countries, especially those with attractive natural resources. World tensions take their toll on the national budget. More highly educated working classes make new demands for improved working conditions and occupational upward mobility. There is also new dissatisfaction with our national inability to preserve the natural environment.

The 1980s and 1990s may not be so much a period when revolutionaries speak out about the quality of life as it is one in which the average citizen is beginning to experience living conditions becoming an increasing challenge. Rather than the steady improvement which we Americans have come to expect — the ability to have an interesting job, own a home, and improve ourselves — more of us are faced with the challenge of simply maintaining our present position. Even more tragic is that the prospects for certain Third World countries, especially in Africa, are incredibly bleak. The land cannot support them, and there is no way that they can generate a basic economy under current conditions. Such populations, if they have the strength to do it, call for a share of the earth's resources. All such countries are ripe for political exploitation.

The Social Consequences of No Policy

Social frustration steadily rises in the 1980s as the decline of manufacturing industries and government cutbacks contribute to increasing unemployment. Without a plan for managed change, the shift of work forces from declining industries to growing ones is apt to be particularly haphazard. There are no effective programs for employee reeducation or relocation. Large segments of our work force become obsolete. This increases the welfare rolls, contributes to inflation, and creates rising frustrations in the population. Mass media use for escapism increases, the content of which contributes still more to frustrations.

Meanwhile, communication and computing technologies continue to be growth industries. It is already evident that this growth is having social consequences. Entertainment television is the number one leisure time activity. Some experts say that it rather than parents are rearing our children and setting our values. Print is declining as an influential medium. There continues to be evidence that the declining use of print is correlateed with declines in reading ability of youngsters. Higher costs of transportation encourage the public to pursue their recreation, education, and work close to home, and sometimes in the home.

Our largest social problem with the new communications technologies is that under a *status quo* policy we create new socioeconomic classes, namely the "communications rich" and the "communications poor." Cable, pay TV, disc, tape, direct broadcast satellite, and home computers do not come cheaply to the consumer. As advertising dollars shift from the mass marketed network television market to cable and other new outlets, the quality of over-the-air, "free" broadcasting sharply declines. Moreover, children reared in homes, and attending schools, with a high rate of technology adoption are far more adapted for life in a communications technology laden society than those who go without. In the twenty-first century, "information" will more than ever in history represent power.

There are also institutional differences in adoption of new technologies. All public institutions continue to suffer in inflationary times, even more in the "tax revolt" climate of the 1980s. Those institutions which have been slow to adopt new technologies — government and especially education — decline substantially in productivity. Given education's decline in the last decade, both in productivity and public support, systems of public education face drastic cutback and possible collapse in parts of the country.

As social unrest grows, it is the everyday fare of the news media. Governmental communications increase in authoritative tone. Telecommunications and computer technologies are used for surveillance, investigation, and control. As social unrest and stratification grow, the lower class, without access to the telecommunications networks, turns to more revolutionary methods of communications. Social frustration and stratification are accelerated by mass market oriented news media. The media are intensifiers rather than mediators of social conflict.

The great social tragedy of a muddling through policy is not only that the great social potentials of the new communications technologies go untapped, but that they intensify social conflict. They present escapism where orientation is needed. They promote oppression where understanding is needed. They intensify and overly dramatize conflict where mediation is needed.

That is to say, our technological miracles could turn on us.

Alternative Scenario: Managing with an Eye Toward Social Benefits

As Daniel Bell forecasts, the citizens of a post-industrial society have a greater demand for human services. A fully developed telecommunications network fulfills many aspects of those demands. The delivery of health, education, financial, and information services is increased effectively through telecommunications.

A national, interactive telecommunications network becomes the most effective basis for democracy ever invented. Problems of national significance are explored in the national media, inviting citizen participation in electronic referenda. A national sense of cooperation emerges as the communications networks facilitate problem definition, spell out alternative solutions, then provide that basis for inexpensive and efficient public participation in decisions. We create a growing sense of *future* as greater numbers of the public engage in "planning ahead."

Public education transforms itself into our most innovative social institution yet by uses of the new communications technologies. Not only do local school systems benefit from instructional program networks and computer-assisted instruction, software, and administrative services, but many of these are directly linked to the home. As the need for lifelong education increases, the market for outstanding courses administered over "pay instructional" networks grows markedly.

Media are used in lifelong education to promote attitudes toward conservation, family planning, and antipollution strategies.

An effectively oriented social policy for communications growth also protects the rights of the individual. Large-scale financial backing of telecommunications networks maximizes their public penetration. (We had already done this successfully in this country with the telephone.) Regulation is also sought to protect the privacy rights of the individual. The "information power" of large data bases (tax records, licenses, health and education records) does not fall into the hands of large bureaucracies. Individuals have rights over the information that others hold on them.

Community planning, even the possibility of new "rural societies" as envisioned by Peter Goldmark (1972) take telecommunication networks into account. Just as common city services are planned, so is the broad range of telecommunications links.

If we were to succeed in managing a future that keeps social benefits in a high priority position, we might then go on to consider new dimensions of social growth. It is one thing for our new technologies to make us physically and socially secure; they could further be the basis for new creativity, new dimensions of human experience and enlightenment. Just as the communications of the Renaissance broke forth with new dimensions of the human spirit, so could the products of the electronic revolution. (This is discussed further in Chapter 20.)

Government Scenarios

Doing More with Less?

Government in the 1980s and 1990s continues in the midst of a paradox of pressures. Tax reduction initiatives are passed by a public which at the same time presses for more services. City, county, and state governments reach their growth limits in terms of financial bases. Having a government go bankrupt is not so much of an oddity. Growth of federal government suffers from its usual role in serving as a political distinction between liberal and conservative positions. Liberals claim we "can do better" while conservatives argue that "less government is good government." Meanwhile, government grows haphazardly. The political system draws so much attention to current crises that concern for the future is often overlooked in the process.

There is consideration of alternative methods of democratic governance as the society becomes post-industrial. Something different from traditional government bureaucracy is sought. Thought is given to new configurations of governance, ones where responsibilities are at a level more relevant to needs, services, and operations. Just as small and inefficient school systems have used transportation to merge themselves into more efficient units, the prospect is investigated of designing local government by use of new communications networks. Such change involves utilities coordination, certain types of law enforcement, business regulation, licensing, tax collections, zoning regulations, libraries, fire and emergency services, to name a few. Some services are offered under contract through agencies other than government, as, for example, firefighting.

New communications technologies lessen the need for large numbers of people to be employed in government. Computers replace about half of the clerical workers. Communications networks allow information to be moved instantaneously anywhere within a governance unit. This is far removed from the days when governmental units were based upon the distance a person could travel in a day. The key challenge is to design systems of governance so as to eliminate duplication, increase resource sharing, and employ automation wherever possible. A key requisite is to protect our democratic heritage.

It is realized that if we are to have a society where social goals predominate, it will be necessary to develop effective methods for defining social goals, gaining public participation, then having indicators of whether goals are being achieved. It is hoped that government could lead rather than be dragged into the post-industrial era. There is recognition that we need leaders who understand the era of limits, the transition to post-industrialism, and the nature of social indicators. It becomes evident that we need talented candidates for public office who understand more about the communications revolution than mounting media blitz election campaigns.

There is a desire to have public decisions of grave importance decided on a more rational basis than through sensationalist news reporting, as the plot materials for light drama on prime time television, or in political campaigns. The public seeks better management of the country. Will government adapt to the future?

The Problems of Government "As Usual"

The *status quo* continues to be a shifting between economizing and sociologizing modes of government as we have vacillated from one administration to another over the last decade or so. This continues to lessen the public's confidence in government to the point where the attitude reduces to the feeling about most administrations that "somebody (anybody!) else could do it better."

The public becomes even more disenchanted with the federal government due to economic stagnation and the inability of the President and Congress to respond rapidly and effectively to national and international problems.

We see failure of many of the new communications networks to live up to expectations. The equipment incompatibilities among them discourage local and regional governments from investing in the potentially wide range of social services. Protectionist legislation is also discouraging to change. In this climate, it is easy for large communications franchise holders to renege on promised services. Competition is discouraged. A slow economy, rising costs of welfare, and increased subsidies to failing manufacturing industries creates a negative climate for innovation. A "let's hold on to what we have" philosophy literally hands economic leadership to other countries, especially in the new technologies.

The lack of a national communications policy makes impossible the creation of an international one. The United States becomes even more of a reactor to proposals for change in international communications than a creator of them. We experience increasing problems from new Third World pressures in the allocation of radio frequencies and for variations in calls for a "new world information order."

Because we do not give priority to national development of telecommunications and computing systems, our government itself becomes increasingly handicapped in its own uses of technology to increase operational productivity. We are faced with "buying it abroad."

Alternative Scenario: Even Government Can Change

One of the more attractive features of Bell's description of post-industrialism is that through managed change the government itself takes on the efficiencies of modern management. To do this, it becomes a much improved adopter of technology, especially communications technologies.

On the local level, the emergence of two-way networks allows considerable cost savings due to consolidation of services. These include fire, police, and medical alarm systems which are tied into local communications networks, usually cable. Such services also stimulate the economic climate for telecommunications investment since the same systems deliver many additional programs and services. Many social services are extended over county and even regional areas, also improving efficiency. Public institutions such as school districts greatly improve their management processes by communications technology adoption and tie-ins with appropriate branches of government (for example, the education agency).

State governments are encouraged to consider communications master plans, for it is likely that the costs of communications be reduced significantly. (Large states benefit from having their own satellites.)

Linkages between states and the federal government are improved through modern telecommunications. Data bases of current legislation directly affecting states are shared nationally. Many federal-state exchanges of reports are done electronically rather than by transporting paper.

Perhaps the greatest innovation is the electronic linkage of the citizens of a democracy. The interaction between citizen and citizen, citizen and government, is revolutionized by modern communications. Of high priority is that the citizen's privacy be respected in this system. The system needs to be designed and operated so that the citizen is protected from surveillance and intimidation. We get "to pull the switch," so to speak.

The United States, which developed many of these new technologies, is now in the position to demonstrate their broad range of economic, social, and governmental applications. This is considered as more than a choice. It is a responsibility.

Fantasies or Scenarios?

All scenarios are fantasies to some degree in their reliance upon imagination and their tendency to exaggerate. Yet these scenarios are purposely intended to stimulate the imagination and to emphasize certain points about our future. We do live in a country where our business, social, and governmental futures highly interact. We are faced with contrasts between reacting to the future as it invades and challenges us bit by bit or planning actively for change. Only by the latter will we take true advantage of the communications revolution. Products of the imagination or not, we will more than likely be benefiting from or challenged by no few of the alternatives suggested in the foregoing scenarios when we put away our noisemakers on the morning of January 1 at the dawn of the twenty-first century.

These are fantasies for serious thought.

An Electronic Renaissance?

CHAPTER 20

Surviving Techno-Impacts

Suppose that in 22,000 B.C. a primitive humanoid who had represented a successful hunt by painting images of prey, self, and the sun on a cave wall in Lascaux also scratched more modest versions of these same images in the dust whenever he wished to mark off his hunting territory. If this had been the invention of writing, what would have been the immediate social consequences? Probably none. Paleolithic life made no pressing demands for a system of writing. Further, if one human were to write in an innovative fashion, who would know exactly what it meant?

Suppose that in 1500 B.C. as skilled artisans first plastered, then carved hieroglyphics on the 100 meter plus entrance tunnel leading to the tomb of Ramses VI, they instead pressed images of the hieroglyphics into wet plaster with carved wooden dies. (Priests and kings did "stamp" their names on seals.) Printing could have been invented 2100 years before it emerged in China or 3000 years before Europe. What would have been the immediate consequences? Probably none. Hieroglyphic tomb inscription was a high and sacred art. Messages were not intended for mortals. Why cheapen the process?

Suppose that in 1453 the power that was already long harnessed by water wheels were used to drive a printing press by use of mechanical devices not much more complicated than those which drive a millstone. Add to that a source of cheap and abundant paper. Such a press might have multiplied the output of medieval printing hundredsfold. What would have been the immediate consequences? Probably none. Not many people could read. The transition from hand copying of manuscripts to their simple reproduction by moveable type was astounding enough. It would take time for society to catch up even with that.

Although we can equate (as in Chapter 2) communications innovation with social change, in past societies it has been a slow process. Those societies reacted slowly to communication innovation; they did not depend upon it.

Suppose that by the twenty-first century every human on earth who has a wrist-mounted communications device can be in contact with any other human via a satellite communications network; that home television has over 100 channels, many of them interactive; that most home appliances are programmable or controllable by our voice; that most mail is sent electronically; that small discs for our home players can hold many thousands of pages of textual information; that an electronic network makes available a university education for anyone willing to pursue it; and that we can join our communities for work, play, education, health care, or inspiration electronically? What then?

Unlike the prehistoric era of cave painters, the ancient culture of Egypt, or the Middle Ages, our society depends heavily upon technological innovation for its growth. As a consequence, we can expect that the most recent era of great change in human communications will have almost simultaneous consequences on our lives. Our society is based upon change, and particularly technological change. That the communications revolution will have an effect upon us is not the critical issue. The challenge will be to manage the *quality* of this change.

How much, for example, should we be wary of the "technology" in communications technology itself? Technology need not be dehumanizing. Dehumanization is not an inherent defect of technology but rather is the result of an oversight or lack of understanding in its applications. Human variables are identifiable and can be entered into technological planning although engineers are notorious for over-simplifying or omitting them. We humans are not as easily manipulated as, for example, electronic circuitry, keyboard design, or manufacturing strategies. Too often design focuses only on immediate results and overlooks long-range consequences. We designed and manufactured automobiles for over a half century before there was any significant public awareness of safety and pollution characteristics. It has only been in the last decade that widespread attention has been given to correcting these problems, and it took public and governmental efforts to do it.

Technological planning *can* include human variables, although it is expensive and complex. We need to become more adept at this process, including the study of long range social consequences of technological implementation. Technology does not have to reduce the human condition to bland efficiency. A systems analysis recipe for a gourmet dish need not result in fast foods!

Another problem is a confusion of means and ends in the application of technology. Doing more with less, increasing efficiency, or attaining a favorable cost-benefit ratio are different as means and ends in technological planning. As *means* we seek these qualities in technological application but they can be kept separate from ends. If you or I wanted to plan two weeks of total leisure, what we eventually experienced as complete relaxation need not be diminished because our plans were carried out efficiently. Properly applied, that which is carefully and technologically planned need not be dehumanizing. We need only to look so far as the work of any successful architect or designer for evidence of this.

That we can fly the 600 miles from Los Angeles to San Francisco in a comfortable 55 minutes is a positive application of technology. The equally long wait for our baggage, if we are lucky enough to have it arrive, is a failure in application.

It is a human mistake when our goals become efficiency or least-effort in and of themselves. This is not a consequence of technology but of our own misapplication. It is a condition worthy of Marcuse's label of "one-dimensional" or Ellul's claim of the technologization of ourselves. But it is also our own fault and avoidable.

To judge the future of a technological society by assumed values of "systems efficiency" and other such mechanical analogies is to extend the confusion of means and ends as well as the open nature of social goals. A technological society has no more inherent limits placed upon goals than any other society. It probably has fewer limitations. Freedom, creativity, and alternative political philosophies can exist as well in a technological society as in any other. The crux is in the selection of goals and these are not derived from technology, at least not directly. They are reasoned from human values, or that which we believe will be favorable to us.

Our problem may not be just a confusion of means and ends in a technological society, but a declining ability to articulate alternative goals. We may technologize ourselves by default. Ultimately if we are to put the communications revolution in technology to positive use, we will have to solve the human goals problem.

What is *good* communications?

If We Can Get What We Want, What Do We Want?

Modern society has done little to emphasize social values in implementations of modern electronic communications technologies. In fact, we have not done so well as those who have preceded us in this society. Our First Amendment, for example, is a quite unique article of government, particularly in how we have interpreted it in times far removed from the era in which it was written. Even the outdated Communications Act of 1934 is farsighted in its philosophy that the public should own the airways and that we should fulfill the commitment "to make available, so far as possible, to all the people of the United States a rapid, efficient, nationwide, and worldwide wire and radio communication service." It is remarkable how valuable these legal precedents have been in a world of electronic technologies which did not even exist 30 years ago.

Except for the postal service and public broadcasting, we have implemented most communications services in this country on a free enterprise basis and one should not expect anything different in a capitalistic society. Neither of those examples is very exciting. We have mostly developed what investors have thought the marketplace would bear. The direct social aim, if any, was to make available to people anything they thought they might need; more specifically, to make available anything for which people might pay. Of course, we have necessarily had regulated monopolies, such as in the telephone business, where competition in main stages of growth might be undesirable. Because of the shortage of spectrum space and the simple need for stations not to drown one another out, we have had to regulate broadcasting. Social motives have probably been too abstract to consider in the early growth stages of communications technologies. It is enough of a miracle to be able to send messages at the speed of light, to link homes with personal two-way communication devices, or to bring entertainment and news over the airways. As when roads were first constructed, the important thing was getting there, not in abstract schemes for benefiting humanity. Steam engines were built without the benefit of thermodynamic theory.

Despite our confusion over values in new communications technologies, their development under a system of free enterprise has been opportune. We do, after all, have the most advanced and reliable telephone service in the world. No matter what your opinions are of the quality of television programming in this country, we create and disseminate many more hours of programming than any other country. We have been and remain the major source of technological advances in computers and telecommunications in the world market. Capitalism, no matter its political counterarguments, has provided a favorable climate for the growth of communications technology in this country. Our basic political system is not the problem — it is that we must employ it better.

Communications technologies have grown so rapidly in our era that we must now begin to pay more attention to their social impact. We must do more thinking about what kinds of communications are beneficial to our way of life. Moreover, we need to be clearer on exactly what we value as our way of life.

Again, the question is: what is *good* communications?

Strictly on the mechanical and physical level, our communications technologies, like others, are valued for low costs, reliability, efficiency, flexibility, and so on. We want our communications technologies to work and work well. In most cases we want to avoid being concerned with any of their technical and operational details. We are more interested in what we can put on our televisions than in how they work. We want our calls to get through; we are not interested in how they get through. This quality in itself is a general value for communications technologies (and some others, of course). Simply put, the less a communications system or component gets in the way of what we want to accomplish with it, the more valued it is as a system. An effective computer system solves problems without its components getting in the way of one another or the whole system getting in the way of the user. Our transatlantic call may cross the ocean by cable or satellite and the land connections to individual telephones may vary in a multiplicity of ways without our ever knowing or caring so long as our call gets through. Local radio stations may originate the program signals from live voice or music, from tape recordings, records or from a network feed without us paying any attention to these differences. But these are simple functional values of the technology itself, almost "engineering" values, not profound human ones.

The deeper value questions of communications technologies are in the domain of human behavior. It is what we can do with communications rather than what it does to us that is ultimately important as a value. *The definition of what is good in communications is what is good for us.* It is not found in the functional characteristics of what have become highly efficient technologies. Value in communications is found in values to us.

Modern social sciences theory in human communication assumes that we are functional users of media, including uses of radio and television which are often described as encouraging passivity. We tend to use the communications resources around us to satisfy our psychological and social needs. Satisfaction comes not only from the content or information obtained via a medium but from experience with the medium itself and sometimes the social circumstances surrounding its use.

A telephone, for example, can be used as a source of information. It also makes us feel safer to have one in our home. Using it to keep in touch with our friends is a source of social satisfaction. Radio gives us news flashes and background music or chatter. An automobile in America is not complete without one; it is a part of commuting or traveling. Sitting around the radio in the 1940s was a frequent family pastime. TV can inform, persuade, or entertain us. But research also shows that many people turn on the set simply to "watch television" as a means to relax. What's on is not always too important. The television set is the gathering place for members of the family, especially when children do not have their own sets. (Do you remember the "TV trays" of the late 1950s and 1960s when we began to bring our whole dinner out to eat while watching television?) Even before the advent of television as a pervasive medium, there was a study which concluded that people read the daily newspaper as much for the ritual of it as to gain information.

Either consciously or subconsciously, we use media to satisfy our needs. We use communications technologies in ways which meet at least some of the psychological and social drives associated with being human. These are not special media needs, but ways that our uses of communications technologies provide us with general need satisfaction. For example, we have a need for information or knowledge, for pleasurable experiences, for recognition from other humans, for an understanding of self, and sometimes simply for temporary escape from the stress of everyday affairs.

One such classification of needs has been proposed by sociologist Elihu Katz and his colleagues (1974). They include *cognitive* (information and knowledge), *affective* (emotional experience, pleasure), *integrative* (confidence, status), and *contact* (relations with or avoidance of others). These types of needs and variations of them have come to be known under the heading of "uses and gratifications" theory in communication. The details of this theoretical area are not the important point here, which is rather the generalization that we attempt to satisfy a variety of our human needs by the use of communications technologies. This provides us with at least one basis for assessing what is of value to us in the use of communications. Good communications is need satisfaction. Valuable communication is that which can potentially satisfy needs.

This line of reasoning leads to several additional generalizations. If we do find ourselves spending increasing amounts of our life in communications-based environments, we should give some thought to the potential of that environment to serve our personal needs. By the same token we should also give some thought to how individuals by their own actions can gain the most satisfaction from this environment. Television, for example, is defined by many social critics as a means for passive escapism. We pop open a beer and settle in (or "out") for the evening. This indeed may be the case for many members in the mass audience, but it is not necessarily the case for all. Television can be a very powerful instrument for conveying information, for stimulating emotional experiences, or for gaining insights about life. The problem in this country is that we tend to make singular use of the television medium for mass entertainment. This bias is so substantial that when we attempt in school settings to use television for instruction, one of the first challenges is to get students and teachers to take it seriously.

In a way, mass entertainment does satisfy certain needs or else there would not be such a big market for it. If there were only one or two channels of television available, perhaps it would be valuable to use it this way — that is, satisfy the broadest audience. The problem has been that as TV channels have proliferated, the market has not had alternative programming for different needs so much as duplication of proven mass entertainment formulas. In one season it is situation comedies, in another it is westerns, and in one season it was jiggling T-shirts. While the networks have tried to emulate one another's success formulas, small independent stations have entered the same market with reruns of past year's successful formulas.

It will be valuable for us as human beings if the new TV channels made possible by cable and satellite are used not to compete in the mass entertainment market but to cater to further human needs susceptible to satisfaction through communications media. A communications environment with *alternatives* should be a fundamental goal. This extends also to the great variety of communications technologies. Computers can solve problems and also play interesting games. The telephone is great for light conversation but can also be a valuable emergency communications device. The radio provides quite satisfactory "audio wallpaper" but it can also be the basis for an extensive public data service.

It is one thing to define good communications as those which serve our alternative needs. It is yet another to evolve our markets and uses of communications in this country to the point where all of this would be economically possible. We will have to serve needs in a sufficiently satisfying way so that people *will pay* for the services. A communications future with rich and rewarding alternatives is as much a challenge to the consumer to support as it is for the communications industries to create.

But we could go further than rich alternatives. Why not new ones?

What Lies Beyond?

Given that our material needs can be satisfied and that we are able to avoid catastrophe, it seems all the more clear that the *psychological* consequences of our application of new communications technologies will ultimately set the stage for the quality of life in the next century. It is on the psychological level that we humans may be able to grow most. If we can control our environment, then why not go beyond where we've ever gone before?

To plot the direction of potential growth, it is necessary to assume a value system, one more basic, it is to be hoped, than found in the uses and gratifications theory discussed earlier. What is it that is most beneficial psychologically to the human condition? What prompts superb human growth? For this we need a value theory.

You may have your own theory on human psychological utopia — "autonomy," "creativity," "saved," "integrated," "enlightened," "realized," or "self-actualized" — and you should feel free to substitute it here. The details of the utopia are not so important as the proposition that the communications environment be designed with psychological growth as a goal.

Consider, for purposes of discussion, the psychological growth theory of Abraham Maslow (1968, 1976). One of Maslow's fundamental premises was that any theory of human needs would be best based upon what we could learn from healthy and successful people. Most traditional psychoanalytic theory had been built upon experiences with patients who were unhealthy, who had problems, who could not cope with the norm. Also, many prior theories of psychological needs attempted to describe broad cross sections of the population but mixed the observations of sick and healthy people. This mixture confounds identification of desired, healthy conditions. Put more practically, Maslow (1976) sought to answer such questions as: What is the good human? What is the good life? How can children be reared to become sound adults?

Maslow's clinical experiences, his comparisons with the observations of others, plus direct research into these questions, led him to propose in tentative form a psychological theory of human needs. It is a psychologically based human value system.

First, like basic human physiological or biological needs, Maslow argued the existence of basic psychological ones. Our psysiological needs are most critical; we must fulfill many of them simply to stay alive. Given their satisfaction, psychological needs become increasingly important to us. We humans actively seek gratification of them. Lack of gratification is injurious to our psychological growth whereas the presence of gratification is therapeutic to us. When we experience consistent patterns of psychological gratification we appear as generally all around healthy individuals. Together these needs and their gratifications reflect a single, untimate value or goal for which we strive. This is *self-actualization* in Maslow's theory.

Self-actualization is not a high flown term to be associated with some of the pop psychology movements which freely use it. It is defined by Maslow in terms of characteristics found in psychologically healthy human beings. Included among these are a clear perception of reality, ability to gain fresh insights, a feeling of personal wholeness and integration, aliveness, full-functioning, a sense of autonomy of selfness, capability for objectivity or transcendence, creativity, ability to merge the abstract with the concrete, and the ability to love. All humans, because they are human, strive for these characteristics. They are the components of growth, full humanness, the fulfillment of which is growth toward self-actualization.

When we are successful in gratifying our psychological needs, we are rewarded with moments of actualization which Maslow calls *peak experiences*. They are feelings of delight or fulfillment, experiences perfect in themselves, ones which validate our existence. Psychologically healthy people who have such experiences exhibit general characteristics of euphoria, a zest for living, joy, calmness, and an ability to deal with stresses and anxieties over problems.

The environment plays a critical role in this theory, for it is the context against which we humans try to realize our potentialities. It encourages or discourages our psychological growth. Life is a contest between the naturalistic forces of our human needs and an environment within which we humans try to realize our psychological growth. Modern life, especially, is a contest between our needs for self-actualization and the psychologically gratifying or denying characteristics of our environment. *Adaptation* is the name of our human game.

For the first time in the duration of our species, communications technologies will allow us largely to control our environment, particularly those components which affect us psychologically.

Like most well known theories, Maslow's concept of a naturalistic value system has not gone uncriticized. He has been accused of everything from a paucity of scientific data to back up his propositions to the release of his own latent psychological desires to evangelize. Perhaps most frequent of all has been the claim of tautology in his research. Are the criteria he used as a basis for selecting "healthy" individuals really the same as the psychological characteristics he claimed later to identify in them? Nonetheless, the concept of basic psychological needs pervades much of contemporary psychological theory. It is used every day by many practicing clinical psychologists.

No doubt we will need value-based planning so that our communications technologies are developed to meet our physical and more material needs. We will want to maintain, if not expand, our social, economic, and political uses of communications networks. We will want to expand applications which benefit our educational, health, and leisure needs. We will want to use communication-transportation tradeoffs to conserve resources of energy and time. We will want to use communications to promote conservation and protection of our natural environment, and to discourage overpopulation.

Yet as we move on all these fronts, we will at the same time be transforming our environment as never before. Barring war, ecological disaster, or other unforeseen calamities, we could be far ahead in the next century in our game against nature. If we can meet the challenge of the era of limits and set a smooth course into an era of post-industrialism, we will be in a position to explore new frontiers in our human existence. For the first time in the history of our species, we may be in a position to create a psychological environment over which we have an unfathomable degree of control.

The new electronic environment is a metamorphosis of the conditions under which life on earth has developed. It erases old dimensions of distance and time. It transcends limitations of the physical environment. In this new environment, almost all of humanity can witness the same experiences simultaneously, or an infinite variety of differing ones. The electronic environment is instantaneously changeable. It can directly link more human minds, minds with ideas, and minds with machines than any communications means we have developed in our 36,000 year spoken or 6,000 year written heritage. It is permeating, energizing, stultifying, mesmerizing, trivializing, delighting, and dulling.

But it is totally artifactual. We create it and we can control it. We therefore have the opportunity to prepare for ourselves an environment which can be tailored so as to encourage our greatest possible human psychological and sociological growth. The communications environment of the twenty-first century should be designed so as to go far beyond satisfaction of our physical needs or even routine psychological ones. It should become *enlightening*. Why not set out on a course which could lead our species to a new level of existence?

Perhaps in some future century the history of the late twentieth century, like that of the fourteenth, will mark a great transition of civilization, a cusp between old and new. It could be called:

the electronic renaissance.

(END)

REFERENCES

NOTE: This section is organized in alphabetical sequence by author. Where an author's name has not been given in a periodical article, the entry appears for the name of the periodical. References to detailed facts and figures, unless they are of critical importance or controversy, are omitted here. They are readily available in many standard publications which report on the communications business.

American Banker. Revolution in telecommunications is broader than electronic funds transfer. December 29, 1978, 5.

Anacker, W. Computing at 4 degrees kelvin. *IEEE Spectrum* May 1979, pp. 26-37.

Andrew, J. Courts ponder status of cable TV to rule on legality of regulation. *Wall Street Journal,* December 29, 1980.

Annenberg School of Communications at the University of Southern California. Continuing education on medical communications. Report of a conference held January 4-7, 1981 in Rancho Mirage, California, in press.

Bargellini, P. L. Commercial U.S. satellites. *IEEE Spectrum* October 1979, pp. 30-37.

Barnes, P. W. Colleges turn to new computers as way to simulate real events. *Wall Street Journal,* November 20, 1980.

Bedell, S. Now it's the three R's — plus Archie and Edith. *TV Guide,* June 9, 1979, pp. 20-22.

Bell, D. (ed.) *Toward the year 2000: Work in progress.* Boston: Beacon Press, 1967.

——— *The coming of post-industrial society.* New York: Basic Books, 1976.

Bishop, J. E. Can a "supercomputer" be built? Team at IBM grows more confident. *Wall Street Journal,* February 27, 1981.

Brown, J. Business as usual at "Liberated" radio. *Wall Street Journal,* January 19, 1981.

Brown, L. R., Flavin, C., and Norman, C. The future of the automobile in an oil-short world. *The Futurist,* December 1979, pp. 447-458.

Bulkeley, W. M. Adapting to computer age sends executives to school. *Wall Street Journal,* January 28, 1981.

——— Competition to equip the paperless office heats up as potential for devices expands. *Wall Street Journal,* March 6, 1981.

Bulthuis, K., Carasso, M. G., Meenskert, J.P.J., and Zalm, P. Ten billion bits on a disc. *IEEE Spectrum,* August, 1979, pp. 26-33.

Chace, S. Despite many obstacles, AT&T's venture into video data puts publishers on edge. *Wall Street Journal,* May 20, 1981.

Cherry. C. *World communication: Threat or promise?* New York: John Wiley, 1971.

Communications News. Warner's QUBE service gets the subscriber involved in programs. April 1979, p. 62.

Comstock, G., Chaffee, S., Katzman, N., McCombs, M., and Roberts, R. *Television and human behavior.* New York: Columbia University Press, 1978.

Cooney, J. E. Cable television is attracting more ads: Sharply focused programs are one lure. *Wall Street Journal,* March 31, 1981.

Crock, S. Radio station format should be governed by market forces alone, high court rules. *Wall Street Journal,* March 25, 1981.

Datamation. The chip revolution . . . a candid conversation. June 1979, pp. 98-107.

Dordick, H. S. Information inequality. *Computerworld,* April 21, 1980, pp.1ff.

Dordick, H. S., Bradley, H. G., and Nanus, B. *The emerging network marketplace.* Norwood, NJ: Ablex, 1981.

Dordick, H. S., Goldman, R. J. and Hanneman, G. J. Telecommunications and vocational rehabilitation: A user's guide to breaking the barriers. Annenberg School of Communications at the University of Southern California for the Office of Research and Demonstrations Rehabilitation Service Administration, Department of Health, Education and Welfare, July 1978.

Dordick, H. S., Bradley, H. G., Nanus, B., and Martin, T. H. Network information services: the emergence of an industry. *Telecommunications,* September 1979, pp. 217-234.

Doyle, D. New decade for U.S. education: Who pays, who gains, who loses? *Los Angeles Times,* December 30, 1979.

Drucker, P. F. *The age of discontinuity.* New York: Harper & Row, 1969.

———— *Managing in turbulent times.* New York: Harper & Row, 1980.

———— The coming changes in our school systems. *Wall Street Journal,* March 3, 1981.

Dumazedier, J. *Toward a society of leisure.* New York: Free Press, 1967.

Dunn, N. The office of the future: Parts I and II. *Computer Decisions,* July, 1979, pp.16 ff.

Ehrlich, P. *The population bomb.* New York: Ballentine Books, 1968.

———— and Ehrlich, A. *Extinction: The causes and consequences of the disappearance of species.* New York: Random House, 1981.

Ellul, J. *The technological society.* New York: Knopf, 1964.

Finely, L. S. You and your friendly computer. *Los Angeles Times,* March 27, 1981.

Gallese, L. R. A digital wave begins to sweep industries: New products emerge. *Wall Street Journal,* May 25, 1979.

———— Computers find wider use in classrooms as small machines help to lower costs. *Wall Street Journal,* June 3, 1980.

Gerbner, G., Gross, L., Eleey, M. F., Jackson-Beck, M., Jeffries-Fox, S., and Signorielli, N. *Violence Profile 8: Trends in network television drama and viewer conceptions of social reality, 1967-1976.* Philadelphia: Annenberg School of Communications, 1977.

Goldmark, P. C. Tomorrow we will communicate to our jobs. *The Futurist,* 1972, 6, 2 (April), pp. 35-42.

Grant, L. Giant market: Computers for home use put to test. *Los Angeles Times,* September 28, 1980.

———— Ma Bell's new "baby" faces tough competition. *Los Angeles Times,* September 28, 1980.

Green, L. A new kind of literacy: computers. *Los Angeles Times,* February 28, 1981.

Harris, K. Home computer prices fall — but where's the market? *Los Angeles Times,* January 13, 1981.

———— Video cassettes: New enterprise found in rentals. *Los Angeles Times,* April 27, 1981.

Harris, R. J. Analysts see motorists passing up long trips for home recreation. *Wall Street Journal,* July 3, 1979.

Hill, A. SBS — A bit of blue sky becomes a reality. *Satellite Communications,* March 1981, pp. 31-34

IEEE Spectrum. Personal computing. September 1978, pp. 86-97.

IEEE Spectrum. Best bits: Applications of microprocessors. July 1979.

InterMedia. Videotex: Words on the TV screen. Vol. 7, No. 3, May 1979 (entire issue).

Katz, E. and Feldman, J. J. The debates in the light of research: A survey of surveys, pp. 173-223 in S. Kraus (Ed.) *The Great Debates.* Bloomington:Indiana Press, 1962.

Katz, E., and Wedell, G. *Broadcasting in the Third World: Promise and performance.* Brainwave measures of media involvement. *Journal of Advertising Research,* 1971, *11,* pp. 3-9.

Katz, E., Blumler, J. G., and Gurevitch, M. Uses of mass communications by the individual, pp. 11-35 in W. P. Davidson and F.T.C. Yu (Eds.) *Mass Communication Research.* New York: Praeger, 1974.

Krugman, H. E. Brainwave measures of media involvement. *Journal of Advertising Research,* 1971, *11,* pp. 3-9.

Krull, R. Program entropy and structure as factors in television viewership. Ph.D. dissertation, University of Wisconsin, 1973.

Leff, L. TV Comes to town: Fads and new wants come along with it. *Wall Street Journal,* October 2, 1979.

——— Firms renting videocassettes worry studios. *Wall Street Journal,* March 27, 1981.

Lesse, S. The preventive psychiatry of the future. *The Futurist,* 1976, *10,* 5 (October), pp. 228-237.

Lesser, G. S. *Children and television: Lessons from Sesame Street.* New York: Random House, 1974.

Lewis, C., Fein, R., and Mechanic, D. *A right to health: The problem of access to primary medical care.* New York: John Wiley, 1976.

Machalaba, D. More publishers beam electronic newspapers to home video sets. *Wall Street Journal,* January 2, 1981.

——— Coming soon: Encyclopedias that can talk. *Wall Street Journal,* February 18, 1981.

Machlup, F. *The production and distribution of knowledge in the United States.* Princeton, NJ: Princeton University Press, 1962.

Mankekar, D. R. *One way free flow: Neo-colonialism via news media.* New Delhi: Clarion Books, 1978.

Marcuse, H. *One-dimensional man.* Boston: Beacon Press, 1964.

Margulies, L. Cable TV rainbow: Can programming match promise? *Los Angeles Times,* October 12, 1980.

Martin, J. *Future developments in telecommunications.* Englewood Cliffs, NJ: Prentice-Hall, 1977.

Maslow, A. H. *Toward a psychology of being,* second edition. New York: D. Van Nostrand Co., 1968.

——— *The farther reaches of human nature.* New York: Viking, 1971 (Penguin edition, 1976 cited).

Masmoudi, M. The new world information order. *Journal of Communication,* 1979 *24,* 2 (Spring), pp. 172-185.

Maxmen, J. *The post-physician era: Medicine in the 21st century.* New York: Wiley, 1976.

McGinniss, J. *The selling of the President.* New York: Trident, 1969.

McHale, J. *The changing information environment.* Boulder, CO: Westview Press, 1976.

McLuhan, M. *The Gutenberg galaxy.* Toronto: University of Toronto Press, 1962.

——— *Understanding media: The extensions of man.* New York; McGraw-Hill, 1964.

Meadows, D. H., Meadows, D. L., Randers, J., and Behrens, W. W., III. *The limits to growth: A report for the Club of Rome's project on the predicament of mankind.* New York: Universe Books, 1972.

Mennie, D. Personal computers for the entrepreneur. *IEEE Spectrum,* September 1978, pp. 30-35.

New York Times. Far off speakers seen as well as heard here in a test of television. April 8, 1927.

Nilles, J. M. *Exploring the world of the personal computer.* Englewood Cliffs, NJ: Prentice-Hall, in press.

Nilles, J. M., Carlson, F. R., Jr., Gray, P., and Hanneman, G. J. *The telecommunication-transportation tradeoff: Options for tomorrow.* New York: Wiley Interscience, 1976.

Perry, J. M. To raise a politician to the heights, try a helicopter and music. *Wall Street Journal,* July 24, 1979.

Plude, F. F. A direct broadcast satellite delphi study: What do the experts predict? *Satellite Communications,* April, 1981, pp. 32-36.

Pogrow, S. In an information economy, universities and businesses compete for workers. *The Chronicle of Higher Education,* March 16, 1981.

Porat, M. U. *The information economy.* Washington, D.C.: U.S. Dept. of Commerce, May 1977 (OT Special Publication 77-12 [1]).

Quaglione, G. The Intelsat 5 generation. *IEEE Spectrum,* October 1979, pp. 38-41.

Ramo, S. *Century of mismatch.* New York: David McKay, 1970.

Robinson, G. O. *Communications for tomorrow.* New York: Praeger, 1978.

(The) Roper Organization, Inc. *Public perceptions of television and other mass media: A twenty-year review, 1959-1978.* New York: Television Information Office, 1979.

Schmidt, R. Telecommunications for the 80s. (Tapes of a conference held December 8-9, 1980.) McLean, VA; Communications Technology Management Corp., 1981

Schramm, W., Lyle, J., and Parker, E. *Television in the lives of our children.* Stanford, CA: Stanford University Press, 1961.

Selim, R. Health in the future: In the pink or in the red? *The Futurist,* October 1979, pp. 329-342.

Shaffer, R. A. Some bet portable terminals will be next consumer rage. *Wall Street Journal,* June 12, 1981.

Siegel, B. Television: It's changing life in Samoa. *Wall Street Journal,* June 14, 1979.

Singer, D. G., and Singer, J. L. Is human imagination going down the tube? *The Chronicle of Higher Education,* April 23, 1979.

Smith, D. Info city. *New York,* February 9, 1981, pp.24-29.

Steigerwald, B. Videodisc: Ultimate weapon or video revolution? *Los Angeles Times,* March 24, 1981.

Sugarman, R. What's new, teacher? Ask the computer. *IEEE Spectrum,* September 1978, pp. 44-49.

Tannenbaum, J. A. Small businesses learn that a computer without software is "dumb hunk of iron." *Wall Street Journal,* April 2, 1980.

—— IBM's new computer model 3081 is announced at $3.7 million plus. *Wall Street Journal,* November 13, 1980.

—— and Bulkeley, W. M. Device makers dream of electronic offices, but obstacles remain. *Wall Street Journal,* March 13, 1981.

Taylor, A. Small computer shootout: The Japanese and IBM are poised to jump into a fast-growing market. *Time,* March 2, 1981, pp. 68-69.

Taylor, R. E. AT&T accord likely to spur drive to overhaul communications law. *Wall Street Journal,* February 11, 1981.

Thomas, L. *The lives of a cell.* New York: Bantam, 1975.

Toffler, A. *Future shock.* New York: Random House, 1970.

Toffler, A. *The third wave*. New York: William Morrow, 1980.

Tuchman, B. *A distant mirror*. New York: Knopf, 1978.

U.S. Government. *The global 2000 report to the President: Entering the twenty-first century* (Vol. I). Washington, DC: Government Printing Office, 1980.

Wall Street Journal. Easing of regulations for radio stations is approved by FCC in scaled-back plan. January 15, 1981.

Warner, M. G. AT&T gets most of mobile phone market in FCC plan: Justice unit, rivals object. *Wall Street Journal*, April 4, 1981.

Weiner, S. Sears beams life into summer catalog for video shopping. *Wall Street Journal*, May 1, 1981.

Williams F. The soviet philosophy of broadcasting. *Journal of Broadcasting*, Winter, 1961-62, pp. 3-10.

———— Social class differences in how children talk about television. *Journal of Broadcasting*, Fall, 1969, pp. 345-357.

———— and Van Wart, G. *Carrascolendas: Bilingual education through television*. New York: Praeger, 1974.

Williams, F., LaRose, R., and Frost, F. *Children, television and sex-role stereotyping*. New York: Praeger, 1981.

Winn, M. *The plug-in drug*. New York: Viking, 1977.

Wolper, D. Docudrama conference. *Emmy*, Summer, 1979.

Yoshihara, N. RCA kicks off a video disc blitz. *Los Angeles Times*, March 24, 1981.

INDEX

ABOUT THE AUTHOR

FREDERICK WILLIAMS is Professor of Communications at the Annenberg School of Communications at the University of Southern California where, from 1972 through 1980, he served as founding Dean of the School. He divides his time between his professorship and an active writing and speaking career on the topic of modern communications, particularly their social consequences. He is past president of the International Communication Association (1977-1978); was elected to be a Research Fellow by the same organization in 1980; and recently completed an international seminar tour of four Arab countries, Pakistan, and India under the sponsorship of the U.S. International Communication Agency. Williams is the author, coauthor, or editor of eight prior books.